ArtScroll Series®

Rabbi Nosson Scherman / Rabbi Meir Zlotowitz

General Editors

DELVING

by
Rabbi Elias Schwartz

Published by

Mesorah Publications, ltd

WITHIN

A master educator
speaks to his talmidim
HEART TO HEART

FIRST EDITION
First Impression . . . February 1996

Published and Distributed by
MESORAH PUBLICATIONS, Ltd.
4401 Second Avenue
Brooklyn, New York 11232

Distributed in Europe by
J. LEHMANN HEBREW BOOKSELLERS
20 Cambridge Terrace
Gateshead, Tyne and Wear
England NE8 1RP

Distributed in Israel by
SIFRIATI / A. GITLER — BOOKS
4 Bilu Street
P.O.B. 14075
Tel Aviv 61140

Distributed in Australia & New Zealand by
GOLDS BOOK & GIFT CO.
36 William Street
Balaclava 3183, Vic., Australia

Distributed in South Africa by
KOLLEL BOOKSHOP
22 Muller Street
Yeoville 2198, Johannesburg, South Africa

Typography by Compuscribe at ArtScroll Studios, Ltd.

Printed in the United States of America by Noble Book Press
Bound by Sefercraft, Quality Bookbinders, Ltd. Brooklyn, N.Y.

Dedicated in memory of
my devoted and beloved son

לעלוי נשמת

צבי יוסף ארי׳ בן אליעזר
Joseph L. Schwartz ע״ה

and also in memory of
my beloved wife

ולעלוי נשמת

מאשא בת ר׳ יוסף
Marcia Schwartz ז״ל

May their neshamos go
higher and higher
in Heaven above
as they are rewarded by Hashem
because of the mitzvos and
maasim tovim being performed
by the many families
and friends they left behind

אברהם פאם
RABBI ABRAHAM PAM
582 EAST SEVENTH STREET
BROOKLYN, NEW YORK 11218

בס"ד יום ב' לסדר וישלח

הנה ידי"נ החשוק והמרומם פ' והבלה ומהלל הרב ר'אליעזר שוואר99
שליט"א, מנהל ישיבת "תורת אמת" ראהך יובל שנים, הראגי ל' קלק
הקונטרסים מסרו לאמנו לבום, תוכן הסרר הוא ליקוט ש'חות והמאמרים
רצ"ו חינוך להגריב לפני התלמידים מזמן לזמן.

ואני רבה קלת ורא'תי כי א'לום רא'ווין הם לגולא[ ]ור
[ ]רכות אליו הנרם הבהרי מסר והנבונה, לכתם יהב לעלביה לדבקת
לאהוב התורה ויר[ ]ו ותכון המצות והדרכות כרגל שאיר, כראו'לבני ישיבה
ורני תורה. הספר נכתב בלשון אנגלית בסנון קל פה מדבר בשאר[ ]ית ופשוטא
הן ות[ ]אסן, כבר וא[ ]ל רסו[ ]ורדברים ה'ולאים מן הלב אל הלב נכנסים לא [ ]ק.

ורגי אמיר ש' יב'י' כאמחבר שימקבל [ ]מקרא סוידו גג בהחנים
רבני האונרים והבורים ולכל בואסקים בקדושת החינוך, ויזכה לאאשר א[ ]זל
הקודך אתנוק בריאות הנוף ומנוהם הנולא ו[ ]אמנה לכבה לאורך ימ[ ]ים!

אליכם פ' יעקב הכהן פ[ ]אם

My dear friend, the distinguished and respected educator Rabbi Elias Schwartz, who was principal of Yeshivah Toras Emes for half-a-century, has shown me portions of his forthcoming book, a collection of his periodic addresses to his *talmidim*.

I have found these essays worthy of being published. They offer insight and guidance; they will inspire the readers to study Torah, fear Hashem and improve their character, as is appropriate for *Bnei Yeshiva* and *Bnei Torah*.

The work is written in English and in a simple conversational style. "Words which come from the heart enter the heart."

May this work be accepted by teachers, parents and all others involved in education, and may my friend the author merit to carry on his holy work in good health, tranquility and joy for many more years.

Avrohom Yaakov HaKohen Pam

ק״ל

Maimonides portrays the incident with Joseph and Potiphar's wife as an example par excellance of יראת שמים, i.e. where the sole deterent from sinning is the fear of G-d.

This requires elucidation. According to the Talmud a supernatural occurrence kept Joseph from transgressing. He saw the face of his father in the window as he was about to sin.

Evidently the Rambam maintains that דיוקנו של אביו — the appearance of the face of the Patriarch Jacob's face in the window — is a description of the fear of G-d that is part of every Jew's psyche. Every Jew has a perception of "his father's face" that is staring at him as he prepares to sin. In the Rambam's lexicon דיוקנו של אביו means יראת שמים.

The past generation has been sorely in need of bolstering the דיוקנו של אביו. Rav Eleas Schwartz שליט״א heard the call and served as Menahel of Yeshivas Toras Emes, where he instilled יראת שמים and אהבת התורה for fifty prolific years in the hearts and minds of thousands.

Read on, dear reader, and you too shall see — דיוקנו של אביו כיצד שוורא של יוסף עלה בא מן החלונות — where a single individual inspired and awakened so many students to do the will of G-d.

I pray that his years in retirement prove to be as fruitful as his active years as menahel, by his writings, which, I am sure, shall inspire and instruct just as his spoken words have done.

דוד קאהן
כו בכסלו תשנ״ג ימי חנוכה
ר׳ אלול ומפל

Torah
Umesorah

160 BROADWAY, NEW YORK, N.Y. 10038 • 212-227-1000

Founded by Rabbi Shraga Feivel Mendlowitz זצ"ל to establish day schools in every Jewish community

National
Society for
Hebrew
Day Schools

ב"ה

לא תתכן כלל הפעלת השכל ללא זיקוק המדות שקדם לה — הרמב"ם במורה הנבוכים

"The mind cannot function properly unless it is preceded by a purification of the מידות*."*

Schmuessen are the vehicles for imparting the value of *mussar* to the yeshiva student. The majestic yeshiva world under the influence of Reb Yisroel Salanter *z"l*, the "K'dosh Yisroel" as his disciples called him, introduced this method of imparting *Tikun HaMiddos* to *Bnei Yeshiva*.

The greatness of the *baalei mussar* was expressed in their monumental spiritual dimensions — their outstanding piety, the vast scope of their Torah knowledge, the oceanic depths of their understanding of Torah, and their deep insights into human nature. All of these qualities would have had a limited influence if their teachings were not shared with the characteristic sincerity and eloquence of the *baalei mussar*, which hold the attention of the listeners and penetrate their hearts.

Rabbi Elias Schwartz, Dean of Yeshivah Mesivtah Toras Emes Kaminetz for 50 years, one of the giants of American yeshiva education, was a trailblazer and pioneer in the establishment of the renaissance of Torah in America. He was a talmid of the *Shlucha D'Rachmana*, Reb Shraga Feivel Mendlowitz *z"l*. "Eli," as he is affectionately known, absorbed the teachings of his Rebbi and the fiery *aish daas* that he imparted.

Guided by Rav Mendlowitz, Rabbi Schwartz undertook a career in yeshiva ketana education in the 1940's in Yeshivah Toras Emes.

His greatness in education expressed itself in his singular intuitive understanding of *chinuch*, his outstanding administrative capacity, his compassion and his understanding of children. He built a *mosad* "*L'shem U'ltiferes.*" His greatest achievement was his uncanny ability to say a *mussar schmuess* to yeshiva elementary and mesivta high school students. He instructed them in the most profound teachings of *Toras HaMussar*, *Tikun HaMiddos*, with a *Chassidish varemkeit* in simple language and with a profound eloquence that penetrated the hearts and minds of these young American students.

This volume, a compendium of his *schmuessen* over a period of fifty years, truly reflects the greatness of his ability to convey the teachings of Torah to his *talmidim* over the decades. His *talmidim* became *Gedolei Torah, Roshei Yeshivos, Talmidei Chachamim* and earnest and sincere, learned and knowledgeable lay people. His voice conveyed the "דרכיה דרכי נועם" of Torah, the sweetness of Torah.

Rabbi Schwartz built an outstanding Torah institution that will teach Torah until *Bi'as HaMashiach*. More importantly, Rabbi Schwartz educated thousands of *Bnei Torah* whose devotion to Torah will hasten the coming of Mashiach בב"א.

Rabbi Joshua Fishman
Executive Vice President
Torah Umesorah

Table of Contents

☙ Middos

∾ Torah

∾ Mitzvah Observance

⋖§ Hashkafah

Acknowledgments

In looking for somebody to type my writings, I was recommended to Esther Sprey and her husband, who computerized the first stage of many chapters incorporated in this *sefer*.

When I was ready to pursue publication, I enlisted the aid of a longtime friend of my family, Sarina Kalker. With her computer background and the help of her son Abraham, she typed the entire *sefer* over a period of two years. Chapters were retyped again and again until they were in their near-final versions.

I owe a grateful thank-you to my children who proofread a great many parts of this *sefer* as soon as individual chapters were completed. A heartfelt thank-you to Libby and Yehuda Schwartz and Faye and Azriel Hoschander for always being there and ready to accept any obligations that I thrust upon them.

A special thank-you to all my grandchildren who encouraged me and always asked:

"Zaydie, when will you finish this book?"

I was constantly encouraged by my sister and brother-in-law, Marty and Miriam Kaplan, and by many personal friends — Annette Langer, Dr. and Mrs. Seymour Lachman, and Rabbi Herbert Russ, just to name a few.

My gratitude to Mesorah/ArtScroll, to Rabbi Meir Zlotowitz and to Rabbi Nosson Scherman, is immeasurable. They insured the timely publication and beautiful design of this *sefer* by dedicating the expertise of their entire staff to this project. Rabbi Sheah Brander's beautiful page design makes this book a pleasure to see and to read.

A special thanks to Rabbi Avrohom Biderman who was a crucial link in getting this *sefer* produced. He is a remarkable individual, working with patience and always with a smile. Mrs. Judi Dick offered important insights and Mrs. Faygie Weinbaum did an outstanding job proofreading this work. My thanks to Dvory Bick, Chaya G. Zaidman and the typesetting/graphics department of ArtScroll.

Rabbi Shimon Finkelman was the editorial coordinator of this *sefer*. His ideas and suggestions were stupendous. His talent for clear and concise writing was of immeasurable help. Working together with him was a labor of love.

❄ ❄ ❄

I owe a world of thanks to the families and individuals who helped me produce this lifework of mine.

To **Mortimer and Barbara Klaus, Lester and Esther Klaus,** and **Arthur and Vivian Klaus,** who dedicated this work to the everlasting memory of their parents **Bess and Samuel Klaus ז״ל,** who set a pattern of devotion to family and Yeshiva Toras Emes Kaminetz that will be difficult to equal.

They understood well the priorities of *tzedakah*: to help yeshivos teach and prepare future generations of Torah Jews.

And in memory of their beloved sister, **Rosalie Klaus Sohn ע״ה,** who is reunited with her parents in *Gan Eden* above.

Morty, Lester, and Arthur are still my *talmidim*. They inherited the warmth of their parents and remain close to me and to the yeshiva.

❄ ❄ ❄

To **Marty and Pearl Sklar, Victor and Frimet Sklar, Lynn Suskower,** and **Estelle Churchman,** who dedicated this work to the eternal memory of **Jennie and Sam Sklar ז״ל.** Sam always referred to himself as a Kohen Gadol of his family. Jennie always responded to me and greeted me with a welcoming smile.

I personally want to thank the children for the mystic bond of friendship, reverence, and high esteem that exists between us.

❄ ❄ ❄

To **Dr. and Mrs. Edward L. Steinberg** who dedicated this work to the everlasting memory of **Molly Steinberg ע״ה,** and in honor of three of her granddaughters תבדלנה לחיים, **Debbie Shimansky, Sherri Herring,** and **Marilyn Lauer.**

I first met Judy and Eddie flying in the sky to Israel. Our friendship is still flying on high.

❄ ❄ ❄

To **Lee Wallach** and his entire family who dedicated this work in everlasting memory of **Mates Wallach** ז״ל, truly a gentle man. He influenced his family to Torah and G-dliness.

❧ ❧ ❧

To **Mrs. Martha Thaw** and her children **Dennis and Sue Thaw, Geoffrey and Nancy Thaw,** and **Sharon and Steven Weinstein,** who dedicated this work to the everlasting memory of **Carl Thaw** ז״ל. I treasured his personal and sincere friendship for half a century and his deep understanding and devotion of how to serve and thank Hashem.

It is also dedicated in memory of his sister, **Regina Blick** ע״ה, a truly religious person devoted to her entire family; she was like a second mother to him.

❧ ❧ ❧

To the **Fuchs family,** who dedicated this work in loving memory of their parents **Jack and Mollie Fuchs** ז״ל and their dear brother and sister-in-law **Saul and Mania Fuchs** ז״ל, who were remarkable individuals and left their stamp upon them.

❧ ❧ ❧

I also want to eternalize several individuals:

Sara and Jack Rosenfeld ז״ל, I thank them for their warm and close friendship;

Bertha and Herman Bresler ז״ל, for their devotion to Hashem, loyalty to Young Israel, and myself; and

Paul Jacobowitz ז״ל who helped this project over a period of years.

❧ ❧ ❧

My personal thanks to **Diane and Irwin Savad,** who have made a name for themselves in Scranton, Pennsylvania for their warmth and gracious approach to the Torah community.

My thanks as well to **Andy Lowinger,** a *talmid* of mine. I am proud of his *chesed,* his graciousness, and particularly his closeness to me.

❧ ❧ ❧

Above all my deep felt gratitude and thanks to HASHEM.

He truly is responsible for this *sefer*. Hashem placed me, directed me, and watched over me while I grew from year to year in my own understanding of what Chinuch in America needs. I hope He approves.

I am what I am because I loved and revered my Rebbeim **Reb Shraga Feivel Mendlowitz, Reb Shlomo Heiman,** and **Reb Chaim Bick** זכרונם לברכה.

I was also privileged to be President of Torah Umesorah's National Conference of Yeshiva Principals and acted as liaison with *all* the *Roshei Yeshivos* in America. I developed and enjoyed a rare closeness with all of these Torah luminaries of the immediate past generation.

They all share in this publication.

Rabbi Elias Schwartz

Brooklyn, NY
Rosh Chodesh Adar, 5756

From the Author

This *sefer,* with *Mussar* and *Hashkafah shiurim, is particularly slanted* for the American yeshiva students.

These chapters include many talks that I was privileged to give in Yeshivas Toras Emes Kamenitz over a period of 50 years.

In addition to my weekly *shmuessen* at the yeshiva, I was invited to various yeshivos (for boys and girls) to address them at regular monthly Rosh Chodesh and other assembly programs. These include (in alphabetical order) Kamenitz Mesivta (before its merger with Yeshiva Toras Emes), Mesivta Ohr Torah (in Queens), Mesivta Tifereth Jerusalem, Yeshiva of Central Queens (boys and girls). I also spoke regularly in yeshivos for Russian students: Be'er Hagola She'aris Yisroel, Sinai Academy, and in Achiezer (a girls' school).

I hope many *Rebbeim,* parents, and Bais Medrash and *Kollel* students will feel enriched as they read, learn, and, I hope, enjoy the diverse and various points discussed.

The word yeshiva generally means any school of learning Torah for either a boy or a girl. Girls schools have so many different names that I felt this would be the easiest way to refer to both.

Although many chapters seem to be directed to masculine readers, it is just as important, in the message carried, to feminine readers as well.

Preface: A Prayer

◆§ Any Endeavor Needs Hashem's Help

Whenever and wherever I speak, I always offer a silent prayer to Hashem. I think of the following *pasuk* (*Tehillim* 106:2):

מִי יְמַלֵּל גְּבוּרוֹת ה' יַשְׁמִיעַ כָּל תְּהִלָּתוֹ

Who can express the mighty acts of Hashem,
[who] can declare all of His praise?

I think of this *pasuk* and I pray:

> Whenever I speak of the greatness of G-d, may at least some of His infinite praises be heard and understood by the listening audience.

This means that I am asking G-d for His help. I am praying that my message will penetrate the minds and hearts of my audience;

- be it a *mussar schmuess* (talk) to a class,
- a lecture to adults,
- a sermon in the synagogue,
- or any other occasion.

I literally pray for two things:

- that I should speak well and convincingly,
- and that my audience should be inspired
  to follow whatever I ask of them.

May the essence of my words be clear and enlightening, so as to be accepted in totality by my listeners.

And now, in writing this *sefer,* I also pray:

> May my words be perceived clearly,
> and may they be found enlightening,
> so as to be accepted by all who read them.
> May my written words inspire my readers
>   to strive for greater heights
>   in their service to Hashem.

Prologue: The Title of This Sefer: Delving Within

There was once an eighth-grade student who was doing very poorly in his studies and forever involving himself in a great deal of trouble. He was not doing well and we were unable to determine the source of his problem. He had many problems, in school and at home.

One Friday, after my weekly *mussar* talk, he followed me out of the *beis midrash.* His eyes were shining and his face was aglow.

He said, *"Rebbi,* that was beautiful. You really touched me. You were terrific. I really enjoyed what you said today."

I looked at this youngster who was such a difficult student and realized that he spoke from the heart. He had come running to me, to tell me that he enjoyed the *mussar shmuess.*

I asked him to come inside my office and said,

"I just do not understand you.

You have two excellent *rebbeim* who are completely devoted to you.

Yet, you are not learning.

Why don't you listen to them as you listened to me just now? Why are you unable to learn? Why can you run over to me and tell me, with such *enthusiasm*, that today's talk meant so much to you; yet you do not listen to your own *rebbeim?"*

His answer was beautiful.

"Rebbi," he said, "there is a big difference between what you are doing and what the *rebbeim* are doing. True, they are fine *rebbeim,* but they are delving deeply into the *Gemara* and the *Chumash,* and the other subjects we study.

"When you spoke, *Rebbi,*
   you were *delving deeply* into *me."*

Listen carefully to the message of this story. Realize what this boy said. I did not think that he was capable of thinking so profoundly. When I repeated this story to his *rebbeim*, they could not believe that he could put forth such a *sevarah*, such a logical, clear, and perceptive theory of what had happened to him that Friday.

That talk had touched his *neshamah*, his *soul*,
reaching deep within him.

He was living with many problems. As far as he was concerned, there was a tremendous division between his studies and *his self*. He had separated learning from himself.

In his mind, his *rebbeim* were delving deeply into *Gemara*, while
I was *delving deeply into him*.
I tried to argue and to reason with him.
"Sure, my *mussar* talks were speaking
directly to the student.
But how will you become a *talmid chacham*,
a *yirei shamayim*, and a *baal middos?*
Only when *I* talk to you and *I* tell you to be one?
Impossible!!
You honestly believe that you will progress
from my talks alone?
Never!!
From listening to your *rebbeim?*
Yes!!
When you study Torah, *that learning* must become
part of your blood stream, part of your inner self.
Constant Torah learning changes you
and develops you into a better person."

That day was a turning point in the life of this student. The *mussar shmuess* sounded a bell within him. We called a conference of two *rebbeim*, this student, and myself. He began to realize that *all of us* were interested in *his welfare* and *his progress*. At that meeting we all tried to touch the innermost recesses of his *neshamah*.

That conference was a turning point in his life.

I met this student several years later at a wedding. He was 22 years old. He was happy to see me and came running over. In the middle of dancing together he said,

"Rebbi, if I invite you to my wedding, will you come?"
"Of course, I will come, please G-d," I replied.

Youngsters attending yeshivos today are indeed fortunate in that their *rebbeim* are truly almost all interested in the students' welfare and personal growth.

- They are not teaching subjects,
  nor are they teaching classes.
- They are teaching *neshamos, individual souls.*

Delve deeply into your Torah studies. Through Torah, you will develop depth in your thinking and your whole personality will change. Torah study has a lasting and profound effect on your general approach to life.

- Let Torah reach deeply within your true and inner self.
- You will create a tremendous change
  in your outlook on life.
- You will develop a Torah approach
  to solve all your problems.
- You will allow the aura of Torah to envelop
  your thinking in all life's problems.
- Your decisions will become Torah decisions.
- You will live more happily.

The dynamics of yeshivah education has improved dramatically over the years. The goals of yeshivah education are to create a complete Torah personality;

- to create a learned Jew, a *talmid chacham* ;
- to create a G-d-fearing Jew, a *yirei shamayim* ;
- to create a *baal middos,* an individual of
  sterling character and stature of whom
  Hashem and the Jewish people are proud.

Whatever topic I speak or write about, my purpose is to make *you* think! You have to think about *your* life. Are you going in the right direction?

- I am not with you in person;
- I cannot tell you whether each thing you do
  is right or wrong;
- You must learn to evaluate *your* own actions.

- You must decide whether a given deed stems
  from the *yetzer tov* or whether it is *maaseh Satan,*
  the work of the *yetzer hara.*

The *Satan,* who is also the Angel of Death, wants to destroy you, spiritually and then physically. He wants to destroy your *neshamah* in any way he possibly can, so that you will not reap the infinite rewards of Torah study and *mitzvos.* The *yetzer hara* is your evil inclination. *You* must learn to fight off the *yetzer hara* in every possible way;

- at school,
- at home,
- at play;
- wherever you are.

You must act with *middos tovos* at all times.

Set an example for others to follow.

It is a unique pride that yeshivah students, both boys and girls, develop an allegiance to their schools and to its teachings, which remain with them even after they graduate.

You should know and *believe* that it is possible that you will be the Torah leader of the next generations. In the same way that you look up to your *rebbeim* and leaders, the youngsters of tomorrow will look up to you.

- Think about your future.
- Weigh the pros and cons of your every action.

You will be on your way to true Torah greatness.

Note: This *sefer* is an attempt to capture the essence of my *mussar* talks as they were given to students of Yeshivah Toras Emes, as well as students of other yeshivos.

However, this *sefer* has meaning and relevance to all Jews (young and old, male and female) who seek to grow and thrive in their *Yiddishkeit.*

May we all grow and go each and every day
מֵחַיִל אֶל חָיִל,
from strength to strength,
אָמֵן, *Amen.*

Middos

1
Middos and Mussar

◆§ *The Purpose of Mussar*

The entire purpose of *mussar* lectures is to develop certain concepts in your mind, to *develop* certain ideas, to *lift* up your sights to strive for the greatness of what a yeshivah student should be.

Do you know what the word *mussar* means?

The word *mussar* (instruction) and the word *tochachah* (reproof) convey a similar thought. They imply:

- Admonishing someone,
- correcting someone,
- solving his problems,
- showing him the right way,
- giving him a "pep" talk,
- teaching him a lesson,
- showing him what he did wrong,
- helping him to become a better Jew.

Rabbi Yisrael Salanter was the founder of what became known as the *Mussar* Movement. He was the one who stressed the idea that every Jew should learn *mussar,* day in, day out.

Every Jew!

He introduced the idea that in every yeshivah, besides learning *Gemara, Chumash,* and *Halachah, mussar* should also be studied.

- *Mussar* makes demands upon a person.
- *Mussar* demands that you should *daven* better — with more feeling.
- *Mussar* demands that you *behave* properly.

There is a famous story of a man who came to Rabbi Yisrael Salanter. Remember, we are going back more than 100 years.

He said, "*Rebbe,* I work very hard all day long. When I come home, it is nighttime and it is dark." (Over 100 years ago we did not have jobs like we have today where most people work from nine to five.)

"I have only a half hour to learn," he said.

"What should I learn in that half hour?

Should I learn *Gemara?*

Should I learn *Chumash* and *Rashi?*

Should I learn *Halachah?*

Rebbe, you tell everyone to learn *mussar.*

Should I spend my half hour learning *mussar* rather than *Chumash, Rashi* or *Mishnayos?*"

Reb Yisrael told him:

"Learn *mussar.*"

The man stood still for a minute. He said, "*Rebbe,* is *mussar* more important than *Gemara?*

Reb Yisrael answered,

"Absolutely not."

"Then why are you telling me to learn *mussar* for the half hour that I have?" asked the man.

The following is a very famous answer, and I want you to remember it.

Rabbi Yisrael Salanter answered: "At first, all you will learn will be that half hour of *mussar.* However, that half hour of *mussar* will inspire you and will make you realize that you can find time to learn for another hour a day. You will learn a half hour of *mussar* and you will learn another hour of Torah as well."

·§ *A Better Way*

The more *mussar* a person learns, the more he comes to realize that it is not important to work from seven in the morning until seven at night, coming home so tired that he has no energy to learn. He will realize that he can make a living working only eight hours a day, so that he will have *additional hours* in which to learn Torah.

This is what *mussar* will do for you! *Mussar* will make demands upon you and tell you:

This is not the way to do it. There is a better way.

When we study *mussar,* our goal is to find this better way. *Mussar* will make *you* think not only of the things you want for yourself, but also that you should take *someone else* into consideration. That someone else could be your mother, your father, your brother, your sister, your friend or, perhaps, even a stranger.

- *Not,* "I do what I want,"
  but, "I *have* to *think* of *someone else.*"
- The individual does not stand by himself in this world.
- *Mussar* will make *you* think.
  It will make *you* react and it will make *you* respond.
- *Mussar* will *refine* your *middos* and your behavior.
- *Mussar* will make you into a finer *person,* a better *Jew.*
- *Mussar* will constantly make
  additional demands upon you.
- *Mussar* will make you into a *baal middos;*
  a person of outstanding character.

This is the primary purpose of the *mussar* talks which I have given over the years.

2
Mussar and Tochachah

ᐳ The Art of Rebuke

What does it mean to administer *mussar* and *tochachah*?
It means:
- to disapprove,
- to admonish,
- to reprimand,
- to instruct.

When you see someone doing something wrong,
- you are obligated to "give him *mussar.*"
- You must try to correct him.
- You must try to convince him that
  he has done something wrong.

- You must do so in a *gentle* manner.
- You may criticize but you are *not to condemn.*
- You may censure but not denounce.
- You may disapprove of his actions,
  but this does not call for a tongue-lashing.
- You may remonstrate
  but you are not to "rake him over the coals."
- You may hint at a fault but you must
  be careful *not to show contempt.*
- You must carefully weigh your choice
  of words in your mind before you speak.
- You may be outspoken when talking to him,
  but do it privately.

- Do not raise a hue and cry against him.
- Do not be overcritical.
- Do not be abusive.
- Do not show dislike.
- Do not speak with derision.

While giving *mussar,* do not make the person feel so low as to destroy him.

Speak to him in a way that will successfully lift him out of the morass into which he has sunk.

⋐§ *Eradicate Hatred*

There are actually two parts to the *mitzvah* of *mussar* and *tochachah.*

לֹא תִשְׂנָא אֶת אָחִיךָ בִּלְבָבֶךָ
"Do not hate your brother in your heart.

הוֹכֵחַ תּוֹכִיחַ אֶת עֲמִיתֶךָ (ויקרא יט:יז)
Rebuke him . . ." (Vayikra 19:17).

Rabbi Samson Raphael Hirsch explains:

If you feel that someone has hurt you by word or deed, it is incumbent upon you to tell him of the injustice done to you. You must clear the atmosphere. Make him realize the wrong he has done.

This puts a very high moral obligation upon us when anyone has wronged us or when we feel hurt or offended. We must not bear a grudge or harbor hatred in any way. We cannot allow what transpired to have the slightest effect on our attitude or feelings towards the person.

- Do not let hatred smolder in your heart.
- Speak out frankly!
  Place the matter openly before the person
  and give him an opportunity to justify his
  behavior or make amends for it.
- Silently bearing ill feelings will
  destroy your own character.
  Make it a policy to discuss
  wrongdoings immediately.
  Do not let them fester in your heart.

The *Avnei Ezel* adds his comments to this important *mitzvah*:

תּוֹכָחָה הַבָּאָה מִתּוֹךְ אַהֲבָה עָשׂוּי לְהַשְׁפִּיעַ יוֹתֵר.
כָּל שֶׁהָאַהֲבָה יוֹתֵר גְּדוֹלָה כָּךְ הַתּוֹכָחָה הִיא יוֹתֵר רְצִינִית

Any admonishment must have two prerequisites:
1. Do not bear any hatred.
2. Remember that you are to admonish with
   love and sincerity.

One must never reprimand another person out of hatred. It will not
have a positive effect.

An admonishment given with love and sincerity will be a
thousandfold more effective.

Only if a person fulfills the first part of the quotation, "Do not hate
your brother in your heart," can he admonish.

In truth, only if you love a person can you help him through
reprimand.

A child will be reprimanded by his parents more often than by any
other person in his life. Differences may ensue because of so much
rebuke. But because of the deep abiding love his parents have for him,
he will eventually accept the admonishments offered.

❧ "Do Not Bear a Sin"

הוֹכֵחַ תּוֹכִיחַ אֶת עֲמִיתֶךָ וְלֹא תִשָּׂא עָלָיו חֵטְא
*"Rebuke, you shall rebuke your fellow and do not bear a
sin because of him" (Vayikra 19:17).*

R abbi Samson Raphael Hirsch explains that not only is rebuke
permitted, but that it is a duty imposed upon us towards anybody
whom we see straying from the path of equity and justice, from G-d's
commandments.

The *Gemara* says that the double use of the word הוֹכֵחַ תּוֹכִיחַ,
Rebuke, you shall rebuke, means:
* You should admonish him again and again.
* Admonish him even more than
  100 times, if necessary.

עִם הַתּוֹכָחָה תָּשִׂים אוֹתוֹ לַעֲמִיתֶךָ אַל תְּשִׂימֵהוּ לְחוֹטֵא
יֵשׁ לִפְנוֹת אֵלָיו בִּדְבָרִים שֶׁיֵּשׁ בָּהֶם כְּדֵי לְרוֹמְמוֹ וּלְקָרְבוֹ (חַוּוֹת יָאִיר)

Chavos Yair interprets the verse in this way:

When you do criticize a person, be sure to make him your friend, equal to you in every respect.

"Do not bear a sin upon him" means:

> Do not let him feel that he is unworthy of your friendship.
> Do not stamp him as a sinner.

If you criticize him in such a way, he will not listen to your words. He will not look upon you as a friend. You will have accomplished nothing.

Even in admonishment, you must lift up the morale of the person, so that he will better himself. He will appreciate what you have tried to do for him and will most likely follow your advice.

If anyone *"yes"es* you all the time and never corrects you or disagrees with you, you can be sure that he is not a true friend of yours. The best friend that a person can have is the one who will try to improve his actions.

⊷§ Cleanse Yourself

Who qualifies best to give *mussar* to another person?
Only an individual who is perfect himself.
As our Rabbis say:

קְשׁוֹט עַצְמְךָ וְאַחַר כַּךְ קְשׁוֹט אֲחֵרִים
"First cleanse yourself, then you can help others."

When a person who was given *mussar* on a particular action realized his error and did *teshuvah,*

> he can then correct others for this same misdeed.

Again, one must first correct himself before criticizing others.

This is alluded to at the *Seder.*

The *Alshich HaKadosh* interprets the first two symbols of the *Seder* as follows:

> • קַדֵּשׁ — *Kadeish*:
> First bring *kedushah* to yourself.
> Sanctify yourself. Perfect yourself.

- וּרְחַץ — *U'rchatz*:
  Wash yourself,
  cleanse yourself of any misdeeds.

After bringing some sanctity into your own life, then:

- מַגִּיד רָחְצָה — *Maggid Rachtzah*:
  You can tell others to cleanse themselves.
  You have set an example for them
  in your own way of life.
  Now, others can follow you.

While the requirement to give *mussar* rests upon every Jew, those best qualified for this task are a father, a mother, and a *rebbi*.

- אָבִי מוֹרִי — My father, my teacher
- אִמִּי מוֹרָתִי — My mother, my teacher
- רַבִּי וּמוֹרִי — My *rebbi,* my teacher.

The same title is given to parents and a *rebbi.* The word *mori* is from the same root letters of the word *moreh* — a teacher. Parents and a *rebbi* are teaching constantly.

Therefore the Torah places parents and teachers in the same category.

בַּכֹּל אָדָם מִתְקַנֵּא חוּץ מִבְּנוֹ וְתַלְמִידוֹ (סנהדרין קה:)

No parent is ever jealous if his child is a better student or is more learned than he.

This is applicable to a *rebbi* as well.

A *rebbi* will never be jealous that his pupil is becoming a greater *talmid chacham* than he is.

✦§ *Between Friends*

A friend is also someone who can give a tremendous amount of *mussar.* Parents and teachers are not around 24 hours a day to monitor our actions.

During recess, while playing:

If you see a friend doing something that you know is wrong,
you carry a heavy burden of responsibility; almost as great as the person who is doing the wrong.
You, as a friend, are obligated to give him *mussar.*

In seeing a wrong being done, you must protest, you must disapprove, you must show your consternation.

ঐ Actions May Speak Louder than Words

The following concerns another aspect of the art of giving *mussar*. We find this same thought in the *Chumash* and *Midrash*. We also find the punishment meted out by Hashem, if one could have given *mussar* and did not.

Pharaoh consulted with three advisors regarding what to do with the Jews in Egypt.

- Bilam advised him to destroy the Jews.
- Yisro ran away. This was his way of expressing his negative feelings concerning the plan. (He later became Moshe *Rabbeinu's* father-in-law, which was a tremendous privilege and honor.)
- Iyov remained silent, and was later severely punished. He suffered in many ways. He lost his wealth and his children. At the end of his life he did *teshuvah.*

Rabbi Yitzchak Zev Soloveitchik, the Brisker Rav, popularly referred to as Reb Velvel, asked:

Why was Iyov punished so severely? We know that G-d punishes measure for measure. Wherein did Iyov merit such a terrible punishment?

The Brisker Rav explained:

Though Iyov did not want to fight or disagree with Pharaoh, nevertheless, he should at least have said:

"*Oy vey.*"
    He should at least have shown his displeasure
        at what was proposed.
    This would have been his admonishment
        against Bilam's scheme.
    He should at least have sighed and said: "Woe is me."
    He should have involuntarily gasped at
        hearing such a vicious plan.

> The *"Oy vey"* would have indicated that it bothered
> him that an entire people were to be destroyed.

Yisro's running away was his way of saying, *"Oy vey."*

It was his cry of *mussar.* He was rewarded for his act of *mussar.*

If the destruction of an entire people did not disturb or pain Iyov sufficiently to cry out against such a dastardly act, then measure for measure, his punishment was the hurt and destruction of his own family.

It is of vital importance for friends to admonish one another whenever necessary. Friends are with each other in moments of relaxation. When there is a carefree atmosphere, things are most likely to go wrong. Generally, when a youngster is, in the company of his parents or *rebbi,* he will behave differently from the way he would when he is with friends.

By ignoring a friend's wrongdoing, several things take place.

- You do not help him to act responsibly.
- You may destroy his character.
- You may hinder his growth.

    He may think that you approve of his behavior.

This is particularly true if he is
    aware that you know he did something wrong and you
    did not try to stop him.

You have the power in your hands to give *mussar,* and you must not hold it back. If during recess you see your fellow classmates ruining or destroying yeshivah or private property, you, as a friend, have the full responsibility to give *mussar.* A person may readily accept advice and correction from one of his peers.

If you see anybody straying from the path of Torah, it is your duty to try to straighten him out. One must never remain silent when he sees somebody deviating from the path of Torah and justice, be they transgressions great or small.

Our Rabbis tell us:

"If one could have kept members of his family or fellow citizens from sinning,
    and he did not do so,
    he is held responsible for their guilt.

Even if his own life is exemplary, he is judged for the fact that he kept silent and did nothing to improve his fellow man.

🪶 "Your Brother"

How should you give *mussar* according to the Torah? The verses quoted above are very clear in their instructions.

The commentators warn us that even while criticizing a person, make sure he remains *amisecha, your* fellow, meaning, your friend.

Do not alienate him or drive him away from you.

Another sentence in the Torah brings out a similar point: וְנִקְלָה אָחִיךָ לְעֵינֶיךָ (דברים כה:ג) כֵּיוָן שֶׁנִּקְלָה אָחִיךָ הוּא

R' Samson Raphael Hirsch explains (*Devarim* 25:3) that after "your brother" is punished by receiving lashes in front of you, remember that he is *achicha,* your brother. You are to show him the same love and respect as before he sinned and was punished.

The word "your brother" is not necessary in the verse. It is superfluous to the meaning of the sentence. But it is placed there to tell us that as soon as the sinner leaves the *beis din,* cleansed of his sin, welcome him back as your brother.

The slate is wiped clean.

Rabbi Hirsch continues, "Your brother" is to receive lashes equivalent to a maximum of "40 minus one." You are not to strike him more than 39 times, lest he become degraded in your eyes.

Rashi expresses it beautifully:

In previous verses, the sinner is called a *rasha,* a wicked person. Once he has received the prescribed strokes, he is restored to your respect,

> he is again your equal,
>
> he is once again "your brother."

The word "your brother" is *not* superfluous. It teaches a most important lesson.

Remember:

> He is no longer a culprit; he is now your brother.
>
> Do not remind him of his sins.
>
> This is the Torah way of giving *mussar.*

The highest degree of *mussar* is to show your friend that it bothers you that his character is being sullied. You are giving him *mussar* only for his sake.

True, you must never remain silent when you see a wrongdoing.

On the other hand, *mussar* must be given kindly and with sensitivity, so that a clear-cut message is given that you care about him, and that you are concerned for him. For he is your brother.

3

Character Growth
and Hakaras Hatov

◆§ The Measure of a Person

We use the word *middos* to describe
- good character
- good behavior
- good manners.

But what is the literal meaning of the word מִדָּה, *middah*?

מִדָּה means *a measurement,* as in מִדָּה אַחַת לְכָל הַיְרִיעֹת, *the same measure for all the curtains* (*Shemos* 26:2).

Do you know how people *measure* you when you speak about your school? Do you know how they measure the school itself?

> They do not know that some of you
> are exceptionally bright.
> They do not know that all of you
> are well versed in *Chumash.*
> They do not know that you know a
> great deal of *Mishnah* by heart.
> They do not know how many *pesukim* of
> *Rashi* you know by heart.
> They are not aware of your scholastic abilities in *Gemara.*

How do they measure the type of person you are?

> They measure you by your manners.
> They measure you by the way you behave
> when you go to *shul* on Shabbos.
> They measure you by the way you speak
> when you go shopping for your mother.

They measure you by seeing whether or not
    you push your way ahead of the next person
    on line because you want to get out faster.
People measure you in very simple ways,
    by whether or not you say:
        Thank you • Excuse me • I am sorry • Please •
        Good morning • Good evening • Good night.

Do you know what else they measure when they speak with you?
    They measure what kind of home you come from.
    They measure your mother and father, even though
        they do not know them. If you speak politely
        and respectfully, then they say to themselves
        that this youngster has grown up in a home
        where the parents teach proper manners.

⊷§ Caught, Not Taught

Rabbi Shraga Feivel Mendlowitz* always said: "It is a mistake to say that you come to yeshivah only to *learn* Torah.
- You come to yeshivah also to learn *from* Torah;
- how to become a *ben Torah,*
- how to act properly, as a *ben Torah* should."

It is quite difficult to teach *middos* through personal criticism. It is quite difficult to constantly correct a person.
- "Control your temper!"
- "Don't yell!"
- "Eat properly!"

Middos are best *not* taught. Rather,
    Middos must be *caught.*

If someone in your house has a contagious virus, you will very possibly also contract that virus. You will catch it from him because you are in his immediate vicinity.

This is how to learn proper *middos*: by being in the surroundings of people who are shining examples of proper character and behavior —

---

* During his lifetime, *Rebbi* insisted on being called *"Mr."* Today, we, his *talmidim,* feel that it is only proper to refer to him as "Rabbi."

and by allowing their qualities to "rub off" on you.

- Watch the way your *rebbi* acts,
- how he talks,
- how he smiles,
- how he controls himself.
- Observe the way your parents behave.

All this is something that carries over to you. It becomes part of your way of life.

You are *caught* up in their beautiful character traits.

אָמַר רַבִּי יוֹחָנָן מִשּׁוּם רַבִּי שִׁמְעוֹן בֶּן יוֹחַאי:
גְּדוֹלָה שִׁמּוּשָׁהּ שֶׁל תּוֹרָה יוֹתֵר מִלִּמּוּדָהּ (ברכות ז:)

R' Yochanan taught us in the name of R' Shimon ben Yochai: *Serving a Torah scholar is greater than the study of Torah* (Berachos 7b).

Staying with a *rebbi,* serving him, watching and absorbing every aspect of his behavior; watching his attitude towards others and studying his reaction to all occurrences, both expected and unexpected, throughout the day,

- will influence
- will inspire

a student as much, and *even more,* than what the student actually learned in his studies.

A *talmid* has to get caught up in the whirl of his *rebbi's* seemingly insignificant activities — there is much to learn from them.

- The lessons learned are of inestimable value.
- These character traits cannot be taught.
- These traits must be observed and then absorbed into your way of life.
- You have to become *caught* up in this beautiful way of life.

Then, these *middos* will become part of your own life style.

⋙ Hakaras Hatov

Hakaras Hatov is a very important *middah. Hakaras Hatov* means to show appreciation to someone who did something for you. It means that you recognize a good deed or a good thing that happened to you and that you are grateful for it. There are many examples which teach us this important *middah.*

The first two plagues in Egypt concerned the waters of the Nile River.

וַיֹּאמֶר ה׳ אֶל מֹשֶׁה: אֱמֹר אֶל אַהֲרֹן קַח מַטְּךָ וּנְטֵה יָדְךָ עַל מֵימֵי מִצְרַיִם
וְיִהְיוּ דָם ... (שמות ז:יט)

Hashem said to Moshe: "Say to Aharon, 'Take your staff and stretch out your hand over the waters of Egypt . . . and they shall become blood' " (Shemos 7:19).

Rashi explains: Since the waters saved Moshe's life when he was placed in a cradle in the water at the age of three months, therefore, Moshe could not cause a plague through the water, neither the plague of blood nor the plague of frogs.

The third plague, lice, came from the dust of the earth. Again, it was Aharon who smote the dust of the earth and there was lice in all of Egypt (ibid. 8:13). Here, too, it was *hakaras hatov* which prevented Moshe from bringing about the plague. Many years before, Moshe had killed an Egyptian who was beating a Jew, and concealed the Egyptian's body in earth. Therefore, it would have been ungrateful of Moshe to have smitten the earth (*Rashi* to *Shemos* 8:12).

This teaches us a great lesson: If it is wrong to show ingratitude to a lifeless object such as a river or earth, then surely one must be careful to show proper appreciation toward his fellow man.

It is quite easy to develop this beautiful character trait.
For example:

Consider the fact that your mother worked all day, went shopping for food, and prepared your supper with the hope that you would enjoy the fruits of her efforts.

When you come home tonight say: "Mom, thank you. This was a delicious supper." Your mother will smile and feel good. This is *hakaras hatov.*

◆§ Avraham Avinu

We learn this *middah* from Avraham *Avinu* as well. Avraham went down to Egypt when there was a famine in Canaan. The Torah tells us that on his return to Canaan, he went back to the very same inns that he stopped at on his way to Egypt.

Why did he return to the same places?

One *midrash* says that he owed some money to these innkeepers. Another *midrash* says that he went back to the same hotels because, when he went down to Egypt, he was poor. On his return, he was much wealthier.

> Avraham wanted to show the people how Hashem had blessed him. This is a manifestation of *hakaras hatov*: to let people see that he was appreciative of how he had been helped by G-d.

Another reason why Avraham went back to the same inns was because he had been treated well at these places. Now that he was a wealthier person, he did not go to a more elegant place.

> "I am coming back to your hotel because you were so good to me."

This is all within the realm of *hakaras hatov,* a very basic *middah,* and a very important one. In fact, the Torah teaches us that people who have no *hakaras hatov* are not worthy of marrying a descendant of Avraham, Yitzchak, and Yaakov.

⋖§ Ammon and Moav

The Torah states:

> לֹא יָבֹא עַמּוֹנִי וּמוֹאָבִי בִּקְהַל ה' . . . עַד עוֹלָם (דברים כג:ד)
> An Ammoni or Moavi can never enter the congregation of Hashem (Devarim 23:4).

They can become converts but they cannot marry a *bas Yisrael.*
   Why?

> Because they did not greet you with bread and water on the road when you were leaving Egypt (ibid. v. 5).

The nations of Ammon and Moav were descendants of Lot, who was Avraham's nephew. Lot had been saved by Avraham when he was captured in war. Lot became wealthy because he lived with Avraham. Yet, Lot's descendants did not show even minimal kindness to Avraham's descendants as they passed by their lands. The prohibition against marrying them is, in effect, saying to them:

"You are the great-grandchildren of Lot. Why didn't you show appreciation to the Jewish people? It was their great-grandfather

Avraham who saved your great-grandfather! How could you not go forth and give them bread and water while they were trekking through the desert?

"You have no *hakaras hatov*; because you lack this basic *middah,* you can never marry a descendant of Avraham."

◈ *Modeh Ani*

Every morning when we wake up, while still in bed, as soon as we open our eyes, we say *Modeh Ani.*

What does *Modeh Ani* mean? — "I thank You."

Whom are we thanking and what are we thanking Him for? We are thanking Hashem for allowing us to wake up in the morning.

Do we take it for granted that we wake up in the morning?

Does one say to himself that everyone who goes to sleep will wake up in the morning? No, such an attitude is wrong.

We thank Hashem for our waking up.

Let us look closely at the words of *Modeh Ani.*

מוֹדֶה אֲנִי לְפָנֶיךָ מֶלֶךְ חַי וְקַיָּם שֶׁהֶחֱזַרְתָּ בִּי נִשְׁמָתִי בְּחֶמְלָה, רַבָּה אֱמוּנָתֶךָ

"I gratefully thank You, G-d, living and eternal King, for You returned my soul within me with compassion. Your faithfulness is very great!"

What does the word בְּחֶמְלָה, *with compassion,* mean?

- Perhaps I was not very good yesterday.
- Perhaps I talked back to my *rebbi* or to my parents.
- Perhaps I sinned in some other way.
- But, Hashem, You are giving me another chance today.
- You have faith *in me.* You believe *in me.*
- You are giving *me* a chance to be better today.

I like to quote a slogan:

"Be better today than yesterday,
not quite as good as tomorrow."

Imagine, just for a minute, if you will really be better today than yesterday.

Yesterday, you were four feet tall spiritually.

Today, you are better. Today, you are four and a half feet tall spiritually.

Tomorrow, you are going to be better than today. You will be yet taller.

As the days go by, you grow taller and taller in your *Avodas Hashem,* in your serving Hashem.

- Each day is an opportunity to learn more Torah.
- Each day is an opportunity to learn about another *mitzvah.*
- Each day is an opportunity to *do* more *mitzvos.*
- Each day you should do something beautiful that you did not do the day before.

If you have ever been on a train at 2:30 in the afternoon when the public schools are dismissed, you will see a gang of boys and girls piling into the train, pushing, shoving, screaming, talking boisterously, at times even fighting. Older people on the train often feel afraid.

However, if yeshivah students are on a train, or on a class trip, there must be a clear distinction between their behavior and that of the others.

- They must practice *middos tovos.*
- They must have good manners.
- They must create a good impression wherever they go.

This, making Hashem's Name beloved to others, is a true way of showing *hakaras hatov* to Hashem for all that He has done for you.

◄§ Reb Moshe

Rabbi Moshe Feinstein (the *Rosh Yeshivah* of Mesivtha Tifereth Jerusalem from 1936-1986) used to go to the cook of his school every Thursday and thank her for cooking delicious meals for the yeshivah students. The cook appreciated and looked forward to this "Thank you."

One Thursday, the *Rosh Yeshivah* had to go to a wedding and did not get a chance to say, "Thank you," since he had left directly from his home.

On Friday, the cook was at home. At this point in time, she was no longer the cook but was a wonderful Jewish housewife getting ready for Shabbos. She received a telephone call from Rabbi Moshe Feinstein. She could not believe that Reb Moshe was calling her!

He said: "I did not thank you last night for the delicious meals you cooked this week and I am calling to say, 'Thank you.' "

What a great person he was! A great person, not only because of his learning, or great in his responsibility for Jews all over the world, but great in *middos,* as we see from his *hakaras hatov.* He showed appreciation to everyone. He did not take anyone or anything for granted.

When you go home each day, make sure to say, "Thank you," to your mother. On Fridays, say, "Good Shabbos," to all your *rebbeim* and teachers. You can also greet the rabbi of your *shul* after *davening.*

And you, too, can say, "Thank you," to the cook in your yeshivah.

> The more *hakaras hatov* we show, the better a person we are, and the more Hashem takes pride in us.

4

Lessons in Behavior and
The Gift of Eretz Yisrael

There are two important lessons we must learn from the *Parashah* of *Metzora* (*Vayikra* Chs. 13-14):

▄§ Social Misbehavior
Evil Gossip — Lashon Hara

The Torah discusses the affliction of *tzaraas,* which in its various forms can affect either a person's skin, hair, clothing or house.

A person who is afflicted with this *tzaraas* is called a מְצוֹרָע. *Chazal* tell us that this word is actually a contraction of two words, מוֹצִיא רַע, *he expresses evil of others.*

He gossips constantly.

He causes arguments and rifts between people.

> מִדָּה כְּנֶגֶד מִדָּה, *measure for measure,* his punishment is that he is to be separated from people. He is to be alone, outside the encampment of Israel.
>
> וְנָתַתִּי נֶגַע צָרַעַת בְּבֵית אֶרֶץ אֲחֻזַּתְכֶם. וּבָא אֲשֶׁר לוֹ הַבַּיִת וְהִגִּיד לַכֹּהֵן לֵאמֹר: כְּנֶגַע נִרְאָה לִי בַּבָּיִת ((ויקרא יד:לד-לה).
>
> G-d says: *"And I will put an affliction of tzaraas in a house in the land of your possession. The one to whom the house belongs shall come and inform the Kohen (priest): 'It seems to me as if there is a nega (affliction) in the house' "* (*Vayikra* 14:34-35).

Rashi comments:

"Even if the owner is a *talmid chacham* and knows the law, he should never proclaim: 'There is an affliction.' He should say: 'It seems to me as if there is an affliction.' " Only the *Kohen* can determine that the discoloration of the wall is an affliction of *tzaraas* which renders the house *tamei*, impure.

The *Midrash* says that the word *tzaraas* comes from צָרוּת עַיִן [*tzarus ayin*], *a begrudging eye,* a combination of jealousy and selfishness.

> A person afflicted with *tzarus ayin* is not good natured and does not want to share his possessions with his neighbors. He has developed a mean, selfish approach in his dealings with others. He thinks only of himself. He does not have a generous outlook; he considers the possessions in his house to be exclusively for his own use.

For example,

A neighbor asks him: "Can you please lend me an axe?" He replies: "I do not have the type of axe you are looking for." In fact, he has what his neighbor is asking for, but he does not want to share with anyone. He is afflicted with *tzarus ayin*.

Torah Temimah sees this hinted to in the words וּבָא אֲשֶׁר לוֹ הַבַּיִת, *The one to whom the house belongs shall come* (v. 35) — the owner's attitude is that everything in his בַּיִת, *house,* is for לוֹ, *himself,* alone.

Therefore, Hashem causes a *nega* (affliction) to appear on the walls of the house, and the owner must call the *Kohen* for his decision. The house must be emptied before the *Kohen* comes. After the *Kohen* proclaims that it is in fact a *nega*, everything in the house becomes *tamei*, spiritually unclean.

When the house is emptied, the neighbor walks by and says: "Oh, so you *do* have an axe. You must have forgotten, when I asked you for one several days ago."

The above verse continues, . . . וְהִגִּיד לַכֹּהֵן לֵאמֹר כְּנֶגַע נִרְאָה לִי בַּבָּיִת [The one to whom the house belongs] shall declare to the *Kohen* saying: "It seems to me as if there is an affliction in the house."

וְהִגִּיד: שֶׁמְּדַקְדֵּק הַכֹּהֵן כֵּיצַד בָּא הַנֶּגַע לְבֵיתוֹ. לֵאמֹר: יֹאמַר לוֹ הַכֹּהֵן דִּבְרֵי כִבּוּשִׁים. בְּנִי אֵין נְגָעִים בָּאִים אֶלָּא עַל לָשׁוֹן הָרָע. (תּוֹרָה תְּמִימָה)
Torah Temimah explains that וְהִגִּיד, [*the owner*] *shall declare*, means that he shall *inform* the *Kohen,* for the

Kohen will question him about the details concerning the *nega*. The term וְהִגִּיד means to be explicit in describing everything concerning the *nega*.

The word לֵאמֹר, *saying,* means that the *Kohen* should speak to the person about the *nega*. He should sympathize with the owner and offer his consolation for this unfortunate occurrence. His discussion with the owner should be in conciliatory tones.

The *Kohen* says:

"*B'ni,* my son, you know that a *nega* comes because you may be doing something wrong.

Perhaps a *nega* came upon your house because you
    refused to share your possessions with your neighbor.
In similar fashion, a *nega* may come upon a
    person's skin because he speaks *lashon hara,*
    evil gossip, against others.
By doing so, he *blemishes* their reputation.
    Therefore, he is punished with a *blemish*
    upon his body. His skin or hair becomes
    afflicted with a discoloration."

In the verse we quoted, we find the word וּבָא, *and he* [the owner] *shall come.* The owner must come himself to speak to the *Kohen.* He cannot send a messenger. *He knows better than anyone exactly what he did wrong.*

The *Kohen* will tell him words of *mussar*:
    "My son, you must change your attitude.
    Did you speak *lashon hara*?
    Did you refuse to help your neighbor?"

Torah Temimah compares this to a *mitzvah* that must be done by the person himself, like the *mitzvah* of *tefillin.* It must be done with the body of the person. No one can fulfill the *mitzvah* of *tefillin* for you.

You can fulfill certain *mitzvos* through others. If one person makes *Kiddush* on Shabbos, everyone can listen, answer *Amen,* and it is as if they too made *Kiddush.*

But *mitzvos* concerning the body of a person cannot be fulfilled by others. The laws regarding *nega* is that only if the person is sick, feeble, or old can he send a messenger, for under these circumstances the individual is unable to go himself.

Therefore, the one who is afflicted with *tzaraas* reports to the *Kohen*. The *Kohen*, in speaking to the afflicted one, will lead him in the direction of *teshuvah*. By speaking softly and sympathetically to the *metzora* (or owner of the house or garment), the *Kohen* will make him realize that he had done something wrong.

Thus, the afflicted person will learn his lesson. He will change his behavior toward his fellow man.

◄§ The Gift of Eretz Yisrael

אֲשֶׁר אֲנִי נֹתֵן לָכֶם לַאֲחֻזָּה

"When you will come to the land of Canaan (*Eretz Yisrael*) *that I give* (*nosein*) you as a possession . . ." (*Vayikra* 14:34).

In the Torah, the words אֲשֶׁר אֲנִי נֹתֵן, *that I give you*,* are always in the *present* tense when referring to *Eretz Yisrael*.

How is *Eretz Yisrael* ours?

It is ours only because G-d gave it, *and gives it*, to us as our possession.*

This should be our approach to Israel *today*. It is ours and will remain ours as long as G-d *wants* it to be ours.

Nobody, then, can take *Eretz Yisrael* away from us.

No United Nations, no Arab nations, and no Western country can take Israel away from us.

כִּי אִם יְמִין ה׳ רוֹמֵמָה לָתֵת לָנוּ נַחֲלַת גּוֹיִם כִּי לֹא בְחַרְבָּם יָרְשׁוּ אָרֶץ. (כְּלִי יָקָר).

The *Kli Yakar* explains this sentence as follows: *Eretz Yisrael* is never to be viewed as a land of *our* possession.

We did not get *Eretz Yisrael* because of our superior army or because of our victory in battle. It is our land because Hashem's Hand was uplifted high to give us a land that other nations were claiming. Only Hashem is our strength, and our power, whenever we speak about *Eretz Yisrael* as being ours.

---

* Throughout the Torah, the expression *that I give you* is always used when speaking about *Eretz Yisrael*.

Torah Temimah asked pertinent questions concerning the opening sentences quoted above:

- Why did G-d foretell that there would be a plague in the houses of Canaan when *Bnei Yisrael* arrived?
- Above all, why is this *nega* destroying our house, making it spiritually impure and unusable?

Rashi explains:

The Emori nations in the land of Canaan feared the oncoming Israelites. They hid their treasures in the walls of their homes. The *nega* was a *gift* to the Jewish people. When the *nega* appeared in the wall, it caused the wall to be broken open, to be replastered, to be repainted; perhaps to be totally replaced. Meanwhile all the hidden treasures were discovered by the Children of Israel.

Remember:

> *Eretz Yisrael* is ours because G-d *gives* it to us as a possession. Therefore, it is not really our possession. It is *always* G-d's.

Remember:

> Everything in the world belongs to G-d. Therefore, *share* your possessions with others.

Remember:

> Do not speak *evil* against your neighbors.
> Do not cause rifts among people.

5

Work, Learn, and Improve!

⇝ *Change Yourself Through Mussar*

The goal of *mussar* is to enable us to realize what to strive for in our service of Hashem. We must begin to practice what we learn in our daily lives, in word, deed, and thought. When we achieve this, we become partners in Divine Creation.

⇝ *Mussar Versus Chassidus*

Rabbi Yisrael Salanter, the founder of the *Mussar* Movement, was a *talmid* of a great *tzaddik nistar* (hidden *tzaddik*), Rabbi Zundel of Salant. One particular encounter proved to be a turning point for Reb Yisrael, and for future generations as well.

One day, Reb Yisrael followed Reb Zundel into the forest to watch the manner in which he prayed and conducted other aspects of his service of Hashem in private. Reb Zundel, like other great *tzaddikim,* would often tear himself away from the world around him to meditate in the stillness of the forest, without interruptions or distractions.

Reb Zundel turned around and saw Reb Yisrael following him. He shouted to him,

"Yisrael, study *mussar*!"

Reb Yisrael understood the full meaning of this three-word statement:

Study mussar! Learn the classic works of *middos* and ethics such as *Mesillas Yesharim, Shaarei Teshuvah* and *Chovos HaLevavos.* Absorb their lessons and acquire greater *yiras shamayim, emunah,* and good *middos. Live every moment according to these teachings.*

Study mussar.

This encounter had such an impact on Reb Yisrael that it completely changed his approach to spiritual development. It was there in the forest that the *Mussar* Movement was born.

> Reb Yisrael is reported to have said that both the *chassid* and the *misnaged* (i.e. the non-*chassid*) deserve to be punished. Why? The *chassid* is at fault if he thinks that he does not need to study Torah since he has a *rebbe;* and the *misnaged* is at fault if he thinks that he does not need a *rebbe,* since he has the *sefer* from which he studies Torah.

Of course, both of these approaches are not valid. Every Jew needs his *sefer,* and every Jew needs his *rebbe.* Both the chassidic and non-chassidic traditions recognize this; it is only their approaches to reaching their common goal which differ.

I remember hearing Rabbi Shraga Feivel Mendlowitz explain one of the differences between *chassidus* and *mussar.* He gave the example of an ant crawling on the ground, making its way slowly to its destination. Suddenly, it came upon a log blocking its path and was unable to go over the log.

The ant had two choices.

- One was to stop in front of the log and go no further.
- The other choice was to go around the log.

The ant decided to go around the log.

Rabbi Mendlowitz said that *chassidus* believes that reaching Hashem is within everyone's reach regardless of what obstacles appear along the way. Should there be an obstacle in the way, it should be circumvented.

- One should go around the obstacle.
- Try to avoid paying any attention to it.
- Move oneself into a *nigun.*
- Sing a song to *HaKadosh Baruch Hu.*
- Feel the happiness of serving Hashem!
- *Do not stand still* in that one place.
- Eventually, the problem will disappear.

Mussar, on the other hand, believes that one should *delve into* and evaluate the obstacle.

Get rid of the obstacle.

- If you see a "log" in the way, then do away with it.
- How? Delve into it until you realize that the obstacle is nothing more than a worthless hindrance.
- It cannot stand in the way of serving Hashem. It must be overcome.
- It *can* be overcome.

Mussar means serving Hashem with your *mind.*

Chassidus means serving Hashem with your *heart,* with your *emotions.*

Chassidus has a very significant place in Judaism. The *Baal Shem Tov* saved hundreds of thousands of Jews whose families had been destroyed by massacres and pogroms. The people felt that their faith in Hashem was weakening.

They were despondent and had drifted away from Torah study.

They were getting lost.

Through the power of song and *tefillah,* emotional uplift, immersing themselves in the glow and warmth of their *rebbe* and his Torah wisdom, trying to *emulate* their *rebbe,* the people were able to raise themselves from their lethargy and once again to serve Hashem with fervor and joy.

Their *rebbe* was a powerful, inspirational force in their lives.

In truth, *chassidim* did, and do, study Torah a great deal. Today, there are tens of thousands of Chassidic *bachurim* studying Torah intensively in yeshivos around the world. One cannot and must not say that *chassidim* do not consider Torah study a priority. *They surely do.* However, they also *sing* their praises to Hashem; they become emotionally involved in His service in a very pronounced way.

In truth, *talmidim* of non-Chassidic yeshivos also sing *nigunim* and strive to serve Hashem with joy and emotion.

Both serve G-d, both strive to achieve *shleimus,* spiritual perfection. Their goals are the same; only their methods differ.

◈§ *"As Long as the Candle Still Burns . . ."*

Reb Yisrael saw that in his time, Torah observance had become a matter of habit for many. It was an *observance* without thought or emotion. The purpose of *mitzvos* is to purify man, but when *mitzvos* are done mechanically, they lack the necessary power to accomplish this.

Reb Yisrael related:

> "I was walking down the street late at night when I saw a candle burning in a window. I looked through the window and saw a shoemaker working. I tapped on the window and said to the shoemaker: 'It is nearly midnight, why don't you go to sleep?'
>
> The shoemaker replied, 'ווי לאַנג אַז דאָס ליכְטְעלֶע בְּרֶענְט, קֶען מעֶן נאָך פאַריכְטעֶן, *As long as the candle burns, one can still work and repair.*' "

Reb Yisrael became tremendously excited upon hearing this response, for he saw in it a lesson for life. Later, he entered the *beis midrash* where his *talmidim* were studying and exclaimed: "As long as the light of the *neshamah* is burning, as long as we are still alive on this world, we can still work to repair and improve ourselves."

◄§ *Changing Yourself*

In our daily *davening* we pray for the day when *Mashiach* will come לְתַקֵּן עוֹלָם בְּמַלְכוּת שַׁ־דַּי, *to perfect the world through the reign of Hashem* (see *Commentary of Rabbi S.R. Hirsch*).

The word לְתַקֵּן means *to fix, to correct, to perfect.* To take a hammer and nails and start to improve an item's appearance is to begin fixing it. But it's only a beginning. The goal is to continue working on improving the item's look until it is a perfect product of which its craftsman can be proud.

In *mussar,* לְתַקֵּן means to fix *oneself,* to help us improve ourselves little by little until each of us becomes an *adam hashaleim,* a person who is spiritually perfect. The purpose of *mussar* is to teach and inspire people to live in complete adherence to the Torah's teachings. In this way, they will lead *happier,* more *purposeful* and more *productive* lives.

> A person may possess a bad *middah,* a negative character trait. It is his task, his mission, to correct that *middah* so that he can become an *adam hashaleim.*

Reb Yisrael would say:

It is more difficult to change a bad *middah* than to learn a difficult topic in *Gemara*. A difficult question in the *Gemara* can be answered. Search through and study the commentaries and you will resolve the difficulties that are bothering you. It may take many hours, even days, but ultimately, you will be successful.

- To change a bad characteristic in yourself, you must look *into yourself*. Nobody can help you unless you are ready and willing to help yourself.
- To change your own personality requires tremendous self-control.

Such change can take months, even years, and it requires dedication and commitment.

This is what *mussar* is all about. Through *mussar* study, you will learn to

study *your self*.

Apply the *mussar* ideas and ideals towards a betterment of *your self*. If you *persevere* in changing a bad character trait, you will have achieved a monumental accomplishment which will affect you and your future generations for all eternity.

In speaking about his *mussar* program, Reb Yisrael said: "I am not going to tell you anything new. I am not approaching *avodas Hashem* in a new way."

In the *Gemara*, when Judean kings did something that previous kings did not do, an expression is often used:

מָקוֹם הִנִּיחוּ לוֹ אֲבוֹתָיו לְהִתְגַּדֵּר בּוֹ

This means that G-d arranged an opportunity (and challenge) for the newly crowned king that he could rise to; a mission for which he was uniquely endowed to fulfill. The new king could breathe fresh life into his people, adding a new dimension of spirituality during his reign.

Reb Yisrael, in his unique way, breathed new life into his people by stressing the study of *mussar* which had been deemphasized by previous generations and was somewhat neglected.

He said:

"Acquiring *yiras shamayim* requires חָכְמָה עֲצוּמָה, *tremendous wisdom*. It is an עֲבוֹדָה כַּבֵּירָה, *a difficult task to accomplish.*

"You must put a great deal of effort into serving Hashem with true *yiras shamayim.*"

זֶה כְּלָלָה שֶׁל מוּסָר

A person puts his *tallis* over his head and thinks that this is his display of *yiras shamayim.* One cannot become a *yirei shamayim* by rattling off his *davening* in the morning or learning something superficially and then going on to another subject. Acquiring *yiras shamayim* requires *effort.*

⪧ Firm and Unchanging

יִרְאַת שָׁמַיִם

Y iras shamayim literally means fear of Heaven. When we speak about *yiras Hashem,* surely we mean fear and awe of Hashem. Why, then, do we use the term *shamayim,* Heaven? What follows is one answer to this question.

The Torah begins:

בְּרֵאשִׁית בָּרָא אֱלֹקִים אֵת הַשָּׁמַיִם וְאֵת הָאָרֶץ
In the beginning, G-d created heaven and earth (*Bereishis* 1:1).

Thus, we learn that heaven was created on the first day.

On the second day, G-d proclaimed: יְהִי רָקִיעַ, *Let there be a firmament* (heaven) . . . . וַיַּעַשׂ אֱלֹהִים אֶת הָרָקִיעַ, *And G-d made the firmament* . . . . . וַיִּקְרָא אֱלֹהִים לָרָקִיעַ שָׁמַיִם, *And G-d called the rakia, shamayim* (heaven) (*Bereishis* 1:6-8).

It is interesting to note that it does not say:

"G-d *created* the *rakia,*" but rather, "G-d *made* the *rakia.*"

Rashi explains:

If heaven was created on the first day, what happened on the second day? It seems to be repetitious.

He answers:

"On the first day heaven was created. However, it was *not* completely set in its place. They were *weak, soft,* and pliable.

On the second day, when G-d proclaimed: "Let there be a *rakia* in the midst of the waters," the *rakia* stood still, strong and immovable in its place.

From that moment on, the *shamayim* has stayed in its place. From the proclamation יְהִי, *Let there be,* the *shamayim* remains forever steadfast.

You could still not see the earth. The water, beneath the heaven, beneath this *rakia,* receded on the third day. One was then able to see the earth.

We see changes in the earth. We see earthquakes, tornadoes, and hurricanes. We see floods which remove the topsoil of the earth. We see changes in the earth. We see changes in mountains.

But the heaven has remained steadfast, from the command of *HaKadosh Baruch Hu* when He said: *yehi rakia.*

This is why we speak about *yiras shamayim. Yiras shamayim* means steadfastness. If we truly feel awe of Hashem, then we should be steadfast and unchanging in our service of Him. Just as the *shamayim* has never changed or wavered since the second day of creation, when it was given its name, so too should we be unwavering in our commitment to Torah.

New generations, new "isms," new theories, new goals, new ideals, and new life styles that evolve cannot and will not change our steadfastness as Jews who are loyal to Hashem and His Torah.

ᵛᶳ *Acting on Instinct*

Rabbi Yisrael Salanter stressed the importance of translating one's learning into action. Torah learning must have a purpose in one's life. In order to translate learning into action, one *must* study *mussar.*

Before Reb Yisrael's time, people were on a much higher level and were able to draw *yiras shamayim* and *mussar* from their regular *Gemara* learning. Now, we must learn *mussar sefarim* to help us reach a higher degree of service to Hashem and acquire true *yiras shamayim.*

Reb Yisrael spoke about the subconscious mind of the individual, his instinctive self. He said that by learning *mussar,* you will come to the degree wherein subconsciously, without thinking, you will translate everything you learn into action. Your learning will become a part of your subconscious.

An example he gave to explain this is as follows:

A certain *rebbi* learned with a *talmid* whom he loved. This *talmid* followed behind the *rebbi* in the streets, for he wanted to learn from his *rebbi's* behavior and emulate it.

The *rebbi* also had a son, with whom he had disagreements very often. His son was not interested in learning.

When asked, the *rebbi* would say that if he had to choose between the two, he would choose his *talmid.*

Yet, said Reb Yisrael:

"If, while this man were sleeping, he was awakened by a cry of 'FIRE,' *he would rescue his son first.* At such a time, a person responds through instinct and it is instinctive for a father to rescue his own child in time of danger."

One must use *mussar* learning to develop his attachment to Torah and *mitzvos* to such a degree that he instinctively acts and reacts in the way of Torah all day, in every situation. One can serve Hashem properly and climb higher and higher as a Torah Jew only if in his subconscious mind, he seeks to fulfill His will.

This, assimilating one's learning into his subconscious, is a condition set forth by Reb Yisrael for acquiring true *yiras shamayim.* When this happens, *yiras shamayim* will flow through his bloodstream and become a part of his very nature.

~§ The Last Laugh

My *Rebbi,* Rabbi Shraga Feivel Mendlowitz, told us, "I do not know how great you will become by attending Torah Vodaath, by being one of my *talmidim* and coming to my classes. I do not know whether I will create *tzaddikim,* but one thing I will accomplish:

הֲנָאָה פוּן אַן עֲבֵירָה וועֶט אִיהר נִישט הָאבֶּען

When you will commit an aveirah it will bother you.
You will derive no pleasure from it."

Of course, an even higher level would be to avoid the sin entirely. That is what Reb Yisrael Salanter referred to. If you want to partake of sweets (i.e. *aveirah*), and have fun, you should first think now of the consequences you will have to face on the morrow.

This can be compared to a sick man with a stomach ailment who must adhere to a rigid diet. If he attends an affair and lets his guard down, and is not strict with what he eats, afterwards he will feel ill and suffer great pain.

Reb Salanter said:

If your learning penetrates into your mind and heart and becomes your natural way of life, then you will be on the road to becoming a true *yirei shamayim*. And with true *yiras shamayim*, one will ponder the consequences before he acts.

This point can be better explained by comparing two similar words:

יִצְחָק – מְצַחֵק

- יִצְחָק is the name of one of our *Avos*. It is a name which embodies *kedushah* (holiness) and *gevurah* (inner strength).
- מְצַחֵק, which literally means *is laughing,* is used by the Torah to describe the behavior of Yishmael when Sarah told Avraham to banish him from their home out of concern that he would be a negative influence upon Yitzchak (*Bereishis* 21:9-10).

Rashi comments there that the word מְצַחֵק refers to immorality, murder, and idol worship — the Three Cardinal Sins.

The two words, יִצְחָק and מְצַחֵק, have the same *shoresh*, root, which, as mentioned above, refers to *laughter*.

- However, יִצְחָק is a holy word and the name chosen for one of our *Avos*.
- מְצַחֵק is the complete opposite, and refers to a wrongdoer.

Where is the difference between these two words? It is their respective tenses.

- מְצַחֵק is in the *present* tense. I laugh *now*.
- יִצְחָק is in the *future* tense. He *will* laugh.

The juvenile delinquent does not think about the consequences of his actions. He laughs *now*. He does not think about *tomorrow*. He will regret what he did today.

יִצְחָק means *he will laugh.* Of course, you can enjoy today, even to the point of laughter, provided that you do not do anything that you will regret tomorrow. This was the difference between Yitzchak and Yishmael. Yishmael laughed for the moment but regretted it later. Yitzchak means that he *will be* happy tomorrow as well. Tomorrow, when he thinks about today's enjoyment, he will still be happy. There will be no regrets. Yitzchak laughs eternally because he was a man who feared Hashem and always thought of the consequences of his actions.

⋖§ A Master Plan

אֵין תּוֹעֶלֶת לִקְרֹא פַּעַם אַחַת

The introduction to *Mesillas Yesharim,* the classic *mussar sefer* by Rabbi Moshe Chaim Luzzatto, states:

Little will be accomplished by learning a *mussar* thought, just *one time.* Rather, it must be reviewed again and again. One should become a *masmid,* a diligent student, in his *mussar* learning.

He should take one idea and review it many times until it becomes part of his thinking, and then a part of his subconscious self. This is how learning and reviewing *mussar* helps a person to become a *yirei shamayim.*

In some yeshivos, 15 to 30 minutes a day are allocated for *mussar* study. Some students learn *Mesillas Yesharim* for years during these sessions. They review it over and over again.

⋖§ The Water and the Rock

When Rabbi Akiva was 40 years old he was an ignorant shepherd. Rachel, a righteous young woman who recognized Akiva's potential, kept urging him to learn. She would not marry scmeone who did not learn Torah.

Avos DeR' Nosson (Ch. 6) tells us: One day, R' Akiva stood by the base of a tumbling stream and noticed a hollowed-out rock. He asked, "Who hollowed this out?" They told him, "The water which drips upon the rock day after day."

He reasoned:

"If water can hollow out solid rock, then surely the Torah whose words are as strong as iron can make an impression on my heart of flesh and blood!" R' Akiva began to learn until he became a great and outstanding scholar, the leader of his generation.

Torah learning, and especially *mussar* learning, is like water dripping upon hard stone. One idea, one thought, that is reviewed again and again, eventually finds its way to the depths of one's heart.

It is difficult to learn a lot of *mussar* at one time. Like medicine, *mussar* should be administered in small doses. One must take *one* thought, *one* idea, at a time. In previous generations, when it came to the month of Elul and all Jews went to *shul* and heard the *shofar* every morning, that was enough *mussar*. One *shofar* blast made them all awaken to the forthcoming days of judgment.

Today we are so involved with material needs and day-to-day living that the *shofar* alone is not enough. Today there is *timtum halev,* the heart has become blocked, hardened. We do not hear the message anymore.

When a businessman is about to invest a large sum of money for his next year's inventory, he devotes a great deal of time. He speaks to other businessmen and marketing consultants before making decisions as to what to buy, how much to buy, and how to advertise his products. He constantly reviews his decisions to make sure that they are accurate.

The same is true of *mussar* study. You must work on *yourself.* You must overcome obstacles in order to succeed. You must do battle with the *yetzer hara.* This requires study, review, thought, strategy— and time.

✑ Be Inspired

While it is possible to study *mussar* on your own, it is extremely worthwhile to hear words of inspiration from someone who has already succeeded in molding his character through Torah learning and *mussar* study.

Rabbi Aharon Kotler was not especially tall physically but was a giant in Torah learning and leadership. He spoke not only with his voice, but also with his eyes. His eyes sparkled with the light of Torah, with a holiness and purity borne from taking words of *mussar* and making them a part of his very being.

Reb Aharon, like other great Torah teachers, would stress to his *talmidim* that a Jew must think about the future, about the *din v'cheshbon* (judgment and reckoning) that every person must face when he leaves this world.

Of course, some people might become pessimistic and downcast if they would contemplate only their misdeeds and the judgment which they will face on account of them.

- Therefore, you need the other aspect as well.
- One must think about the infinite rewards he will receive in the next world and of the joy which serving Hashem brings us in *this world.*
- Thus, he will become uplifted.

Although women do not have the *mitzvah* to learn Torah for its sake alone, the need to learn *mussar* applies to them as well. Rabbi Yisrael Salanter states: "The subject of *mussar* is unlike any other. Whereas . . . women are exempt from the obligation to study Torah . . . such is not the case with *mussar* — no one is exempt" (*Ohr Yisrael* Ch. 3).

There are many lectures given by knowledgeable yeshivah and Bais Yaakov graduates so that women, too, can be inspired throughout their adult years.

Those who have already graduated yeshivah have attained a certain level of *avodas Hashem.* Yet, all their lives, they continue to attend *mussar* lectures by great *roshei yeshivah* and *rebbeim.* In this way, they are continuously inspired and constantly grow. A little bit of *mussar* learning helps the individual in his everyday life in any field and helps him grow every day. However, when one stops learning, he is at a standstill, he stagnates.

You must forever study or listen to another *vort,* another *mussar* idea so that you will not become lethargic in your *avodas Hashem.* When hearing a new thought or reviewing one you have already learned, you will tell yourself,

"Look, there is still room for me to improve. I must continue to work on myself."

A man once came to Rabbi Yisrael Salanter and said that he could only spare a half hour a day to learn."

"Should I learn *Gemara* or should I learn *mussar*?" he asked. "Surely *Gemara* is far more important than *mussar.*"

Reb Yisrael answered:

"But the greatness of *mussar* is that if you would learn *mussar* for a half hour a day, you will find another hour to learn *Gemara.*" Such is the power of *mussar*.

Often when a person says the *Shema,* he thinks that G-d is the Master of the entire universe.

But, he forgets that G-d is also *his* Master.

Do not think only in terms of grandiose things, that G-d is the Creator of the world. When you say *Shema,* think of *Ol Malchus Shamayim,* that you accept upon *yourself* that G-d is *your* Master and you must do the things He commands you to.

Reb Yisrael said that before he studied *mussar* he used to find fault with others, not himself.

"Now that I am learning *mussar*, I see only my own shortcomings. I do not see other people's shortcomings."

This is the greatness of *mussar*:
- Work on *yourself.*
- Study *mussar* regularly —
- Improve yourself constantly.
- Continue to delve sincerely and thoughtfully into your inner self.
- Aspire to reach perfection in your service of Hashem.

❧ Torah

6

The Power of Torah

The Respect Due to Torah
You, too, Can Become an Outstanding Talmid Chacham and Even a Great Torah Luminary

The following story is related about Rabbi Akiva and his development:

Akiva was a shepherd to Kalba Savua, one of the wealthiest men in Yerushalayim. Kalba Savua had a daughter, Rachel, who chose to marry Akiva, and this made Kalba Savua very unhappy, to say the least.

Akiva was 40 years old, and unlearned in Torah, but he was a very honest and diligent worker. Rochel saw greatness in Akiva, and when asked for her hand in marriage, Rachel agreed, on one condition: that he go learn, and try to master the intricacies and depth of Torah.

Akiva did not feel that, at the age of 40, he was capable of becoming a *talmid chacham.* However, one day he passed a stream of water flowing over a cliff. At the bottom of the cliff was a rock which had an indentation in its smooth, solid surface.

Akiva stopped short, looking and staring at the steady dripping of the water.

He realized that if he would persevere, and learn "drop by drop," day after day, he could, and would, become a *talmid chacham,* as Rachel has foreseen.

Rachel's father was aghast at this *shidduch* for his beloved daughter. He tried to prevent the engagement but to no avail. Kalba Savua finally made a *neder* (vow) that he would disown Rachel if she persisted in marrying Akiva.

Rachel did marry Akiva with the condition that he go to the yeshivah and learn. This Akiva did faithfully and totally.

◄§ *A Proper Outlook*

The couple lived in poverty, sleeping on straw. The *Gemara* tells us that Akiva realized that his wife came from the wealthiest home in Yerushalayim, and he felt terrible that she was reduced to sleeping on straw, which constantly entangled itself into their hair.

אָמַר לָהּ אִי הֲוַאי לִי רָמֵינָא לֵיךְ יְרוּשָׁלַיִם דְּדַהֲבָא (נְדָרִים נ:א)

He said to her, "When I am able to, I will make you a beautiful piece of jewelry, a tiara of gold depicting the beauty of Yerushalayim." (Indeed, he eventually did give Rachel this elegant ornament [*Shabbos* 59a].)

The *Gemara* goes on to relate that Eliyahu *Hanavi* came to Rachel and Akiva in the form of a human being and asked them if they had a little straw to spare for him. *Rashi* and *Ran* explain that Eliyahu wanted them to feel a bit better with regard to their poverty, knowing that there was someone who had even less than they, who did not even have a piece of straw.

It is human nature for a person not to feel downtrodden when he has a bit more than someone else.

In our daily *davening,* at the very end of the first paragraph of *Aleinu,* we say:

וְיָדַעְתָּ הַיּוֹם וַהֲשֵׁבֹתָ אֶל לְבָבֶךָ כִּי ה' הוּא הָאֱלֹקִים בַּשָּׁמַיִם מִמַּעַל וְעַל הָאָרֶץ מִתָּחַת אֵין עוֹד.

"You should know this day and take to your heart that G-d is the Lord of Heaven above, and also on the earth below; there is none other."

In a play on words:

- *Shamayim,* heaven, refers to *ruchnius;* heavenly, spiritual values of life.
- *Eretz,* earth, refers to *gashmius;* physical and material values of life.

I: When thinking of heavenly and spiritual matter,
    always look *above* you.
- This person does more *mitzvos* than you.
- This person learns more than you do.
- He devotes more of his leisure hours to Torah.
- This person gives more *tzedakah* than you do.

In *mitzvos* and *ruchnius,* look *above* you.
- Try to be as good as that other person is.
- There is room for improvement
    in *your* serving Hashem.

II: In earthly and material matters,
    look *below* you.
- That person is missing many more comforts than you.
- He cannot afford all the material things
    you are able to buy.
- He cannot go on a vacation as you do.

In material comforts, look *below* you.
- Be satisfied with what you *do* have.
- Thank G-d for all His blessings
    bestowed upon you and yours.

With these two thoughts as guides for your life, you will become a happier person. You will also become a finer and more respected individual.

⊷ Rachel's Selflessness

Rachel told Akiva that she wanted him to begin learning immediately. Akiva left home for 12 years to learn with Rabbi Eliezer and Rabbi Yehoshua, the greatest sages of the time. At the end of 12 years he returned to his home, to his wife, Rachel. By that time he had already become learned and was a great rabbi.

He overheard someone (whom the *Gemara* calls "*Chad Rasha,*" a wicked person) berating Rachel in the following manner:

"It is a good thing that your father threw you out of the house. It was the right thing to do. Why did you not marry someone equal to you? (The *Ran* says that Akiva did not come from an "outstanding family." He did not have a "good family" background.)

"Akiva left you living like a widow. You have been separated from your husband for 12 years. You go around in tattered clothing. . .."

Rachel's answer was splendid:

"If my husband were to stay away for another 12 years and continue his studies in greater depth, I would be satisfied!"

We see in this reply Rachel's **mesiras nefesh,** utter self-sacrifice. *"Let him learn another 12 years.* I will continue to sleep on straw and wear tattered clothing." The *Midrash* says that she had beautiful hair, which she cut off and sold, in order to have money to sustain herself.

Upon hearing these words, Rabbi Akiva did not even enter the house. He returned immediately to the yeshivah to learn for an additional 12 years.

Note the *mesiras nefesh* of Rabbi Akiva as well. Rabbi Akiva felt that Rachel might feel worse if he came and left; if he came home for only a short while before returning to the yeshivah. Rabbi Akiva was also afraid that once he entered the house and saw the conditions under which his wife was living, he would not be able to leave her.

ও Study Without Interruption

One of my *rebbeim* offered still another explanation as to why Rabbi Akiva did not even visit his wife:

When one learns regularly and steadily, the power of his Torah study increases daily. The logic of Torah study, its philosophy and inspiration draws you closer to Hashem. The Torah becomes emotionally, mentally, and scholastically a part of you, so much so that you do not want to leave your Torah studies. Torah becomes part of your life, and as such, your life becomes completely bound up in Torah. There is a *continuous* craving to learn more and more Torah.

True, Rabbi Akiva could have stayed a few days and then returned to the yeshivah to learn for another 12 years. But there would have been a great difference in his learning. There would have been *two separate* 12-year periods rather than *one* 24-year period *without any interruption.*

≈§ All of It Is Hers

At the end of 24 years, Rabbi Akiva returned as a great *Rosh Yeshivah* with 24,000 *talmidim* in tow.

Remember, all this occurred soon after the *Churban Beis HaMikdash,* the destruction of our Holy Temple. Our people had lost the *central* point of *kedushah*; they had lost the *Beis HaMikdash.* The entire city of Yerushalayim had been pillaged and plundered by the Romans. The Romans wanted to destroy and bury it, leaving no trace of this holy city.

- The Jews remained united because they had a treasure that no other nation had.
- *They had the Torah!*
- Torah remained the *central* point of their lives.

At the end of 24 years, Rabbi Akiva traveled with all of his *talmidim* because none of them wanted to miss one word of their *rebbe's* Torah. People came from near and far to greet this now great and famous *talmid chacham* and *Rosh Yeshivah.*

Rachel, too, went to see this great man, Rabbi Akiva, who was her husband.

Kalba Savua was also going to meet this *gadol,* but he had no idea that this was his son-in law, the son-in-law whom he had rejected. Kalba Savua hoped that this great *Rosh Yeshivah* could annul his vow. He was now older; 24 years had passed. Kalba Savua wanted to welcome his daughter into his home once again.

The same person who had berated Rachel years before asked if she was going to meet the *Rosh Yeshivah.*

Rachel answered,

"Yes, and I will be welcomed."

When Rachel tried to get near Rabbi Akiva, the *talmidim* surround-ed him and cordoned him off, so that Rachel was not able to see him. However, Rabbi Akiva saw her from where he was sitting and said:

הַנִּיחוּ לָהּ, שֶׁלִּי וְשֶׁלָּכֶם שֶׁלָּהּ הוּא! (נדרים נ.) תּוֹרָתִי וְתוֹרַתְכֶם שֶׁלָּהּ הִיא:
עַל יָדָהּ הוּא כָּל מַה שֶּׁלָּמַדְתִּי – הִיא נָתְנָה לִי עֵצָה לְמֵיזַל לְבֵי רַב. (רש"י
וַר"ן)

"Let Rachel come here and stand by my side. All the Torah that I have learned, and all the Torah that I have taught you, *belongs to her.*

"To her belongs all the merits and privileges that have been earned through all the Torah for which I have worked so hard. The Torah learning that I labored at for 24 years, that I handed over to you, *belongs to her,* and not to me.

"Rachel, my wife, advised me and encouraged me to go to the yeshivah to learn" (*Nedarim* 50a).

Rachel followed a tradition beginning with our mother Sarah. Jewish wives and mothers have always had a major role in guiding their families. There is no nation in the world that gives their women as much *kavod,* honor, as the Jewish nation. There should be no such thing as a woman feeling inferior. Every mother in Israel should be involved in *chesed* and in rearing her family, so that she should be completely and *soul-fully* satisfied with her position and importance. It is important to bear this in mind nowadays, in a world where feminism is a major issue.

For example, when Sarah saw that Yishmael was having a bad influence on Yitzchak, she told Avraham to send Yishmael away (*Bereishis* 21:9-12). The two boys could not live together in one house.

Yishmael was doing wrong and would ruin Yitzchak. The *Midrash* says that he transgressed the three cardinal sins: idol worship, immorality, and murder.

At first Avraham felt badly about this until Hashem said:

כֹּל אֲשֶׁר תֹּאמַר אֵלֶיךָ שָׂרָה שְׁמַע בְּקֹלָהּ (בראשית כא:יב).
"Everything that Sarah tells you to do, *shema bekolah,*
listen to her voice" (*Bereishis* 21:12).

She visualizes the future better and more clearly than you do.

One of the commentaries points out the following:
- *Shema Yisrael* is the essence of faith in G-d,
- and is a most important part of our daily *davening*.

In a play on the two words *shema bekolah*, G-d said:
- "Whenever Sarah speaks, the *Shema* is *bekolah*, the *Shema* is in her voice.
- Sarah always speaks with the utmost of faith in what G-d would want done.
- You can literally hear the call of *Shema Yisrael* in her voice as she speaks.
- You can literally hear the *Hashem Echad*, the oneness of G-d in her voice, in her chosen words.
- Therefore, listen to her. Follow her advice."

At the same time that Rabbi Akiva was expressing his gratitude to Rachel, Kalba Savua was approaching Rabbi Akiva from a different direction and he did not see his daughter. He asked the great sage to annul his vow, which Rabbi Akiva did. How?

He asked Kalba Savua: "Had you known that your future son-in-law, Akiva, knew how to learn, or would one day become a renowned *talmid chacham*, would you have made such a vow?"

Kalba Savua answered: "If I had known that he would know the *alef beis*, I would not have made such a vow. He was an ignorant shepherd at the time. He knew absolutely nothing."

As a result, the vow was annulled.

◆§ Never Too Late

Rabbi Akiva seemed to be "nothing" until he reached the age of 40. We can learn a tremendous lesson from this. Today, youngsters begin yeshivah as early as the age of three or four. Some do not learn well, nor do they accomplish what is expected of them. However, there is hope for everyone. One can begin to learn at *any* age. Simple, unlearned Akiva became the great Rabbi Akiva even though he started to learn after the age of 40.

There are many *baalei teshuvah*, who never learned in their youth, who are returning to G-d. They begin learning, living, and practicing

Torah in later years. They have found satisfaction and success in their newly found spiritual lives.

- You must have the *will* to learn.
- You must find the power and the drive to *want* to learn.
- You must have the *mesiras nefesh* to learn!
- Without *mesiras nefesh* for Torah, you cannot become a *talmid chacham*.

It can be done!

You can do it!

Do not ever give up!

⋖ Proper Honor

What happened that caused so many of Rabbi Akiva's *talmidim* to die between Pesach and Shavuos?

Our Rabbis tell us:

לֹא נָהֲגוּ כָּבוֹד זֶה בָּזֶה

They did not respect one another.

They did not honor one another.

The *talmidim* of Rabbi Akiva were, indeed, great. *Chazal* say that they did not speak with proper respect to each other. This seems to have been some very minute transgression; yet the punishment was so great.

It is difficult to understand what happened.

Rabbi Yaakov Yitzchak Ruderman, the *Rosh Yeshivah* of Ner Yisroel in Baltimore, explained this phenomenon at a convention of Torah Umesorah as follows:

Rabbi Ruderman asked:

"How can we understand this statement? Surely such outstanding students of the great Rabbi Akiva must have respected one another."

Rabbi Ruderman cited a *Gemara*:

אָמַר ר׳ יוֹחָנָן: י״ב תַּלְמִידִים הָיוּ לוֹ לְרַבִּי אוֹשַׁעְיָא וְי״ח יָמִים גָּדַלְתִּי בֵּינֵיהֶן וְלָמַדְתִּי לֵב כָּל אֶחָד וְאֶחָד וְחָכְמַת כָּל אֶחָד וְאֶחָד (עירובין נג.א)

Rabbi Yochanan said:

"Rabbi Oshaya had 12 students. I spent 18 days amongst them. I examined and delved into their hearts. I studied their feelings and actions towards one another. I gained a knowledge of each one's intellectual powers and of each one's wisdom" (*Eruvin* 53a).

Rashi explains:
> "I gained an insight into the differences in their abilities to grasp the depth of the *Gemara*.
>
> "I also realized the differences in the wisdom they each attained, and how much more learned one was than the other."

Rabbi Yochanan spent 18 days judging, examining, and evaluating only 12 students. He harnessed all his powers of discernment to observe carefully how each student spent the day. He wanted to survey and inspect each individual action with a penetrating look. He wanted to perceive their individual differences and approaches. He wanted to look closely, to view these 12 students in all phases of their lives. Thus, Rabbi Yochanan spent 18 full days with them.
> What did he examine? How did he evaluate them?
> He examined their hearts as well as their minds.

Rabbi Ruderman asked:
"Why did Rabbi Yochanan devote 18 days to study and evaluate each student? How do you examine the hearts as well as the minds?"
The following was his answer:
> "One has to give honor and respect to every *talmid chacham*.
> How much *kavod* do you give
> - to a *talmid,*
> - to a *rebbi,*
> - to a colleague, or,
> - to a friend?
> Each person, according to the level of greatness that he has achieved, requires a specific degree of *kavod.*"

In order to judge the greatness of a person you must study him in depth. You must not only evaluate his Torah learning, but you must search out his heart as well.
- What kind of *middos* (character traits) does he have?
- What kind of a *mentsh* is he?
- Is he arrogant?
- Is he humble?

Therefore, you must evaluate each and every person individually. Each person may deserve a *different* degree of *kavod*:

- for his Torah learning,
- for his Torah learning combined with *yiras shamayim;*
- for his Torah learning combined with *derech eretz;* or
- for his Torah learning combined with exceptional *middos*.

There are many different levels.

This is the reason Rabbi Yochanan spent 18 full days at Rabbi Oshaya's yeshivah.

- He observed carefully how the *talmidim* behaved.
- He observed carefully the way they conducted their daily lives.

Commenting on the death of Rabbi Akiva's students, Rabbi Ruderman said:

"They did not give each other the *proper kavod*. Of course, they honored and respected each other. Perhaps they did not give each other the *true* and *proper kavod* according to their *individual greatness; according to their individual merits*."

I added a personal thought:

זֶה לָזֶה – זֶה בָּזֶה

- The words *Chazal* quote are not:
  "They did not extend honor *zeh lazeh, to one another.*"
- The exact words quoted are:
  "They did not extend honor *zeh bazeh, into one another.*"

The *inside* of each individual must be evaluated. You must know him thoroughly in *all* of his actions.

The *talmidim* of Rabbi Akiva were remiss in not evaluating each other in depth. Each one's beautiful Torah way of life went unnoticed, and he did not receive the proper *kavod* he truly deserved.

If the respect they gave each other was somewhat superficial, their actions towards each other were also superficial.

These actions showed a lack of understanding of the true value of their Torah as well as their character. Such deficiencies can, G-d forbid, lead to the destruction of *Klal Yisrael*. This is what brought about the terrible punishment meted out to Rabbi Akiva's students.

This resulted in the period of mourning between Pesach and Shavuos.

- All Israel must respect a student of Torah,
  a *talmid chacham.*
- Yeshivah students must always be *exemplary*
  in all of their actions towards their *rebbeim,*
  teachers, parents, friends, etc.
- Without giving proper *kavod* you are denigrating
  the greatness of Torah.
- Respect and honor everyone.
- Evaluate the level of respect and honor
  that each individual is entitled to.
- Be careful of *your own* character rating
  in the eyes of others.

This will bring *Mashiach.* quickly and soon, in our time, please G-d.

7

Ahavas Torah — Love of Torah

✍ *Five Minutes of Eternity*

W hat does love of Torah mean?
My *Rebbi* and *Rosh Yeshivah,* Rabbi Shlomo Heiman, used to say:

> If you observe a child who has been exposed to Torah learning, and you see that his eyes start to shine when he asks a question, or he is thrilled when he understands the answer to a troubling question in his studies, know that these are the signs of *his love* for Torah.

My *Rebbi* passed away 17 Kislev, 1945. My *Rebbi* was a *Rosh Yeshivah.* He was not teaching high school students or elementary school children; his *talmidim* were young men of post-high school age. But he noticed that every time the bell rang, the high school students ran to get a court to play. He saw how they enjoyed playing ball. Friday, after the 12 o'clock dismissal, they could play for hours.

My *Rebbi* used to say that he knows that boys love to play ball. And, he would continue, "If you can develop this kind of love in a child for Torah learning, then that youngster is on the road to becoming a *talmid chacham.*"

Some boys feel this love of Torah already in their junior high school year. There are boys in these grades who, whenever they have a spare moment, open a *sefer;* they are always learning, always reviewing. When they come to *shul* early, they learn, reviewing the *Gemara* they study in class. It is beautiful.

My *Rebbi,* R' Shlomo, used to say very often:

"Rabbi Akiva Eiger, the great outstanding *Gaon* of his generation, became a *talmid chacham* in five minutes."

Yet, we know this is impossible. Surely, Rabbi Akiva Eiger learned Torah day and night.

Rebbi explained:

"When Rabbi Akiva Eiger came to *shul* early, he never allowed a minute to go to waste. He would immediately take a *sefer* and begin to learn. If he only came five minutes early, he did not waste those five minutes."

Five minutes here, five minutes there, added to his learning and his stature.

In *Rebbi's* time they did not have the express elevators we have today, elevators that whisk you up to higher floors in a few seconds. In those days, you might spend as much as *five minutes* in an elevator each time that you entered one.

Rebbi said:

"Every business man who is a *ben Torah* should always have a *sefer* with him, whether it be a *Chumash, Mishnayos, sefer* of *Halachah,* etc.
- When he has five minutes to spare,
  the minutes should not be wasted.
- The *sefer* should be opened and the
  extra minutes should be used for LEARNING."

It is amazing to see how these minutes here and there add up to hours; and how they add up to your learning ability.

This is how Rabbi Akiva Eiger became as great as he was.

Do not waste precious minutes!

Rebbi said, "Becoming a *lamdan,* a Jew who is proficient in deep *Gemara* learning, is an ongoing process, day by day."

He once asked, "Who is a *lamdan?*

Is it a person who *knows how* to learn?"

Rebbi said,

"No, this does not fulfill the true meaning of a *lamdan.*"

He continued: "Who is a *ganav,* a thief?

Is it someone who *knows how* to steal?

Certainly not! Everyone of us *knows how* to steal!
- This *does not make* you a thief.
- A thief is one who *actually steals.*"

Likewise, a *lamdan* is not one who *knows how* to learn, but one who *actually learns,* day after day, hour after hour. He enjoys learning

Torah and avails himself of every possible opportunity to open a *sefer* and study Torah.

Rebbi would say that sometimes the *cheshek,* strong desire, to learn comes in the high school years, especially in the first year of *beis midrash.*

> "And once he starts learning, nothing will stop him from further developing this love for Torah."

When I was a young man, most of the boys of the Mesivta went to evening college classes. When I entered the *beis midrash,* I too was going to college. However, when I came to R' Shlomo's *shiur,* I developed such a love for him and he instilled in me such a love for Torah, that I stopped going to college for many years. I spent all day learning.

> This is what *ahavas Torah,* love of Torah, can do for you.

⤳ With Yiras Hashem

The Amshinover *Rebbe,* is a Chassidic *Rebbe* who lives in Bayit Vegan, *Eretz Yisrael.*

He is a *talmid* of mine.

When he was four years old, his great-grandfather R' Shimon called me and said: "Rabbi Schwartz, if you do not mind, I would like to come to see you. I want to talk to you. I want to ask you something about your yeshivah."

I immediately replied: "It will be my pleasure to meet with you concerning the goals and curriculum of the yeshivah. However, *I* will come to *your* home to discuss curriculum with you."

We made an appointment for *Motzaei Shabbos.* That Shabbos was the one immediately preceding the month of Elul.

As a former student of Torah Vodaath, I modeled my classes and selected *rebbeim* for my staff according to my own experiences under the great leadership of my *menahel,* Rabbi Shraga Feivel Mendlowitz, and my *Rosh Yeshivah,* Rabbi Shlomo Heiman. There were very few yeshivos in Boro Park and none on a par with ours. There were no chassidic yeshivos in the Boro Park or Flatbush neighborhoods. All chassidic parents sent their children to us.

When I came to Reb Shimon on *Motzaei Shabbos,* he and his son-in-law, Reb Sheah, both asked questions concerning our yeshivah's goals in Torah learning.

I told them what my *Rebbe,* Reb Shlomo, had said concerning developing a love for Torah.

I said:

> "I will be more than satisfied if I can be successful in instilling such *ahavas Torah* in the hearts and minds of all my *talmidim.*"

Reb Sheah became the Amshinover *Rebbe* after Reb Shimon passed away. He later settled in *Eretz Yisrael,* in Bayit Vegan.

He said to Reb Shimon: "Today we blessed the month of Elul and we prayed to Hashem

. . . שֶׁתְּהֵא בָנוּ אַהֲבַת תּוֹרָה וְיִרְאַת שָׁמַיִם

that *our lives* shall be blessed with and that *within* us, there shall be *ahavas Torah* and *yiras shamayim.*

These are two very different requests.

Yiras shamayim means awe. The way we show awe of G-d is by faithfully adhering to His every command.

But when we seek a life of Torah, we do not ask for *yiras HaTorah,* that Hashem instill in us awe of Torah, but rather, we ask for *ahavas Torah, love* of Torah.

I added, "In that blessing, our request for *ahavas Torah,* love of Torah, precedes *yiras shamayim,* awe of G-d.

"To attain proper *yiras shamayim,* we must first develop in ourselves *ahavas Torah.* Only after we have developed within ourselves true love of Torah can we achieve true and lofty *yiras shamayim.*"

I also said that we speak about *yiras Hashem* and *ahavas Hashem.* Though *yirah* is commonly translated as *fear,* this is not really accurate when speaking of *yiras Hashem.*

I have always explained *yirah* as "awe." We must develop a sense of awe in responding to Hashem's commandments. *Yiras Hashem* can perhaps best be explained as a blend of fear and reverence.

> To stand in awe of Hashem is to experience the highest respect for Hashem; to feel a total submission to His will, to stand ready to obey and fulfill every *mitzvah.*

ר׳ אַהֲרֹן מִקַּרְלִין אָמַר: יִרְאָה בְּלִי אַהֲבָה אֵינָה שְׁלֵמוּת,
אַהֲבָה בְּלִי יִרְאָה אֵינָה וְלֹא כְּלוּם

Rabbi Aharon of Karlin said: *Yirah,* awe, without a sense
of *ahavas Hashem,* love of Hashem, is lacking; a blend of
both is required — awe, tempered by, and permeated
with, love.

But,

love of Hashem, without a sense of being awestruck; love
of Hashem, without being overwhelmed by Hashem's
greatness; love of Hashem, without a sense of awe and
reverence for Hashem — is absolutely nothing.

Love of Hashem means to love Hashem's ways and to strive to
emulate them.

Awe of Hashem is a recognition of His greatness and is reflected by
a willingness to put the love of G-d above your personal desires.

We need both.

Awe and love interwoven as one.

Perhaps this is why we pray for both in one breath. We pray to be
blessed with a life consisting of love of Torah coupled with awe of
Hashem.

We demonstrate our love of Hashem through our love for His Torah
and his *mitzvos.*

It is this love which will insure our developing proper *yiras Hashem.*

The Amshinover *Rebbe* smiled softly and blessed me:

זָאלְעֶן אַלֶע תַּלְמִידִים פוּן אַלֶע יְשִׁיבוֹת אוֹיסוַואקְסֶען מִיט אַ לִיבְּשַׁאפְט
פַאר תּוֹרָה — מִיט אַהֲבַת תּוֹרָה

"May all the students of all yeshivos grow up with this
all-embracing love for Torah."

This was the blessing I received from R' Shimon and I want to share
it with all my students.

In order to grow in Torah,
you must develop a love for Torah.

◆§ *"Our Father, Merciful Father"*

Every day, in our morning and in our evening prayers, we recite a
blessing concerning Torah and our love for learning Torah.

Twice a day we beseech Hashem for His help in developing within
ourselves a love for Torah.

It is interesting to note that in *Shacharis,* in the blessing of *Ahavas Olam* (or *Ahavah Rabbah*), which is recited immediately before *Shema,* we beseech Hashem:

אָבִינוּ אָב הָרַחֲמָן הַמְרַחֵם רַחֵם עָלֵינוּ

"Our Father, Merciful Father, Who acts mercifully, have mercy on us.

What is the blessing we ask of You, O G-d?

We do not ask for wealth, nor do we mention material or physical requests of any kind.

וְתֵן בְּלִבֵּנוּ בִּינָה לְהָבִין וּלְהַשְׂכִּיל לִשְׁמוֹעַ לִלְמוֹד וּלְלַמֵּד לִשְׁמוֹר וְלַעֲשׂוֹת וּלְקַיֵּם . . .

"Instill understanding in our hearts, the ability to understand and elucidate,

- . . . to listen
- . . . to learn myself
- . . . to teach others, to help others learn
- . . . to guard my teachings
- . . . to do, to actively fulfill

אֶת כָּל דִּבְרֵי תַלְמוּד תּוֹרָתֶךָ בְּאַהֲבָה

all the words of your Torah's teaching with love.

וְהָאֵר עֵינֵינוּ בְּתוֹרָתֶךָ וְדַבֵּק לִבֵּנוּ בְּמִצְוֹתֶיךָ

May our eyes sparkle and shine with Torah.

Enlighten our eyes, attach our hearts to Your commandments.

וְיַחֵד לְבָבֵנוּ לְאַהֲבָה וּלְיִרְאָה אֶת שְׁמֶךָ – לְמַעַן לֹא נֵבוֹשׁ וְלֹא נִכָּלֵם

Unite our hearts to love and revere Your Name so that we *may never feel shame* or humiliation."

Why does a Jew ask for all these blessings each and every day of his life?

- Not because he wants to be recognized as a *talmid chacham,*
- not because he wants to be respected and looked up to by everyone,
- not because he wants to take advantage of the physical pleasures of this world,
- not because he wants to receive a "pat on the back"

- Only so that he should never feel inner shame or humiliation, for lack of knowledge in Torah.
- Only so that he can fulfill his mission on this world by attaining his potential as a Torah scholar and keeper of the Torah through love and attachment to its *mitzvos.*

You are asking for all these blessings, not for the sake of Hashem. *"Do it for my sake, please, G-d."*

Some people might ask for wealth, for successful financial ventures. They want to go on vacation. They want two cars. Thet may want to take a trip around the world. They may want to enjoy themselves, to have a good time.

Our prayer is entirely different.

There are two parts to this prayer:

The first part, which we have discussed, concerns Torah in all its aspects:

- We should love Torah and we should fulfill the Torah's commandments;
- not only to learn but also to teach and to put our learning to practice.

The second part of this prayer concerns

- our love for *Eretz Yisrael,*
- our yearning for the Redemption,
- our love for Hashem
- and Hashem's love for us.

It refers to קִבּוּץ גָּלֻיּוֹת, *the ingathering of the exiles* when *Mashiach* will come.

"Bring us in peace from the four corners of the world and lead us with upright pride to our land; for You bring about salvations, Hashem.

You have chosen us from among every people and tongue. You have brought us close to Your great Name forever, in truth; so that we may praise You and proclaim Your Oneness with love; Blessed are You, Hashem, Who chooses His people, Yisrael, with love."

A profound love for Hashem and His Torah is echoed in this *berachah,* which is a prayer for spiritual enlightenment.

Let our hearts concentrate upon the lofty goals expressed in this beautiful prayer and not be distracted by worldly desires.

✂§ The Evening Prayer

I n *Shacharis,* we pray for Torah and *geulah,* redemption. In daytime, when everything is bright and beautiful, and we feel redemption beckoning as the sun appears on the horizon, we pray for these two most important *needs.*

In the *Maariv* prayer, at night, when it is dark, and we are in *galus,* exile, we pray only for Torah.

Even if we are scattered throughout the world, we remain bound together as a nation of Hashem through
the *strong bonds* of *Torah.*

Though we are still in *galus,* and we may not be worthy of Redemption as of yet,

- We still have Torah and *mitzvos.*
- They are our life and the length of our days;
and we will meditate about them day and night.
- Torah will forever keep us alive as Jews.
- Through our allegiance to Torah, we will never
forget our traditions and our past.

- If the Jew has Torah, he will never get lost.
- If the Jew has Torah, then he has a bit of *Eretz Yisrael* in
him as well.

מָה אָהַבְתִּי תוֹרָתֶךָ כָּל הַיּוֹם הִיא שִׂיחָתִי (תהילם קיט:צז)

O, how I love Your Torah! All day long it is my conversation (Tehillim 119:97).

Rabbi Samson R. Hirsch explains this sentence:
O how I have come to love Your teachings, it is my meditation all day.

Because Hashem's Torah extends to every aspect of life, and there is no moment that does not derive value and purpose from His Torah, therefore, Torah is the theme of my speech and meditation all day long.

Rabbi Eliezer ben Shamua applies this sentence to his disciple,

Yosef HaBavli, to whom Torah learning was his joy and whose face shone when he heard a Torah thought (*Menachos* 18a).

This is true *ahavas Torah.*

Develop within yourselves a love for Torah learning. With proper Torah learning, we will better understand our responsibilities in serving Hashem properly.

Most yeshivah elementary schools have four hours of Torah sessions each day. Years ago, that was all the time that was devoted to Torah studies. Today, some yeshivos have added another hour, or more, to this part of the curriculum.

My slogan for all of you to follow is:
- Do not be a four-hour Torah learning Jew.
- Be a 24-hour Torah *living* Jew.

Develop for yourself a *seder* (order) to meet a friend as your *chavrusa,* your study partner, on Shabbos afternoon. Review your studies for the week. Attend an *oneg Shabbos* get-together, where the atmosphere is Torah oriented.

What I am asking is that you should grow daily in your love for Torah learning. Live up to your potential. Rise to the challenge of becoming as great as you *can* become — the sky's the limit.

Preparation for your future through Torah education will insure the future generation with Jewish identification and our people's continuation as loyal, committed Torah Jews.

8
Keys to Torah Learning

◆§ Three Fundamentals

To succeed in Torah and become a *talmid chacham,* it is necessary to focus on three fundamental aspects of Torah study:

1. Strive to become a בָּקִי בְּשַׁ״ס, one who is fluent in the entire Talmud. For this, one must have at least one daily *seder,* learning session, in which he covers ground quickly, rather than delve into every nuance of the *Gemara.* In this *seder,* one should learn *Gemara* with only the commentary of *Rashi.* Learn fast and learn a great deal. Cover ground, in order to increase your general knowledge of the Talmud.

   This is what *Daf Yomi* is accomplishing today. With *Daf Yomi,* you learn a *blatt* (two sides of a *Gemara* page) *every* day. You keep on moving. Sometimes there is simply no time to delve properly into the *blatt Gemara* that you are learning. This, indeed, is a drawback. But in the meantime you are learning a *blatt* of *Gemara* daily, and in seven and a half years you will finish all of *Shas,* the *entire* Talmud. Thus, you will have gained general knowledge in all areas of *Gemara* and *Halachah.*

2. You must also have a daily *seder* for learning *Gemara* בְּעִיּוּן, *in depth,* with *Tosafos* and other commentaries; with *Rishonim* and *Acharonim* (Earlier and Later Commentators). You must work hard and study with intensity. To learn בְּעִיּוּן means to learn with great *depth* and effort.

   In this method of learning, every conceivable question is asked and every conceivable answer is explored. The pros and cons of each explanation are suggested and weighed by you and your *chavrusa* (learning partner). Listen carefully to the way he understands the *Gemara*. Argue with *him relentlessly* if you honestly disagree with his line of thinking. Muster all your strength and ability to explain to him *your sevarah*, your thinking, your logic, your understanding of the *Gemara*. This is *limud b'iyun* in its ideal form.

Rabbi Shraga Feivel Mendlowitz, the *menahel* of Yeshiva and Mesivta Torah Vodaath, insisted that our two primary *sedarim*, fixed daily learning sessions, be very different from one another.

In the morning, we heard a *shiur* (lecture) from our *Rosh Yeshivah*, Rabbi Shlomo Heiman, *b'iyun*, in depth. We learned slowly. If we learned 20 *blatt Gemara* in the entire *z'man*, semester, it was considered a tremendous amount. It was considered a *z'man* well spent, a period of accomplishment.

In the morning, we would prepare the *Gemara* by ourselves. *Rebbi* would then give his *shiur* from 11:00 to 1:00. Following this, we would review the *Gemara*. This session could sometimes focus on only a few lines of *Gemara*. We reviewed these few lines with countless *mefarshim* (commentaries). Learning *Gemara* in yeshivah sharpens your mind and develops your thinking. If you learn the *Gemaras* taught in yeshivah well, you will be able to learn other *Gemaras* on your own, without a *rebbi*.

- The yeshivah can only teach you to sharpen
  your mind and *develop* your thinking.
- The yeshivah will give you a strong foundation
  in fundamental *Gemara* reasoning.

In this way, for the *rest of your life* you will be able to learn new areas of *Gemara* on your own.

Rabbi Mendlowitz said that the students should have a second *seder* each day to learn *Gemara* without *Tosafos*, or other *mefarshim*, only *Rashi*. This was our *seder* for the afternoon, generally from 3 to 5 o'clock. He wanted us to try to learn 100 *blatt Gemara* each year. This was done in order for the student to acquire *yedios*, general knowledge, in most areas of *Shas*.

3. You must learn *lishmah*, not for glory or for the selfish pleasure of besting your learning partner, but with the sincere desire to

know Hashem's Torah. When it comes to *emes*, truth, you have to honestly judge who is right, you or your *chavrusa*. If you decide that your *chavrusa* is right, then you must accept his understanding of the *Gemara* and drop your own explanation of the matter. Say to your *chavrusa*: "You are right." You have then attained clarity and truth in your learning. This is Torah *lishmah.*

◄§ Wars Which End in Love

There is a verse in the Torah which refers to the travels of the Jews in the Wilderness:

עַל כֵּן יֵאָמַר בְּסֵפֶר מִלְחֲמֹת ה', אֶת וָהֵב בְּסוּפָה וְאֶת הַנְּחָלִים אַרְנוֹן
(במדבר כא:יד)

Therefore it is said in the Book of Wars of Hashem: The gift of [the Sea of] Reeds and the rivers of Arnon (Bamidbar 21:14).

In a play on these words, our Sages expound (*Kiddushin* 30b):

- The word וָהֵב (*gift*) is related to אָהֵב, *to love.*
- The word סוּפָה (*Reeds*) is related to the word סוֹף, *end.* (We may suggest that the word אֶת in the verse refers to the Torah which was written with all the letters of the *Aleph-Beis,* from א to ת.)

R' Chiya explains these words by saying that even a father and a son, a *rebbi* and his student, who are battling constantly, seemingly like enemies, as they argue over the true meaning of the Torah which they are studying, will eventually resolve all their differences. The Torah will bring them close to one another until they will understand, agree, and feel true, mutual love.

In yeshivah, you will often see two *chavrusos* battling each other. One might even say to the other: "You do not know what you are talking about! That is not *pshat,* the true meaning. What are you saying?" One would think that they are the worst enemies in the world.

But from אָהֵב, *their love of* אֶת, *the words of our Holy Torah,* they will come to love each other בְּסוֹף, *in the end.*

They will have come to an understanding and a clarity in the *Gemara,* and they will love each other because of their battling as they strove to arrive at the truth in Torah study.

This also can be applied to differences that can exist between parents and children. Parents and children do not always understand each other. Often, they disagree over important matters.

This is also true of differences that sometimes exist between a *rebbi* and his student. A *rebbi* is never satisfied. He is always making additional demands upon his students. He wants them to be more attentive. He wants his students to constantly review. The students, not realizing their *rebbi's* intentions and genuine concern for them, may rebel against him.

To those uninitiated in this process of learning, one might think that there will never be *shalom* between these two sides.

> But, if Torah is involved, the learning will bring them together in gratitude and love.

I always feel that in today's day and age, where we have problems with the "generation gap," the Torah is truly the *bridge* between generations.

Even when we have difficulties or misunderstandings between parents and children, they can be overcome. If on Shabbos, they sit together at the table and discuss a *dvar Torah,* then, at the very least, they are *talking* to each other. There is *communication.* There may be no communication regarding other problems, but *not* as far as Torah is concerned. In the end, the family members understand one another and there will not be any friction between them.

If you will learn well, learn with a desire to learn, and learn in depth, you will have a vast knowledge in Talmud. This will help you in understanding *mussar* and you will become a better Jew and a true *yirei shamayim.*

9

Learn to Your Potential —
And G-d Will Help You to Exceed It

◆§ Make It Your Torah

The following *pasuk,* about learning Torah, describes how to reach your potential and how to learn even beyond your ability.

כִּי אִם בְּתוֹרַת ה' חֶפְצוֹ וּבְתוֹרָתוֹ יֶהְגֶּה יוֹמָם וָלָיְלָה (תהילם א:ב)

But his desire is in the Torah of HASHEM, and in His Torah he meditates day and night (Tehillim 1:2).

Man's striving is in G-d's Torah. A person's goals and desires should involve him and propel him toward G-d's Torah to such a great extent that he thinks, meditates, and learns His Torah day and night.

כָּל הָעוֹסֵק בַּתּוֹרָה הקב"ה עוֹשֶׂה מַה שֶׁחָפֵץ (עבודה זרה יט:א)

The *Gemara* explains: If a person's *yearning* is for excellence and progress in G-d's Torah, then G-d will fulfill *cheftzo,* his desire. If you are totally immersed in Torah, then G-d will help you and grant you your goals in learning and other needs in this world (*Avodah Zarah* 19a).

When Hashem sees you struggling and persevering to master a Torah lesson,

> when He sees that you refuse to give up,
> then Hashem will extend His helping hand.
>> You *will* learn.
>> You *will* do well.
>> Just do not give up.

In the *pasuk* quoted above, the literal meaning of the word בְּתוֹרָתוֹ, *in His Torah,* means *in Hashem's Torah.*

However, in the *Gemara,* Rava interprets the word differently. He says that it refers to the *person's* Torah: *His desire is in* HASHEM's *Torah, and in his own Torah he meditates day and night.*

When does it become his (the individual's) personal Torah?
When does it become *your* Torah?

- When you learn, meditate and review Torah day and night, it becomes yours.
- You make a *kinyan* — you acquire — G-d's Torah. It becomes your possession, if you devote time and effort to delve into it, day and night.

After the student toils to understand it, it is considered as *his* possession, *his* Torah.

Rabbi Samson Raphael Hirsch comments:

He finds his goals and his striving only in the Law of G-d. In Torah, his personal goals have been set and his paths marked out ... His constant and most intense thinking moves in the direction of making G-d's goals become his *own* "Divine Law," day and night.

It becomes *his* Torah.

- During the day, the Torah is the guide for his thinking, for his desires and for his actions.
- The night is also devoted to the study of Torah. His leisure hours are utilized to enrich and to ennoble his mind and his emotions.

יֶהְגֶּה pertains to the meditations of the heart and also to speech. It refers to a developed thought ready for expression.

יֶהְגֶּה is also the very specific expression denoting the thoughtful *study* of Torah. This is not attained through mere thoughts without words. It requires even from one who *studies* alone, the precise *verbal* expression of the thought which is being brought to life.

וּבְתוֹרָתוֹ יֶהְגֶּה יוֹמָם וָלָיְלָה

Rava says:

- At first it is called G-d's Torah. As you continue learning, it becomes *your* Torah.
- This is a gift to you from Hashem.

As you sit in class and listen to your *rebbi,* it is G-d's Torah being interpreted and explained to you by G-d's messenger on earth, the *rebbi.*

G-d speaks to us through the voice of a *tzaddik,*
through the voice of a *rebbe.*
- When you add hours to the *rebbe's* lesson,
- when you review the *shiur* on your own time,
- when you explain the lesson of the day
to your *chavrusa* (learning partner),
it becomes *your* Torah as well.

When you listen to a *mussar shmuess* from me, it is *my mussar* that you hear. When *you* repeat my *mussar* thoughts to your family at the Shabbos table, or if you repeat my talk to a friend,
it becomes *your mussar shmuess* as well.

Thus, when you learn Torah day and night, it becomes *your* Torah.

⇜ Learn According to Your Ability — Live up to Your Potential

A verse in *Tehillim* states:

גָּרְסָה נַפְשִׁי לְתַאֲבָה אֶל מִשְׁפָּטֶיךָ בְכָל עֵת

My soul is shattered with yearning for Your laws always (*Tehillim* 119:20).

David *HaMelech* is saying:
My soul yearns to learn, my soul lusts to acquire more Torah.

The word גָּרְסָה, *shattered,* is related to גֶּרֶשׁ, *ground* (*Vayikra* 2:14), which refers to the coarse grinding of grain, the "chewing" of the kernels into food.

Rashi explains the term as follows:

When you grind wheat kernels and chaff into a cereal, to be used as a food, there are two stages. The first stage is placing the wheat into a mill which breaks up the wheat into two or four pieces so that it is ready to be eaten. It is a coarse cereal, with many large, lumpy pieces in it. This must be chewed carefully.

It may not be too tasty.

The second stage is טְחִינָה which is also translated as *grinding*. However, with טְחִינָה, the wheat is ground very fine, so that you can eat it and swallow it very easily.

It tastes just fine.

The *Gemara* (*Avodah Zarah* 19a) discusses David's use of the term גְּרְסָה as opposed to טְחֲנָה in the verse where he speaks of his yearning for Torah.

In Torah learning, the "grinding" implied by טְחֲנָה would mean the spiritual "breaking up" and digesting of instructional matter, so that it can be easily absorbed and better understood. It would mean mastering the learning thoroughly and deeply.

However, King David proclaims:

הָיְיתִי שׁוֹבֵר לְפִי הַיְכֹלֶת אַף עַל פִּי שֶׁאֵינִי טוֹחֲנָה הָדֵק לִיכָּנֵס בְּעוּמְקָהּ

(רַשִׁ''י)

My soul studies with an insatiable learning.

David broke off coarse chunks (גְּרְסָה) of "Torah matter." At first, he toiled to understand the broad basic concepts, even while he could not grasp their deeper "finer" meanings for such was his thirst for Torah. Later, he reviewed his learning and subjected these basic concepts to an even *finer* analysis.

Rashi then explains the term לְתַאֲבָה, *with yearning,* in the *pasuk.*

The term תַּאֲוָה (ו and ב are sometimes interchangeable) usually refers to a powerful desire. The *Gemara* derives from here that a Jew's *neshamah* should desire Torah so much that he will always learn according to his ability, even when he cannot "grind the wheat too finely."

- Even when he cannot delve deeply into his learning,
- even if he does not understand the finer and
  deeper meanings of the Torah, nevertheless,
    he still yearns to learn to the *best* of his *ability.*
- Even if an individual cannot master the lesson
  100 percent,
    he should persevere and continue to learn.

Rava seems to say:

As long as I break down the *Gemara* as much as I am able to, even if I do not reach עוּמְקָהּ, the *depth* of the lesson, I have fulfilled Hashem's will.

- Live up to *your* potential.
- Utilize all of *your* abilities.

In the *Gemara* we are discussing, Rava teaches that at all times, a person should learn, even if he forgets, even if he does not understand the Torah in depth.

We find this same idea in two places in the Torah concerning two outstanding personalities, Yosef *HaTzaddik* and Moshe *Rabbeinu.*

Pharaoh appointed Yosef as a viceroy over all of Egypt (*Bereishis* 41:44).

The *Gemara* describes what occurred:

> R' Chiya, son of Abba, said in the name of R' Yochanan:
>
> The ministers asked Pharaoh:
>
>> "Are you going to appoint a slave to rule over us?"
>
> Pharaoh answered:
>
>> "I see majesty in Yosef's bearing."
>
> The ministers then stated:
>
>> "There is a tradition in Egypt that a king must know 70 languages."

אָמַר רַבִּי יוֹחָנָן . . . בָּא גַבְרִיאֵל וְלִמְּדוֹ וְלֹא הֲוֵי קָגָמַר הוֹסִיף לוֹ אוֹת אַחַת מִשְּׁמוֹ שֶׁל הקב"ה (תּוֹרָה תְּמִימָה בְּרֵאשִׁית מא:מד)

Hashem sent the angel Gavriel to teach Yosef all the languages,

> but he could not learn them;
> it was too difficult for him.

עֵדוּת בִּיהוֹסֵף שָׂמוֹ בְּצֵאתוֹ עַל אֶרֶץ מִצְרָיִם (סוטה לו:ב)

Gavriel added the letter *hei* from G-d's Name to Yosef's (making it יְהוֹסֵף — see *Tehillim* 81:6) and he mastered all of the 70 languages (*Sotah* 36b).

Let us consider. Yosef was brilliant. He was able to plan and execute the storing of food during the years of plenty so that there would be enough to eat during the years of famine. This was a difficult administrative process. Throughout the land, granaries had to be built and prepared for grain storage.

How was it possible that Yosef could not learn 70 languages?

He had a good mind and

> he had a very good *rebbi,* an angel from Hashem.

Perhaps this *midrash* wants to teach us a very important lesson (as we shall soon see).

The *Midrash* tells of a similar incident with Moshe *Rabbeinu:*

The Torah states:

וַיִּתֵּן אֶל מֹשֶׁה כְּכַלֹּתוֹ לְדַבֵּר אִתּוֹ בְּהַר סִינַי שְׁנֵי לֻחֹת הָעֵדֻת

And He [G-d] gave to Moshe, when He finished speaking to him on Mount Sinai, two Luchos [Tablets] of Testimony (Shemos 31:18).

Rabbi Yochanan said:*

וַיִּתֵּן אֶל מֹשֶׁה (שְׁמוֹת לא:יח)

אָמַר ר׳ יוֹחָנָן . . . מֹשֶׁה לוֹמֵד וּמְשַׁכְּחָה עַד שֶׁנְּתָנָה לוֹ בְּמַתָּנָה (נְדָרִים לח:א)

During the 40 days that Moshe was in Heaven to receive the *Luchos*, he was taught the *entire* Torah. But he repeatedly forgot his learning. He was taught again and again, and constantly forgot, until Hashem *gave* him the Torah as a *gift;* a gift of memory, and he no longer forgot.

The word וַיִּתֵּן, *and He gave,* comes from the same root as מַתָּנָה, a *gift.* Finally, Hashem gave the Torah to Moshe as a *gift.*

This *midrash* is difficult to understand.

Can this really pertain to Moshe?
- He was exceptionally gifted.
- He was blessed with extraordinary abilities.
- He was our greatest *Rebbi* and leader.
- Everything we learn and know,
  Moshe taught to *Bnei Yisrael.*

Torah Temimah comments:

There is no doubt that Moshe *did not* forget naturally. It is inconceivable that he was overpowered by the common human trait of forgetfulness. This could not happen to Moshe.

Rather, there was a special *Hashgachah,*
  a special Divine intervention, that *caused* Moshe to forget.
  G-d *purposely* made Moshe forget.

The following (from *Yerushalmi, Horios* 3:8) is also said in the name of the *same R' Yochanan,* who was quoted above regarding Yosef's inability to learn:

Why did G-d do this?
Why did He make Moshe forget?

---

* It is interesting to note that Rabbi Yochanan in *Sotah* 36b concerning Yosef's disability with regard to learning 70 languages is also the same Rabbi Yochanan in *Nedarim* 38a concerning Moshe's disability in learning the Torah until it was given to him as a gift. It is also the same R' Yochanan from *Yerushalmi Horios* 3:8.

כְּדֵי לְהַחֲזִיר אֶת הַטִּפְּשִׁים

So that this will serve as an answer to all those who cannot learn well, to all those who initially find it difficult to learn and to understand, to encourage those with learning disabilities never to give up.

No one should ever say:
"Why should I struggle so much in my learning of Torah?
- I learn, I review, and still, I forget.
- I learn, I review, and still, I do not understand it fully."

We say to all these individuals:
- "Moshe also forgot; yet he learned again and again, until Hashem gave Torah to him as a gift.
- And Yosef also could not master the 70 languages until the angel Gavriel added a letter from G-d's Name to Yosef."

The *Gemara* teaches,
- Even if one learns and forgets, he must never give up. Keep on plugging and working!
  You will succeed! (see *Avodah Zarah* 19a).
A person who perseveres will know how to learn.

Through striving to learn and a desire to be spiritually bound to Hashem's Torah, he will overcome all obstacles.

Both Yosef and Moshe *seemingly* encountered difficulties in learning, yet they eventually succeeded.

Hashem stepped into the problem and imparted understanding to them.

Both Yosef and Moshe serve as role models for us.
- We, too, will succeed.
- We must not give up!
- G-d will step in and help us, too.

⋑ Never Give up — Hashem Is on Your Side

I often speak about סִיַּעְתָּא דִּשְׁמַיָּא, *siyata dishmaya* (Divine assistance).

If a person truly desires to learn, then he is granted *special assistance* from the *Almighty* Himself.

Rava is telling us:
> No student should say, "I am the weakest in the class.
> I cannot be helped."
>> • Some students may be smarter.
>> • Some students may have greater capabilities
>> (better minds). They may have greater
>> powers of concentration.
>>> This does not mean that they will become
>>> greater *talmidei chachamim.*

I have found throughout my experiences as a *menahel* that the ultimate success of students cannot be predicted at an early stage of their Torah lives. I know many students who did not do well in their yeshivah days. I have kept in touch with most of these students through their *mesivta* and *beis hamedrash* years. In many instances, things took a turn for the better somewhere along the way.

Suddenly, they thrived. They bordered on being in the top third of their group.

> How did they accomplish this? They never gave up!

They reviewed *many more times* than the "better" students. As a result of their constant reviewing, the lessons were much clearer to them and remained with them for the rest of their lives.

> If you don't give up, Hashem will meet you more than
> halfway.

In the *beis hamedrash* of Mesivta Torah Vodaath, there was one student, Yaakov, who could not learn as well as the other students. He simply was not as bright as the others.

But he was a *masmid* (diligent). He reviewed the *shiur* that the *rebbi* gave. He reviewed 10 to 15 times *each day.* The rest of us studied and reviewed five times a day, at most.

Yaakov had never really participated verbally in the *shiur.*

One day, when we were learning *masechta* Bava Kamma, our *rebbi,* Rabbi Shlomo Heiman, posed a question. As we all pondered this, Yaakov started to speak.

He said: "Last year, we learned *Bava Metzia. Rebbi,* you said a *sevarah,* a beautiful thought which resolved a difficult question. With that same *sevarah* we can answer the question which *Rebbi* is asking today."

Yaakov repeated the *sevarah* brilliantly. We all sat up and took notice of Yaakov's explanation.

Yaakov remembered because he studied and *reviewed more often* than we had.

From that time on, Yaakov participated in all the *shiurim*. Eventually, he became a *rebbe* in a renowned *beis hamedrash*. He became known as a great *talmid chacham.*

He never gave up. Constant review, *chazarah,* made him into what he became.

We have a slogan in Toras Emes which I repeat regularly:

> Review tonight the lessons you learned during the day.
> Then, you will be O.K.
> It is the only way.

⋅ఽ *Rebbeim Can and Must Help*

At a staff meeting at Yeshivah Toras Emes, an interesting thing happened.

At the beginning of the new term, I suggested to my *rebbeim* that they approach their new class with an open mind.

I said:

"Judge your new students yourself. Do not review your students' past records for the first two weeks or so. Perhaps a student who had not done well with a *rebbi* last year will do better this year."

At a subsequent teachers meeting, I remarked:

"I am thrilled with Moshe's progress this year. He did quite poorly last year. Each *rebbi* has his own method of teaching, and I want to commend his present *rebbi* for awakening and inspiring Moshe to a new future in learning. Perhaps this year's *rebbi* has a different approach in teaching. It proves once again

> we must never give up on a student."

Moshe's previous *rebbi* bristled. He felt that this was not possible. He said:

"Moshe had an I.Q. of 90 on his Intelligence Test. He is a borderline learning-disability problem."

Moshe's present *rebbi* argued that this is not so. After a few weeks into the term, he had looked up Moshe's record and found that his I.Q. was 110, and he was doing just fine.

In the ensuing discussion, we brought in Moshe's records, and his *rebbi* said: "See, his I.Q. is 110."

The previous *rebbi* looked at the record and exclaimed:

"110 is his locker number, but his I.Q. is 90!"

A hush fell over the room.

I said:

"This just proves what I have been saying all along. You judged him as a 90 I.Q., and perhaps gave up on him. You felt that he was unable to keep up with the class and could not do the work properly.

"Moshe's present *rebbi* gave him a fresh start and treated him as a normal student. In devoting time to Moshe, the *rebbi* ignited a spark in him that had been dormant. Moshe responded beautifully to his new *rebbi.*"

(Moshe may have been a late bloomer. He did well in his succeeding years at the yeshivah.)

- This the power of a *rebbi.*
- A *rebbi* carries an awesome responsibility.

In *Hallel,* we say:

הַהוֹפְכִי הַצּוּר אֲגַם מָיִם

G-d has the power to change a rock so that it becomes a pond of water (*Tehillim* 114:8).

Rabbi Samson Raphael Hirsch explains:

G-d changes *tzur,* the most compact solid rock, into a pond, for the collection of fresh waters.

This sentence refers to an incident which occurred in the Wilderness. Israel was thirsty and clamored to Moshe and Aharon for water. Hashem told Moshe to *speak* to the rock and water would flow for his thirsty brethren. Moshe was hurt by the attitude of *Bnei Yisrael,* and he hit the rock instead of talking to it (*Bamidbar* 20:7-11).

There ensued a debate between the rock and Moshe. The rock refused to give forth water.

When G-d created the world, He created four major elements:

1. אֵשׁ — fire
2. מַיִם — water
3. עָפָר — earth
4. אֲוִיר — atmosphere

The rock said:

"G-d created me from the element of עָפָר, *earth.* I cannot change into another element, into מַיִם, *water.*"

When Moshe struck the rock a second time, it was to preserve his honor that water came forth. However, had Moshe spoken to the rock, the Holy One, Blessed is He, speaks through the throats of righteous people. The rock would have changed into water immediately, since Moshe Rabbeinu was on the *madreiga,* on the level of שְׁכִינָה מְדַבֶּרֶת מִתּוֹךְ גְּרוֹנוֹ, The Divine Presence speaks through his throat.

Hashem created the rock, and His command, through the spoken word of Moshe, would have been heeded by the rock. It would have changed into water immediately.

Let us utilize this incident to learn another skill in teaching.

Sometimes we have a student whose mind is *tzur,* as solid as a rock. Torah — which the *Midrash* compares to water — does not seem to penetrate.

We are confronted with an educational problem. We want to change the "rock-head" into a different element, the element of Torah, the element of water. Can it be done? Certainly.

We can make a play on words. The *pasuk* says:

הַהוֹפְכִי הַצּוּר, *Who changes the rock.* We can *change* הַצּוּר, and read it backwards, to spell רוֹצֶה, *desire.* With Hashem's help, with His words being spoken through the throat of the *rebbi,* we can change the *tzur* child into a *rotzeh,* one who desires to learn.

- Captivate his mind.
- Inspire him and motivate him.
- Create an atmosphere of *wanting* to learn.
- Make the lesson interesting so that the child
  will listen avidly and want to make progress.
    If a child wants to learn, he will learn.
    He can become a *talmid chacham.*

This requires a creative and dedicated *rebbi.* This forces the *rebbi* to prepare so well that the teaching comes alive.

- Being a *rebbi* is truly an awesome responsibility.
- The future of our nation is dependent
  upon our children, and therefore,
    lies within the hands of the *rebbi.*

❧ Learn Torah or Learn From Torah — A Set of Torah Notes

תורה־מורה

The word Torah comes from the word *moreh,* to teach.

When Yaakov was going down to Egypt, he realized that this would be our first *galus,* exile. He sent Yehudah ahead of the rest of the families *lehoros* (*Bereishis* 46:28).

וְאֶת יְהוּדָה שָׁלַח . . . לְהוֹרֹת לְפָנָיו גּ'שְׁנָה (בראשית מו:כח)

to *organize* a *place* of *learning.*

Yehudah was to plan, to prepare, and to build a place for learning Torah. He would build a yeshivah *before* the family of Yaakov, including his other sons and grandsons, came down to Egypt.

Rabbi Samson Raphael Hirsch adds this beautiful thought concerning the word "Torah":

The word "Torah" comes from the same *shoresh,* root, as וַתַּהַר, *and she conceived.*

A seed is planted. The seed then grows and becomes a living, viable child.

- Torah is the planting of a seed.
- Torah is G-d's blueprint, His set of notes.

From this blueprint, from the growth of the seed of Torah planted in our minds starting from our youngest years, we can grow in stature and learning.

We learn the Written Torah. We then proceed to Torah *She'baal Peh,* the Oral Torah, the vast Talmud, which elucidates and elaborates upon the Written Torah. Throughout our lives, we continue to build up our knowledge of Torah.

- The Talmud gives meaning to obscure words and passages in the Written Torah.
- It reveals the hidden thoughts of Hashem.
  Without this elaboration,
    the Torah would remain a closed Book.

For instance:

There are 39 types of *melachos,* forbidden labors, that we are not allowed to do on Shabbos. These *melachos* are *not* written in the Torah. Furthermore, *melachah* is not forbidden on Shabbos unless it was done with intent. This, too, is not written in the Torah.

The Torah is *our set* of *notes.*

The Talmud is the explanation and further elaboration of the Torah's notes. Through Talmud study, everything becomes clear to us.

Sometimes you attend a lecture, a *shiur,* given by a *gadol,* and you take notes. You cannot write every word. You write many key words and many key phrases. Later, when you read your *notes,* you can remember and *review* the *entire* lecture.

The Torah is our *set* of *notes,* of *G-d's laws.*

From a word here, and a word there, in the Torah, there is an entire *masechta* named Shabbos. This *masechta* explains all the laws pertaining to Shabbos.

Besides the 39 basic *melachos,* there are thousands of other laws, derivatives, concerning that which we may not do on Shabbos.

The Torah is our set of notes. The Talmud explains these notes and clarifies them for us.

We hope to plant the seed of Torah learning in you. We pray that the seed will flourish so that you will be able to open any *Gemara,* pick up any *sefer,* and learn it by *yourself; without* the aid of a *rebbi.*

You can grow, and continue to grow, until you are *crowned* with the title of *talmid chacham.*

> You *earned* the title through your *perseverance* in learning and your belief that, with Hashem's help, you would succeed.

✍ Mitzvah Observance

10

The Meaning and Beauty
of Tefillah

I. Tefillah vs. Prayer

◆§ There Are Differences

What exactly are the powers of *tefillah*? Let us begin answering this by posing another question: What does the word *tefillah* mean? The literal English translation of *tefillah* is "prayer"; in truth, however, this word encompasses *much, much* more.

We must understand that there is a *vast difference* between the term *tefillah* and the English word "prayer." Most people use these words interchangeably.

Rabbi Samson Raphael Hirsch offers a very beautiful and different concept of *tefillah*:

> If *tefillah* is prayer, then it should revolve around what the person is praying for.
>
> What *I* am praying for may not be what *you* are praying for.

A poor man may be praying for one thing and a wealthy man may be praying for an entirely different request.

A person who has trouble with his children may be praying for a solution to this problem, while a person who does not have this problem may be praying for something else.

> In other words, if *tefillah* originates from inside your heart, then each individual's *tefillah* should be different. This would result in a multitude of *tefillos*, with different

texts. *Tefillah*, then, would simply be a way for beseeching Hashem for solutions to specific problems.

- Each individual would formulate *his own text.*
- And each individual would *daven* whenever *he feels the need to.*

If this would be the primary purpose of our daily *davening,* then we would not have a structured *tefillah.*

Why, then, *do* we have structured *tefillos,* with, specific texts composed by *Chazal,* in addition to specific chapters of *Tehillim* which are part of our daily *tefillos?* And why do we have set time periods in which to recite each of the daily *tefillos?*

The answer to this is that *tefillah* is not mere "prayer."

It is incorrect to assume that what we call *tefillah* emerges from me to Hashem; from inside of me, from my heart.

What emanates from my heart to Hashem should rightfully be called prayer, not *tefillah.* There are two proofs for this concept:

1. The time of *tefillah.*

You *do not daven* whenever you want to.

Tefillah means that there are special times for *davening.* You must get up in the morning and *daven* at a specified time. What if you do not feel like *davening* that day? It is of no avail. You *must daven* every day. It is one of our *mitzvos.*

2. There are regular set *tefillos* that must be said.

(Note: In the *berachos* of our *Shemoneh Esrei* you can add your own words if you have a special request.)

What is this *tefillah* that we say every day?

What is the power of our *tefillah?*

Rabbi Samson Raphael Hirsch explains the concept of *tefillah* beautifully:

- "Prayer" originates in your heart.
- *Tefillah,* however, begins with directives *from Above,* which enter our hearts and shape the way in which we will serve Hashem *all day long.* It is in accordance with these directives that we then offer our *tefillah* to Hashem.

This will be elaborated upon thoroughly in the following section.

II. Tefillah: Judging Oneself

The root of the word תְּפִלָּה, tefillah, says Rabbi Hirsch, comes from פלל, to judge. In Bereishis we learn that Avraham went to live in Gerar. Avimelech, the king, sees Sarah and has her taken to his palace. G-d appears to Avimelech and warns him not to touch or harm Sarah.

Hashem says: "Return Sarah to Avraham so that he will pray for you (וְיִתְפַּלֵּל), and you shall live" (Bereishis 20:7).

Rabbi Hirsch comments that the word וְיִתְפַּלֵּל means to judge, from the root letters פלל. Thus, Avraham will judge Avimelech's request and will pray for him.

When the Torah discusses the amount that should be paid for damages, it states: וְנָתַן בִּפְלִלִים, And he shall pay it by order of judges (Shemos 21:22).

The Hebrew word for judges is פְּלִלִים, from the root פלל.

A judge effects justice and righteousness. With the help of Hashem, he penetrates all phases of a dispute. With true justice, he brings about harmony and resolves argument.

When we daven to Hashem, we focus on G-d's truths as taught in the Torah, and we direct all phases of our lives towards fulfilling our mission as His servant. Whatever we ask for in Shemoneh Esrei is to help us achieve this goal, which is the purpose of our being on this world. With this approach, all our wishes become one lofty desire and we gain true inner harmony. Thereby, we gain for ourselves the harmonious even tenor of our whole existence for G-d. Thus, our daily davening is a kind of self-judgment and therefore, the Hebrew term for davening is לְהִתְפַּלֵּל.

There are two versions in praying to G-d.

- A prayer from *within* yourself, *from you to G-d.*
- There is also a *tefillah*-prayer. We shall soon see that this is a prayer from *without* yourself, *from G-d to you.*

A *tefillah*-prayer is, in reality, a most *complete contrast* to what is generally called prayer.

Tefillah, then, does not begin as an outpouring from within, for it is only after we have *judged* our inner selves and rededicated ourselves to being true servants of Hashem that our words of prayer can rightfully be called *tefillah.*

By contrast, a prayer that *does* begin from within, that is seen more as a personal request, is referred to as a בַּקָשָׁה or תְּחִנָּה.

For example:

וָאֶתְחַנַּן אֶל ה׳ . . . (דברים ג:כג)

And I implored Hashem (Devarim 3:23).

Rabbi Hirsch explains that the word וָאֶתְחַנַּן, *And I implored,* is related to תְּחִנָּה, *request.*

With this word, Moshe *Rabbeinu* begins to relate how he beseeched Hashem for permission to enter *Eretz Yisrael.* While Moshe's every word, thought and desire was directed toward serving Hashem, he saw this request as a personal beseeching on his own behalf.

> *Tefillah* is a prayer that is a renewed intake and penetration of truth which comes from *outside* oneself.

Tefillah, therefore, means to work on and to prevail on our *inner* selves.

In his commentary to the *Tachanun* recited on weekday mornings, Rabbi Hirsch expresses it this way:

תְּחִנָּה is a prayer beseeching G-d for help.

תְּפִלָּה is a prayer seeking spiritual purification
   and proper understanding.

- *Tefillah* means to raise ourselves to a higher level;
- to bring our inner selves to recognize the Torah's truths
- and to make greater resolutions regarding our service of Hashem.

This is why we have fixed times and prescribed texts for our *tefillah* prayers. In this way, Jews come together three times a day every day, to dedicate themselves anew to Hashem's service. It is only through such *tefillah* that we earn the right to also express our personal בַּקָשׁוֹת, *requests.*

◄§ *Personal Beseeching vs. Personal Awakening*

When a person's heart is filled with pain or anxiety, he needs to find his own way of expressing himself. Each person has different needs for which to beseech Hashem.

- One person may pray for good health.
- Another may pray for wealth.

- A third prayer may ask for a job.
- A fourth may simply seek His mercy regarding a personal problem.
- Another request might be for recognition from one's peers.
- Success concerning a forthcoming venture might constitute another prayer, etc.

These prayers fall under the category of תְּחִנָּה and בַּקָשָׁה.

Someone arises in the middle of the night and finds that a loved one was just taken to the hospital.

He pours his heart out to Hashem.

He recites *Tehillim.*

"Please, G-d, accept my prayers and heal this person."

That is *techinah.*

These individual prayers are all different from each other. They may affect people in many different ways.

However, *tefillah,* with its *set* words, to be said at *set* times, is entirely different. It serves to awaken us, to help us realize our responsibilities toward Hashem.

Tefillah serves to forever keep us fresh in serving Hashem. One can truly say that the less we feel inclined to *daven,* the greater is our need to involve ourselves in *tefillah.* And the more we strive to say our *tefillos* with *kavanah* and *feeling,* the greater their effect on us will be.

◄§ Pesukei D'Zimrah

All of *Pesukei D'zimrah* (the chapters of *Tehillim* and other verses from *Tanach* with which our morning prayers begin) describe the powers of Hashem in this world.

In the *Ashrei* prayer, we express the powers of Hashem in the form of praises. We praise all the outstanding attributes of Hashem concerning His relationship with man.

In the third paragraph following *Ashrei* (*Tehillim* Ch. 148), we call upon all of creation to declare Hashem's praises:

Praise Hashem from the heavens, from the earth, and from everything in the world: fire, hail, snow, wind, mountains, trees, beasts and cattle, princes and judges of the earth, both old and young, should join together in praising Hashem, for His Name alone will have been exalted.

When you say these words, uplift yourself with the thought that you, too, should sing Hashem's praises daily.

Judge yourself as you involve yourself in *tefillah*:

- Are you doing this?
- Do you praise Hashem through your actions and activities from day to day, from moment to moment?
- You, too, must praise Hashem constantly as all of nature is constantly doing.
- The way in which you declare Hashem's praises is by living according to the Torah's teachings.

◆§ Bircas Krias Shema

In the prayers that we say as part of *Bircas Krias Shema* (following בָּרְכוּ), we speak of the ministering angels who sing Hashem's praises:

וְכֻלָּם מְקַבְּלִים עֲלֵיהֶם עֹל מַלְכוּת שָׁמַיִם זֶה מִזֶּה

They all accept upon themselves the yoke of the kingdom of heaven from one another, and lovingly grant permission to one another to sanctify the One Who formed them . . .

וְנוֹתְנִים (בְּאַהֲבָה) רְשׁוּת זֶה לָזֶה

They grant permission (with love), to one another . . .

Each angel helps the other to sanctify Hashem's Name.

Judge yourself! Do you help others in their service of Hashem?

The paragraph immediately preceding *Shema* primarily concerns Torah learning and the future Redemption. We entreat Hashem to help us to succeed in our study of Torah. We beg Him to help us to understand the Torah in depth, and that we may perform His *mitzvos* with love.

We also pray for the redemption of all Israel from the four corners of the earth, so that all Israel may be brought back to our beloved homeland, *Eretz Yisrael*.

In discussing these prayers, one feels the vital need to pray with sincerity.

Through sincere *tefillah,* you will become imbued with the idea that you, along with everything else in this world, belong to Hashem.

With this frame of mind, your *tefillah* will be far more intense and it will have a decided effect upon you. All this serves as an introduction to our saying of the *Shema,* our קַבָּלַת עוֹל מַלְכוּת שָׁמַיִם, *acceptance of the Yoke of Heaven.*

> You will then be ready to accept G-d as the Master of the World as well as the Master over *yourself.*

❧ The Shema

When reciting *Shema,* every Jew feels a spiritual surge and a sense of uplift.

When we say the words ה׳ אֱלֹהֵינוּ ה׳ אֶחָד, *Hashem is our God, Hashem, the One and Only,* we accept upon ourselves the yoke of His rule. We resolve ourselves to serve Hashem constantly and consistently, in accordance with His Torah.

Judge yourself!

- Are you reaching for high standards in your *avodah,* service, of Hashem?
- Or are you satisfied with being mediocre?

Attempt to constantly raise yourself to a higher level of service, little by little, step by step.

When we cry out: ה׳ אֶחָד, *Hashem, the One and Only,* we raise our thoughts and resolve to be one, together with Hashem.

Bircas Krias Shema, as well as *Shemoneh Esrei,* were composed by prophets and great Sages of the *Anshei Knesses HaGedolah,* Men of the Great Assembly, who lived at the start of the second *Beis HaMikdash* era.

> These words, from *without ourselves,* demand our complete attention and *kavanah.* We try to elevate ourselves to the thoughts behind all these words and then become more devoted to staying on a course leading to:
> - G-dliness,
> - purity,
> - and *kedushah.*

III. My Words and My Thoughts

The *pasuk* which follows the last blessing of *Shemoneh Esrei* is very beautiful.

יִהְיוּ לְרָצוֹן אִמְרֵי פִי וְהֶגְיוֹן לִבִּי לְפָנֶיךָ ה' צוּרִי וְגֹאֲלִי (תהילם יט:טו)

"May the *words* of my mouth and the *thoughts* of my heart find favor before You, Hashem, my Rock and Redeemer" (*Tehillim* 19:15).

This sentence deals first with the *words* of one's mouth and then with the *thoughts* of his heart. In reality, however, a thought *precedes* the spoken word. A person first has to *think* about what he is going to say and then he expresses his thoughts. Why does the *pasuk* reverse this order?

The *Gemara* explains why *Chazal* arranged the order of *berachos* of *Shemoneh Esrei* in the exact order in which we recite them. As Rabbi Chaim Volozhiner writes (in *Nefesh HaChaim*), the words of *Shemoneh Esrei* and their order have a plain, obvious meaning and a deep, mystical meaning as well. They are infused with *kedushah* (sanctity) and we cannot possibly improve upon them.

In respect to *Shemoneh Esrei,* our *words* are even more important than our *thoughts*.
- These words are filled with holiness.
- These words are filled with beauty.
- These words cannot be improved upon.

It is our hope that our thoughts will be
- just as great,
- just as holy,
- just as beautiful.

Therefore we conclude with a *pasuk* in which we say to Hashem:
May these beautiful and *purest* of *words* that we have just expressed be acceptable to You.
We hope and pray that the *thoughts* of our mind shall live up to the *meaning* of these holy words.

⋖⸱ Reflection and Introspection

In addition, our *tefillah* contains many *t'heelos,* praises of G-d, which radiate to us so that G-d's greatness can be reflected in us. When we *daven,* we proclaim our recognition of G-d in our midst.

Our daily *tefillah* aims to provide us with peace of mind and strength for life.

- If we are permeated with awe of and faith in G-d,
- if we are striving towards ever greater *kedushah,* sanctity, in our personal lives,
- if we are guided through life by Hashem, by accepting upon ourselves עֹל מַלְכוּת שָׁמַיִם, the yoke of subservience to Hashem,

then, by saying the *Shema,*

- we will secure for ourselves a closeness to G-d.
- We will have attained the right to the certainty that Hashem *listens* to us (שׁוֹמֵעַ תְּפִלָּה) when we stand before Him as we recite *Shemoneh Esrei* three times daily.

In our *tefillah,* we not only ask for His favor, graciousness, and mercy, we also thank Him for listening to us.

There is so much we can accomplish within ourselves through proper *tefillah.* We must develop the proper approach to *tefillah* so that it will enable us to spend our day gainfully and serve Hashem according to His truths, as taught to us in His Torah.

- All the words that we say should penetrate our hearts.
- The words we say should make demands upon our hearts and minds.
- They should have a profound effect upon the way we live our lives.

We must develop the ability to judge ourselves.

- Are you living up to the precious words of *tefillah* that you say each day?
- Are you striving to plumb the depths of meaning and inspiration that lie within these words?

It is crucial that everyone give attention to learning *peirush hamilos,* the meaning of the words of our sacred *tefillos.*

IV. Proper Concentration

In the days of Rabbi Yisrael Salanter, some 150 years ago, they undoubtedly *davened* better than we do today.

A Jew named Yaakov came to Reb Yisrael and said:

> "Rebbe, it takes eight minutes to say *Shemoneh Esrei.* How is it possible for me to concentrate on every word of *Shemoneh Esrei?* In these eight minutes, I start to think about where I have to go today, with whom I have an appointment and how to settle a business deal. How can I concentrate for the full eight minutes?"

This encounter took place in the spring when the circus had come to town.

Reb Yisrael said: "I want you to go to the circus. I want you to watch the tightrope walker and tell me what happens."

Yaakov returned from the circus later in the day.

Reb Yisrael asked: "So how long did it take the aerialist to walk across the thin wire?"

"Exactly eight minutes," Yaakov replied.

Reb Yisrael then asked: "Did he slip? Did he fall?"

Yaakov responded: "He concentrated with every ounce of his concentration on walking across that wire. He *did not look* at anything else. He *did not think* of anything else. His entire mind was on placing one foot in front of the other, and to balance himself properly."

"Why did he concentrate so much?" asked Reb Yisrael.

"Had he not concentrated totally on the wire, he would have fallen and could have been killed."

Reb Yisrael then said to Yaakov: "You see, a person *can* concentrate for eight minutes."

"Yes," Yaakov replied,

> *"if his life depends on it."*

Reb Yisrael smiled, and said: "In *Shemoneh Esrei,* you ask Hashem for many vital needs: wisdom, redemption, healing of the sick, peace, and much more. When you start to *daven,* say to yourself, 'I must say every word with proper *kavanah.*

> " '*My life depends on it.*

" 'I must not think of anything but the meaning of the words I am uttering.

" 'I should not attempt to finish *Shemoneh Esrei* in two or three minutes flat. I must really concentrate when I pray to Hashem.' "

Picture 1,000 people *davening* together. They *daven* quietly; one does not disturb the other as a beautiful, serene atmosphere prevails.

It is similar to a symphony orchestra. Everyone is *davening* to Hashem and the murmur of voices are in concert with each other.

But as soon as they have concluded *Shemoneh Esrei,* some individuals start talking to each other as they stroll around the *shul.* Suddenly, the concert, the beautiful symphony, is shattered; the talking is disquieting. The individuals who are still *davening* are disturbed.

If you understand that your life depends upon it, you will *daven* better, and you will not disturb the *davening* of others. If you realize that the words of *Shemoneh Esrei* are demanding self-improvement of you, and you think about what you are saying, you will pour your heart into your *tefillah.*

After you finish, you will say to yourself: "I must live up to everything I just uttered before Hashem. I must become a better Jew."

This is the true greatness of *tefillah.*

All my years as a principal, I put enormous emphasis on teaching the meaning of the *tefillos.* I would deliver a short *dvar Torah* to my students every day, at the *minyan,* which centered around the meaning of our *tefillos.*

Many of my students came to the *minyan* regularly, for three years or more. As a result, they have a deeper understanding and appreciation of *tefillah.*

V. An Audience with Hashem

Tefillah is an opportunity to have an audience with מֶלֶךְ מַלְכֵי הַמְּלָכִים, *the King of kings.* Not everyone can go and visit an earthly king whenever he wants to. Not everyone can ask for an audience with the president. Even those who are granted such appointments often have to wait months before their meeting can take place.

- *Tefillah* is a very personal moment between yourself and Hashem.
- Concentrate on what you are saying.
- G-d alone is listening to *you.*

Davening Shemoneh Esrei three times a day represents a personal appointment between you and Hashem.

This is the way to look upon *Shemoneh Esrei,* every time you recite it. This is the way to look upon *tefillah,* in general.

With this approach, your *tefillah* will have a pronounced effect upon your life. You will grow to become a *yirei shamayim,* a *baal middos,* and you will study Torah with greater dedication.

VI. Open Your Heart to Hashem and His Torah

הוּא יִפְתַּח לִבֵּנוּ בְּתוֹרָתוֹ וְיָשֵׂם בְּלִבֵּנוּ אַהֲבָתוֹ וְיִרְאָתוֹ

May He (G-d) open our heart through His Torah and place in our heart love and awe of Him.

One Simchas Torah in Mesivta Torah Vodaath, our *menahel* and *Rebbi,* Rabbi Shraga Feivel Mendlowitz, joined us as we were singing the words: ... הוּא יִפְתַּח לִבֵּנוּ בְּתוֹרָתוֹ, *May He open our heart through His Torah* ... (from וּבָא לְצִיּוֹן).

Rebbi approached one of the older students in the *beis midrash* and opened his jacket, then *pointed* to the boy's heart and said the next few words of this song. ... וְיָשֵׂם בְּלִבֵּנוּ אַהֲבָתוֹ וְיִרְאָתוֹ.

Rebbi said:

> "It is not enough for our hearts to be open; the word וְיָשֵׂם means *and [may He] place.* After an opening in your heart has been created, you must pray that something be *placed* inside that opening; and that "something" is love and awe of Hashem.

We pray that Hashem open our heart and place love and awe inside it. But there is much we can do aside from *tefillah* to ensure that this occurs.

- When you go into a classroom to study Torah, you have inserted the key into the lock that will open your heart.

- When you sit down, open your *sefer,* and find the place, you have opened the door further.
- When you concentrate on the words you are being taught, and allow the words to penetrate within your *neshamah,* you have begun to *fill* your heart with love and awe of Hashem.

VII. In Your Heart or upon Your Heart

In the *Shacharis tefillah,* we find three quotations concerning spiritual growth and our heart:

1. As mentioned above, in וּבָא לְצִיּוֹן, we ask:

הוּא יִפְתַּח לִבֵּנוּ בְּתוֹרָתוֹ וְיָשֵׂם בְּלִבֵּנוּ אַהֲבָתוֹ וְיִרְאָתוֹ

May He open our heart through His Torah and place in our heart love and awe of Him.

2. In the first paragraph of *Shema* we say:

וְהָיוּ הַדְּבָרִים הָאֵלֶּה אֲשֶׁר אָנֹכִי מְצַוְּךָ הַיּוֹם עַל לְבָבֶךָ (דברים ו:ו)

Let these words that I command you today be upon your heart (Devarim 6:6).

3. In the blessing recited after *Shema* and before *Shemoneh Esrei,* there is a sentence which I say aloud every day when I lead the yeshivah *minyan:*

אַשְׁרֵי אִישׁ שֶׁיִּשְׁמַע לְמִצְוֹתֶיךָ וְתוֹרָתְךָ וּדְבָרְךָ יָשִׂים עַל לִבּוֹ

Praiseworthy is the person who obeys Your command-ments and places Your teaching and Your word upon his heart.

Why, in the first quotation, do we pray that love and awe of Hashem be placed

in our heart,

while in the next two quotations, we speak of His holy Torah as being

upon our heart?

Rabbi Mendlowitz explained the differences beautifully.

1. The first quotation refers to a general approach to learning Torah. The sentence begins with a plea that Hashem will open the door of our heart so that Torah can enter *therein.* The love and awe of Hashem that we pray for at the sentence's conclusion is needed to help us attain this goal of having the Torah permeate our hearts.

2. The *pasuk* from *Shema* (וְהָיוּ הַדְּבָרִים ...) is followed by the command וְשִׁנַּנְתָּם לְבָנֶיךָ, *Teach them thoroughly to your children.* To be
ideally suited to teach Torah to children, a person has to be so
immersed in Torah that it fills his entire heart, spills over *upon* it,
and thereby enters the heart of his students or children. This is
why the Torah states, *Let these words that I command you today be*
upon *your heart.* Teach them thoroughly to your children.

> עֶס זָאל אִיבֶּערגִיסֶען אִיבֶּער דֶער הַארץ
> If you have so much Torah in your mind and heart that it
> overflows over your heart, then you can teach your
> children.
>
> This abundance of Torah will enable you to teach
> others as well.

3. The third quotation, *Praiseworthy is the person who . . . places*
Your teaching and Your word upon his heart, follows the same idea:

> Praiseworthy is the person when his heart overflows with
> Torah. This person can serve as a role model. This person
> has so much Torah that he can share it with others,
> perhaps with all of *Klal Yisrael.*

It is not enough to be a learned Jew *for yourself.* Torah should be
overflowing from your heart. In this way, you will *reach* out to others.

This is the reason why I would say this sentence out loud every day.

This is the reason why I would walk around the entire *minyan* as I
said this sentence.

> I wanted to awaken in each and every *talmid* a desire to
> *daven* with greater *kavanah.*

Most people recite the *pasuk* "Shema Yisrael . . ." out loud and with
kavanah, meaning that they concentrate, at the very least, on the plain
meaning of the words (see *Shulchan Aruch, Orach Chaim* Ch. 61).
However, once they complete the next sentence, ... בָּרוּךְ שֵׁם כְּבוֹד, and
their voices are lowered, people often "zoom" through the rest of
Shema. Please bear in mind that though the *halachah* states that בָּרוּךְ
שֵׁם כְּבוֹד ... should be said softly, the remainder of *Shema* may be said
out loud. Every word must be said clearly.

And try your very best to say each word with proper *kavanah*,
concentration. To *daven* with *kavanah* means to *daven* with understanding, sincerity, and *hergesh*, feeling.

"*Kavanah*" has another very important meaning, as we shall see.

VIII. Kavanah: Direction

When I traveled to *Eretz Yisrael* for the first time, in 1961, I immediately learned to ask:

בְּאֵיזֶה כִּווּן אֵלֵךְ

"*B'eizeh kivun* (כִּווּן) *eileich?*" "In which *direction* should I go (to get from one place to another)?"

Thus, I learned that the word כַּוָּנָה also means *direction.*

Many Jews in America today are yeshivah graduates and know the פֵּרוּשׁ הַמִּלּוֹת, the meaning of the words in our *tefillos.* However, many old-timers and *baalei teshuvah* do not know the *meaning* of the words they say in their prayers. One may arise every morning, put on *tallis* and *tefillin,* and have no notion of what he is saying.

Would you say that his *tefillah* is not worth anything?

- He does not know *kavanah.*
- He does not know the *peirush hamilos;*
  he does not know what he is saying.
- He does not understand the *tefillos.*

What does he accomplish with his *tefillah*?

I once said that perhaps the plain, simple Jew, who is not a learned Jew but starts his day with *tallis, tefillin* and sincere *davening,* merits that his *tefillos* are accepted by Hashem just like those of a learned person.

I wish I had the *kavanah* that Rabbi Moshe Feinstein had in his *tefillah*! Reb Moshe's *tefillah* was on a much higher plane than that of you or me. As the leader of our generation, his thoughts in *tefillah* had much more depth and meaning than ours.

Yet, here I am saying that a much simpler Jew, an Orthodox Jew who never learned in his youth, and who does not know the meaning of his *davening,* might merit that his *tefillah* be as acceptable before G-d as the *tefillah* of a learned Jew.

How is this possible? Dare we express such a thought?

There is such a thing as saying, "Thank You," to Hashem.

When Reb Moshe said, "Thank You," to Hashem, he knew exactly what he meant; "Thank You" came straight from his *heart.*

But what does "Thank You" mean when the person who is saying it does not even know what he is saying?

Remember, the word *kavanah* means *direction.*

Why do simple, unlearned Jews get up every morning to *daven*? They know that it is a *mitzvah* to *daven.*

וּלְעָבְדוֹ בְּכָל לְבַבְכֶם, *and to serve Him with all your heart (Devarim* 11:13), refers to *tefillah,* to the *mitzvah* of *davening.* אֵיזוֹ הִיא עֲבוֹדָה שֶׁהִיא בְּלֵב? הֱוֵי אוֹמֵר זוֹ תְּפִלָּה (תַּעֲנִית ב:א). When the simple Jew arises in the morning, he directs himself to Hashem.

> "Hashem, I do not know what the words of *davening* mean. But You want me to *daven.*
>
> "Therefore, I will *daven* to You, Hashem. It is hard for me, Hashem, to stand before You in prayer, uttering sentence after sentence, paragraph after paragraph, without understanding anything at all. But I will do it, Hashem, because
>> this is what *you want!*
>>
>> Therefore, this is what *I will do!*"

This is, perhaps, the *greatest* intent that a person can have, to *daven* with perfect faith in Hashem, and only because Hashem *wants* us to *daven* to Him.

The key word for such *kavanah,* intent, is *direction.*

"I get up in the morning and the first thing I do is to put on my *tallis* and *tefillin.* I do not go to work until I have prayed. I do not go and talk to my friends. I do not sit down to eat. In my *davening,* I *direct* myself for one half-hour or more to You, Hashem."

This is why I say that it is conceivable that the *tefillah* of such a person is as acceptable as that of a most learned person.

This *tefillah,* that an ordinary person directs to G-d, is his *kavanah.* It is most acceptable to Hashem.

IX. Minyan — Its Importance and Greatness

It is most important to *daven* with a *minyan,* a quorum of ten men. There are many reasons for this:

1. When a multitude of people declare,
> "Long live the King,"
   this has greater impact than if one person offers praises in one place while another individual offers similar praises elsewhere.

Ten or more Jews together form a powerful group in a spiritual sense and bring the *Shechinah* (Hashem's Presence) into their midst.

2. There are many parts of *tefillah* that can be said only with a *minyan*. These include: *Kaddish; Borchu; Kedushah;* and *Krias HaTorah.*

   Davening with a *minyan* ensures fulfillment of these important *mitzvos.*

3. Our Rabbis tell us that whereas an individual's prayers may not always be accepted, prayers of a *tzibur,* community (i.e. a *minyan*), are never rejected.

Rabbi Mendlowitz offered a beautiful parable concerning this:

There was a small but wealthy village near the sea. Never had this village been visited by the king of the land.

One year, in celebration of the village's 100th anniversary, its villagers petitioned the king to honor them with a royal visit. Their request was granted.

The villagers attended a mass meeting to discuss the format of the celebration. This was to be a great day! The village council decided that each villager would contribute one jewel. From these jewels, they would fashion a scintillating, exquisite crown which would be presented to the king as a gift.

However, there was one villager who could not afford such an expensive contribution. Therefore, he roamed the seashore day after day in search of a stone that could be used in the crown. One day, he found a perfectly round, transparent pebble. The rays of the sun glinted through this pebble in full brilliance.

The villager presented his stone to the council as his contribution to the crown. Many people scoffed at him until a wise man spoke up:

"Surely, if the entire village lined up before the king, and each villager presented his one jewel in paying homage to the king, and this villager would present his pebble, then, most probably, the lone villager would be jailed for ridiculing the king, no matter how good his intentions may have been.

But,

> if this pebble will be part of a crown, in which all the jewels cast their lustrous glow together, then this villager's pebble would also be an acceptable contribution."

Rabbi Mendlowitz explained:

If each individual's prayers come before the Heavenly Throne and are judged on their own merit, then perhaps some of these prayers will be considered mere "pebbles," and will not be acceptable. However, if all our prayers come before Hashem collectively, then they form a crown of exquisite beauty and are acceptable to the King of kings.

When one comes to *shul* to *daven,* his intentions are surely good. Yet, his *kavanah* may be so lacking that his *tefillah,* on its own merit, carries very little weight in Heaven.

But,

> if my *kavanah* is acceptable in *Shemoneh Esrei,* and someone else in the *minyan* has proper *kavanah* in answering אָמֵן to every *berachah,* and a third person's *kavanah* is good throughout the *Shema,* * then their prayers wing heavenward together and form one beautiful sparkling crown; collectively, all their prayers are acceptable.

This is why many *tzaddikim* recommended saying the *pasuk* וְאָהַבְתָּ לְרֵעֲךָ כָּמוֹךָ, *Love your fellow as yourself* (*Vayikra* 19:18) every morning before *davening.*

- If there is love and understanding for one another,
- if there is a bond of friendship that unites us,
    then our prayers can count for one another.
- The crown of *tefillos* that are recited by a *minyan* is most beautiful.
- The prayers of a multitude of people are always great in the eyes of Hashem.

X. We're Counting on You —
Remember Who You Are!!

Surely, when you start *davening,* you will remember that the word *kavanah* means *direction,* as I explained it. Direct your words to Hashem.

---

* *Shulchan Aruch* states that for a person to fulfill the *mitzvah* of *Shema,* he must at least concentrate on the meaning of the first *pasuk* and . . . בָּרוּךְ שֵׁם כְּבוֹד.

Yet, I want a great deal more from you, dear *talmid*:

- I expect you to come to *minyan* regularly and daily: *on time.*
- I expect you to listen to the meanings of the *tefillos* as I explain them every day.
- I urge you to *daven* with *kavanah*: with sincerity and understanding of the prayers you say.
- I urge you to strive to the best of your ability to involve your entire being in your *tefillos.*

As we say in *Nishmas* on Shabbos morning:

כָּל עַצְמֹתַי תֹּאמַרְנָה ה׳ מִי כָמוֹךְ (תהילם לה:י)

All my bones shall say, "Hashem, who is like You?" (*Tehillim* 35:10).

Remember, if you start the day off right, with proper *tefillah,* you will learn better as well.

I want, I hope, and I pray that each and every one of you will grow up to be in a position to inspire others so that they will want to emulate

- your love of Hashem,
- your love of Torah,
- your love of *mitzvos,* and
- your love of *maasim tovim* (good deeds).

In such a person, the world will perceive a happy, warm, and sincere Jew.

We need more people like this in our world. It is not easy to be such an individual.

May G-d grant that of the many people who will read these pages, at least some, perhaps even many, will resolve to be this kind of person.

May G-d grant that of the many people who will read these pages, *you* will be among those who will resolve to be this kind of person.

11

Kibbud Av Va'eim —
Respect for Parents

כַּבֵּד אֶת אָבִיךָ וְאֶת אִמֶּךָ §•

The *mitzvah* of כַּבֵּד אֶת אָבִיךָ וְאֶת אִמֶּךָ, *to honor and respect one's father and mother,* is one of the most important *mitzvos* we have. Let us understand the depths of this complex *mitzvah.* Allow me, first, to point out to you some of the major points of this *mitzvah.*

The Ten Commandments, which were inscribed upon *Shnei Luchos HaBris,* the Two Tablets of the Covenant between G-d and Israel, are divided into two sets of *mitzvos.*

•§ *Between Man and G-d*
בֵּין אָדָם לַמָּקוֹם

On one of the *Luchos,* five *mitzvos* between man and G-d were inscribed:

1. I am Hashem your G-d. . .
2. You are not to have any other gods. . .
3. You must not take the Name of G-d in vain.
    You must not swear in vain.
4. Observe the Sabbath Day. . .
5. Honor (and respect) your father and mother.

◄§ Between Man and Fellow Man
בֵּין אָדָם לַחֲבֵרוֹ

The commandments on the other Tablet are *mitzvos* between man and his fellow man.

One may then ask, why is the fifth commandment of honoring parents in the first group? Is it not a *mitzvah* between man and his fellow man?

The answer is that by giving *kavod* to your mother and father you are automatically giving *kavod* to Hashem. Your parents teach you all the *mitzvos* of the Torah. They teach you about Hashem, that there is a G-d in the world. They teach you about Shabbos and not to swear falsely or in vain.

- By honoring your parents and their teachings,
  you will be honoring Hashem.
- By honoring them, and living their way of life,
  you will automatically be fulfilling all the *mitzvos*
  of the Torah as you try to emulate them.
- By listening to them, you will learn all about
  Torah, *mitzvos,* and *maasim tovim.*
- By seeing your father put on *tefillin* and attend Torah
  classes, you will automatically begin doing this as well.
- By watching your mother prepare for Shabbos and
  Yom Tov, and watching her light candles, you will
  be inspired by the beauty of living a Torah life.

The continuous transmission of Torah and tradition is ensured by the influence of the home. Through this means, we learn to fulfill the entire Torah. Therefore, this *mitzvah* is in the group of command-ments between man and G-d, for through this *mitzvah* we will learn to fulfill all *mitzvos* between man and G-d.*

---

* In today's times, some individuals may seek substitute parents. We have so many *baalei teshuvah* whose parents did not teach them Torah and *mitzvos.* Not everyone sees *mitzvos* being observed in their homes. Therefore, they must adopt a teacher from whom they will be able to learn.

In their quest to understand what it means to be Jewish, these *baalei teshuvah* seek a role model to emulate. In this way, they find the road to G-d and to *Yiddishkeit.*

כַּבֵּד אֶת ה׳ מֵהוֹנֶךָ

We are commanded to honor G-d with everything He has blessed us with. We are also commanded to honor our parents.

Our Rabbis tell us that since the expression כַּבֵּד, *respect,* is repeated in relation to G-d and also in relation to parents, then,

> when we show our respect to our parents, we are literally giving Hashem respect as well.

⋅§ Gratitude Without Limit

We see the prominent position that "respect for parents" has, in developing proper ways of fulfilling Torah concepts.

A great deal of the upbringing of children falls on the shoulders of the mother. Many fathers are either working or otherwise occupied with daily responsibilities. The mother is the one to remind her son to *daven,* recite *Modeh Ani* and *Shema,* and make the appropriate *berachah* before he eats. Our mothers are not there just to cook meals for us or clean up after us. The respect we owe her cannot be overestimated.

We equally owe a great deal to our fathers. We go to *shul* with them. We generally review our Torah studies with them. Their learning and general behavior are an inspiration.

The aspiration of our parents to "teach us properly" is constant. They pray that their goals and their hopes for their children will be fully realized.

Respect means that we have to follow their teachings while they are alive. We must give them even greater *kavod* after they, G-d forbid, pass away.

> Why? Because when they are alive, they are right in front of us. We see them all the time. We have ample opportunities to show them our love and our respect.
>
> If they are no longer with us, we must remember that every *mitzvah* we do on this world brings added greatness and luster to them in the world above.

⚜ Their Image Before You

There is a story told about a 12-year-old boy who left Europe to go to America at the turn of the century. His father cautioned him that in America he would find it difficult to purchase kosher food. In 1900, there were no *hechsheirim* (kashrus certification) on food. He also discussed keeping Shabbos, and putting on *tefillin* regularly, once he reached his *bar mitzvah*.

His father suddenly paused. He said to his son, "Can I foretell every problem that you will face in America? Should a problem arise that I did not warn you about, do not say to yourself that since we did not discuss this particular problem you can do whatever you want. On the other hand, who knows if we will ever see each other again? [They did not.]

"My best advice to you is as follows:

When you have a problem, ask yourself: 'What would my father or mother advise me to do? Will I bring *kavod* to them in Europe (if they are still alive)? Will whatever I do bring *kavod* to them in Heaven above, if they are no longer alive?'

"By doing this," said the father, "you will not make mistakes."

⚜ The Greatest Honor

When Yaakov *Avinu* went to Charan at the suggestion of his parents, he stayed to learn at the Yeshivah of Shem V'Eiver for 14 years. He was away from home for an additional 22 years. For 20 of those years he was working for his uncle Lavan, whose daughters he ultimately married.

Measure for measure, in the same way that Yaakov was away from his parents for 22 years, Yosef was separated from his father Yaakov for the same number of years.

The question is raised: Why wasn't Yaakov punished for the 14 additional years that he was away at the yeshivah? He was away these 14 additional years and could not fulfill the *mitzvah* of honoring his parents!

The answer is beautiful and significant.

Sitting in a yeshivah and learning Torah for 14 years was the greatest *kavod* he could have given his parents. They were overjoyed that he was laying the foundation to live in a foreign country by first fortifying himself with Torah learning and direction.

He learned two important lessons:

1. Shem had lived through the generation of the *mabul*, when the people had no respect for one another. It was truly a state of anarchy.
2. Eiver had lived through the generation that built the tower of Babel, as an attempt to wage war against G-d.

Yaakov learned from them how to deal with wickedness against people and arrogance against G-d.

Before leaving for a strange country, and before living with Lavan, Yaakov went to study how to deal with all sorts of problems and people that he would encounter.

By stopping at the yeshivah, Yaakov was fulfilling the *mitzvah* of respect for his parents. He was fortifying himself so as not to stray from his parents' righteous teachings.

We should consider our parents the most important people in our lives. They have helped us develop and brought us closer to Torah and *mitzvos.* Whatever we are as we grow up, we owe to them and to their teachings.

There are many little ways in which we can give *kavod* to our parents. The greatest way of course is how we act in yeshivah. We spend more time in yeshivah than we do at home. If a child's behavior is exemplary in the yeshivah, the parents are complimented for raising a wonderful person; this is the greatest *kavod* you can possibly give your parents.

The *Gemara* uses the expression אַשְׁרֵי יוֹלַדְתּוֹ, "How fortunate are the parents who gave birth to such an outstanding child."

⋖§ Care and Concern

There is an amazing *Gemara* (*Kiddushin* 31a) which states:

Avimi, the son of Rabbi Avuhu, said:

There is a son who serves his father a banquet meal every night, and yet, that son will never have *Olam Haba*; that son will not receive credits or rewards.

There is another son who makes his father toil in a mill, which is very laborious work. (One had to turn huge stones, which in turn ground the wheat into flour.) This son will be rewarded with *Olam Haba*.

Rashi comments very simply:

The son who serves his father a seven-course meal does so with a frown on his face. He is not pleasant when preparing the meal. He hardly speaks to his father.

On the other hand, how does the son who sends his father to the mill deserve *Olam Haba*? He eases the burden by speaking pleasant words to his father and he tries to make it as easy as possible. He encourages his father with his words of care and concern.

Both *Rashi* and *Tosafos* quote a beautiful *Yerushalmi*:

The father who was treated to such outstanding meals was overwhelmed. He once asked his son how he managed to prepare such lavish meals every single day.

The son answered him: "It is none of your business. You are old and decrepit. You just go ahead and eat."

His response showed his father that it was difficult for him to prepare the meals and that he was unhappy doing it.

This type of son will not get a share in *Olam Haba*.

Then they quote another incident wherein the father was an elderly person. In those days, the king demanded that all citizens should work a certain amount of time in the king's palace. The father received his notice to serve in the palace for two weeks. The son worked in a mill. The son was worried about his father and said to him:

"Abba (Father), you never know what kind of work you will do in the palace. You might have to work long hours. The work might be menial. Take my place at the mill and I will go to the palace in your place. You will have regular hours. You will be able to rest whenever you please."

This son was concerned about his father's welfare and well-being. Although he suggests that his father do laborious work at the mill, he will receive *Olam Haba*.

From this *Yerushalmi* we learn an important lesson:

It is not *what* you do,

but *how* you do it, that counts!

This is why *Sefer Bereishis* is important. We could have had one *Chumash* that listed all 613 *mitzvos* in order.

But no!

We have *Sefer Bereishis* to teach us the historical and social development of *Klal Yisrael* from the beginning of creation, and through the lives of Avraham, Yitzchak, and Yaakov. The Torah describes their lives, and how they lived and served Hashem.

> We need *Chumash* not only to tell us about the *mitzvos*, but *how* to do the *mitzvos*.

- Avraham taught us *chesed*;
  how to interact with all people.
- Yitzchak taught us *mesiras nefesh*; that we
  must be prepared to give up our lives in serving G-d.
  He was prepared to be a *korban*, a sacrifice to G-d.
  He taught us *avodah*, how to serve Hashem,
  completely and sincerely.
- Yaakov taught us the importance of learning Torah:
  Only through Torah can we know how to live our daily
  lives, according to Hashem's will. How to do a *mitzvah*
  is as important as the doing of the *mitzvah*.

רַב יוֹסֵף כִּי הֲוָה שָׁמַע קַל כַּרְעָא דְּאִמֵּיה, אָמַר אֵיקוּם מִקַּמֵּי שְׁכִינָה דְּאָתְיָא (קידושין לא:)

When Rav Yosef would hear the footsteps of his mother coming into the room he would say: "I shall arise before the Divine Presence. The *Shechinah* is coming with my mother" (*Kiddushin* 31b).

Rav Yosef equated his mother with G-dliness. When he listened to his mother, he was listening to Hashem.

A feeling of *kedushah*, spiritual uplift and holiness, entered together with his mother.

◆§ *Two Outlooks*

A student, Yisroel, came into my office one day and complained that his mother was constantly "bugging" him, criticizing him, picking on him and telling him what to do. There were many disagreements.

I told Yisroel that for the next three days, he should write down when he thinks his mother is "bugging" him; he should keep a record of each disagreement.

The list went as follows:
- "Hang up your coat."
- "Did you do your homework?"
- "Put your briefcase away."
- "Wash up for supper."
- "Make a *berachah.*"
- "Did you *bentsh?*"
- "Daven *Maariv.*"
- "Recite *Krias Shema,*" and so on.

I reviewed the list and discussed it with Yisroel. I told him:
"The items you listed are things that have to be done.
"From now on, do everything on your own, without having to be told.
- Hang up your coat.
- Do your homework.
- Wash up for supper etc.

Do all this on your own. Let me know the results."

Yisroel approached me a few days later. He was ecstatic. "Thank you so much.
You straightened out my mother for me.
She doesn't tell me what to do any more. I do it on my own. Everything is wonderful at home, peaceful and quiet."

I stared at Yisroel for a full minute and said very quietly but forcefully, "I did not straighten out your mother.
I straightened you out.
"You were the problem all along. You did not know how to appreciate your mother. You did not understand the depth of the *mitzvah* of *Kibbud Av Va'eim.* You did not act responsibly.

"Your mother was merely trying to bring you up in the right *derech,* in telling you what to do. She was doing her job in calling your attention to your own responsibilities."

⋖§ A Chain Reaction

There is a famous story told about the *mitzvah* of *Kibbud Av.*
There was once a family who had an elderly father living with them. All went well for many years. They ate together in a carpeted

dining room. As the father grew older and more feeble, he started making a terrible mess at mealtimes. The daughter and son-in-law saw how uncomfortable the father was, since he was dirtying the carpet and expensive tablecloths, and was surely embarrassed by this. To avoid further embarrassment they sent him out to the kitchen to have his meals there.

He no longer ate with the family.

He ate alone.

They did this out of the kindness of their hearts, thinking that he would be more comfortable.

Once in the kitchen, things ran smoothly, until his hands began shaking badly. He dropped china and glasses, which smashed on the hard tile floor. The son-in-law thought of a plan to ease his father-in-law's discomfort. He went down to his workshop and carved out a wooden plate, spoon, and fork. He presented it to the old father, explaining that even if these would fall, they could not break.

Once, upon returning from vacation, the son-in-law and daughter of this old man were approached by their very own young son and were presented with a beautifully wrapped "welcome home" gift.

When they opened it, they were astounded to find

- two wooden plates,
- two wooden forks,
- and two wooden spoons.

When the father asked his son for an explanation, he was told:

"This is for you and Mommy when you grow old and begin to shake. I am just preparing for the future."

Although their intentions were good and they wanted to avoid embarrassing their old father, they apologized immediately, realizing their grave mistake.

They saw that the way they were treating the old man was exactly the way they would be treated when they would grow old. They told the old father that he would now be eating with them in the dining room again, and he should not worry about spilling or breaking things.

The father thanked his son for bringing to his attention what he had done wrong.

The Torah commands us, "Honor your father and mother so that your days may be long upon the land which Hashem, your G-d, gives you" (*Shemos* 20:12). You will be rewarded and granted a long life.

Why will you live long if you fulfill this *mitzvah*? Because your *parents* will live long if you treat them with love and take good care of them, as the story above illustrates.

The way you treat your parents sets an example for the way your children will treat you. If you treat your parents well, they will live long and happily, due to your kind treatment.

> In turn your children will give you the proper *kavod* and you, too, will live longer.

And the *mitzvah* continues on and on from generation to generation.

Today, there is a world-wide *baal teshuvah* movement. When someone returns to the observant Jewish fold, he is obligated to fulfill the *mitzvah* of *Kibbud Av Va'eim,* even if his parents are not *frum.*

There was a very dynamic *Rebbi* who influenced a group of students to observe Shabbos, *kashrus,* and many other *mitzvos.* They eventually enrolled in a yeshivah, much to their parents' disapproval. They kept kosher on their own and tried not to desecrate Shabbos.

One of the students went to a *shiur* Friday night, and was locked out of the house by his parents. They did this to force him to ring the bell. The student sat outside until two a.m., when the parents finally relented and opened the door.

This group had tremendous *mesiras nefesh* for *mitzvos* but they never forgot how to respect their parents.

I told them to do errands for their parents, shop for them, and set a good *"yeshivah bachur"* example.

Over the years many of these homes became kosher homes. Many fathers began putting on *tefillin* when the time came for their sons to do so at *bar-mitzvah* age.

This is what *Kibbud Av Va'eim* is all about.

> It goes both ways:
>> In doing their best to honor and respect their parents, they were able to influence their parents to join with them, to come closer to Hashem and His Torah.

12
מַחֲשָׁבָה, דִבּוּר, מַעֲשֶׂה
Thought, Speech, Action

Under the various sections of this chapter, again and again, we are reminded of the importance of service to Hashem in Thought — Speech — Action.

I. Shabbos

◄§ *The Song of Shabbos*

מִזְמוֹר שִׁיר לְיוֹם הַשַּׁבָּת (תהלים צב:א)
"A psalm, a song for the Shabbos day" (*Tehillim* 92:1).

Physical creation was complete at the end of the sixth day, but the spiritual development of mankind will continue until the End of Days, until the arrival of *Mashiach,* speedily in our time.

On the seventh day, on Shabbos, our day of rest from the work week, we are stirred to sing to Hashem. Man's soul is liberated from its weekly shackles. Cleansed and purified, we can sing and praise Hashem.

How can we serve Hashem? In these ways:

1. מַחֲשָׁבָה, *thought.*
2. דִבּוּר, *speech.*
3. מַעֲשֶׂה, *action.*

Every *mitzvah* we do, each one of the 613 *mitzvos,* as well as all the *mitzvos d'rabbanan* (from our Rabbis), will fall into one of these three categories: thought, speech, action.

לְהַגִּיד אַמְרֵי שִׁיר בִּשְׁלֹשָׁה כּוֹחוֹתֵינוּ: בְּפֶה – בְּמַעֲשֶׂה – בְּמַחְשָׁבָה
(תִּפְאֶרֶת יִשְׂרָאֵל תָּמִיד ז:ד)

Tiferes Yisrael, in his commentary to *Mishnah Tamid* (7:4), expresses the same idea. He comments on *Tehillim* Ch. 92 which we recite every Shabbos, and which was sung in the *Beis HaMikdash* every Shabbos:

"It is good to thank Hashem and to sing praises to Your Name, O exalted One. To relate Your kindness in the dawn and Your faith in the nights. Upon ten-stringed instrument and lyre, with meditation accompanying the harp" (vs. 2-3).

These *pesukim*, says *Tiferes Yisrael*, refer to three כּחוֹת, *abilities,* through which we serve Hashem.

לְהַגִּיד בַּבֹּקֶר חַסְדֶּךָ, *To relate Your kindness in the dawn,* describes the כֹּחַ of דִּבּוּר, *speech,* through which we express Hashem's praises.

עֲלֵי עָשׂוֹר וַעֲלֵי נָבֶל, *Upon ten-stringed instrument and lyre,* describes מַעֲשֶׂה, *action.* We use our *fingers* to play musical instruments, a most lofty way of serving Hashem through action.

עֲלֵי הִגָּיוֹן בְּכִנּוֹר, *With meditation accompanying the harp,* describes the מַחֲשָׁבָה, *thought,* which the servant of Hashem engages in while he is *listening* to the music, especially the moving sounds of the harp. His *thoughts* are lifted up higher and higher. He is carried away into higher spheres of מַחֲשָׁבָה, as his soul is enraptured by the beautiful music.

Irrespective of the mood in which the Shabbos may find us as it enters our home, the Shabbos will always inspire our minds and captivate our hearts.

Our actions and emotions come closer and closer to Hashem, as we serve Him throughout the Shabbos day. Therefore, in the Song of the Shabbos Day, King David inspires us to draw close to Hashem in thought, speech, and action.

Distinctions

T here is a vast difference between the three powers described above.

The thought process is, in essence, the most delicate and most finely tuned of these three qualities of man.

- It encompasses perception and intuition.
- It is the process that triggers our emotions.

To describe a fleeting thought which flashes across your mind in a split second can take hundreds of words.

For example:

A mother is standing at the window. She sees her child dashing across the street. At the same time she sees a car speeding down the street.

In that *fleeting moment of thought,* she is horrified.

The mother shrieks: "Oh! *Ribono Shel Olam!*"

Imagine the thoughts that pass through her mind.

To describe this moment of horror takes countless words. It is impossible to capture the fears and agonizing thoughts of that mother. How does one express, in mere words, the anxious heartbeat of a mother at that horror-stricken moment?

An architect might contemplate various ways of building a magnificent structure when suddenly an idea hits him. The thought can be *instantaneous.* Yet, to describe such a thought would take a great deal of time and many words. It would necessitate his writing numerous pages and drawing countless diagrams. He would then have to consult engineers and various construction experts to develop this thought of his before he even begins acting upon it.

The *thought* could have lasted *one* moment in his life. It could take months, or possibly years, of *speaking* and discussion before his idea (thought) can be translated into action.

When he finally reaches the point of *action,* to gathering all of the materials necessary, and then to actually building this edifice, many years might be needed.

Thus, there are definite distinctions between the three powers with which we serve Hashem.

II. Moshe Rabbeinu's Farewell Address

We find this same thought in Moshe *Rabbeinu's* final address to the Jewish people.

11. כִּי הַמִּצְוָה . . . לֹא רְחוֹקָה הִוא,
The mitzvah is not far from you.

12. לֹא בַשָּׁמַיִם הִוא . . . .
It is not in the heavens.

13. וְלֹא מֵעֵבֶר לַיָּם הִוא.
It is not on the other side of the ocean.

14. כִּי קָרוֹב אֵלֶיךָ הַדָּבָר מְאֹד: בְּפִיךָ וּבִלְבָבְךָ לַעֲשׂתוֹ.
The Word (of G-d) *is very close to you. It is* בְּפִיךָ,
in your mouth (speech), וּבִלְבָבְךָ, *and in your heart*
(thought), לַעֲשׂתוֹ, *to do it,* to fulfill it (action).
(*Devarim* 30:11-14)

With these words, Moshe tells *Klal Yisrael* that there is no *mitzvah* that is too difficult for them.

> *It is close to you. It is through your speech, your thought, and your action* that you can fulfill everything that Hashem wants you to.

In truth, most *mitzvos* we perform (through action) are preceded by a *berachah,* which involves *kavanah,* concentration (thought), and speech. Thus, most *mitzvos* involve the three ways of serving Hashem, *machshavah, dibur,* and *maaseh.*

III. Modeh Ani – מוֹדֶה אֲנִי לְפָנֶיךָ

◆§ *Start the Day off Right!*

How do you wake up in the morning? As soon as we awaken, our *thoughts* turn immediately to thanking Hashem for the return of our soul. Our Rabbis tell us that each night a part of the *neshamah* returns to Heaven and gives an accounting of everything it did that day. It is noteworthy that our Rabbis also teach that before retiring for the night, we should make a *chesbon hanefesh,* a spiritual accounting of all our actions of the day, and note both our *mitzvos* and our transgressions.

When our *neshamah* is returned to us and we awaken, we should be filled with a desire to thank Hashem for this. Our first *thought* should be to serve Him.

We then serve Him through *speech*, by saying *Modeh Ani*. We voice our thanks to the Almighty for having returned our soul to us. We thank Hashem for granting us another day of life, for having faith in us, that we will be better today than we were yesterday.

Immediately thereafter, we serve Hashem with *action*, by washing the traditional *negel vasser*: taking a cup of water and pouring it on each hand three times.

One of the reasons for washing *negel vasser* is that when the *neshamah* leaves us at night, we become *spiritually unclean*.

> G-d has created us with a definite purpose in mind. In life, we can reach the highest degree of *kedushah*, holiness, and *taharah*, purity, through the performance of *mitzvos*.

When the *neshamah* leaves us at night, and we are in a state in which we cannot perform *mitzvos*, we lose some of this holiness and become spiritually unclean. This is also the reason for the washing of our hands, in this same manner, when one returns from a funeral or from a cemetery. In life, there is *kedushah*; in death, when there no longer are *mitzvos* to perform, there is spiritual impurity.

When the *neshamah* returns to us in the morning, this spiritual impurity leaves and remains only on the fingers.

Our Rabbis have taught us that only by washing our hands in this manner do we rid ourselves completely of this spiritual impurity.

Rabbi Samson Raphael Hirsch offers another reason for the washing of our hands in this manner:

He does not define the words *netilas yadayim* as washing the hands, but as *lifting up* the hands. As we wash our hands according to the dictates of *halachah*, we, so to speak, raise them from the level of lower physical nature to their higher spiritual purpose. This teaches us that our actions throughout the day should be "lifted up" to Hashem and dedicated to Him. Just as our first action of the day is done according to prescribed law, in the same way will all our actions of the day follow the prescribed law of the Torah.

It may have taken you some time to read this, but the actual performance each morning takes but a minute.

Upon awakening, your first *thought* is to thank Hashem, You *say Modeh Ani,* and your first *action* of the day is the washing of the hands.*

In your first minute of awakening, you serve G-d with *thought, speech, and action.*

Our *Chachamim* were great. They composed the *Modeh Ani* and did not include G-d's Name in it. Therefore, this prayer can be said even while our hands are spiritually unclean. Immediately after the *Modeh Ani,* we follow the above-mentioned procedure, thereby washing away our spiritual uncleanliness and completing, in the very first minute of our day, our service of Hashem in all three possible ways.

You fulfilled all facets of life, in your service to Hashem, in your very first minute, upon waking up.

A most important blessing we say each morning is *Elokai Neshamah,* in which we utter Hashem's Name and offer praise for His having returned the *neshamah* to us after a night of sleep.

- A new day!
- Another day to do *mitzvos*!
- Another day to serve Hashem!

But since you are not yet completely spiritually and physically

---

* Even after washing your hands, you are still not ready to pray. Upon awakening, you must go to the bathroom to cleanse your body; you must wash your hands and face properly to prepare for prayer. You must brush your teeth, not because the dentist said so, but because your mouth may be full of saliva. You may have a foul smell from the entire night of sleeping.

After these preparations, you are permitted to say G-d's Name; you are ready to say prayers properly.

The *Nusach Ari Siddur,* used by many people, does not start *davening* with *Mah tovu* as we do. It begins with the *berachah* for washing hands, *al netilas yadayim.* This is followed by the *berachah, Asher Yatzar,* which is said after going to the bathroom, thanking G-d for creating man, as He did.

בָּרוּךְ אַתָּה ה' . . . אֲשֶׁר יָצַר אֶת הָאָדָם בְּחָכְמָה, *Blessed are You, Hashem, Who fashioned man with wisdom, and created within him many openings and cavities. If one of them were to be ruptured or blocked, it would be impossible to survive. . .*

Immediately following this *berachah, Nusach Ari* comes back to the most important *berachah* of the morning, *Elokai Neshamah.*

אֱלֹקַי נְשָׁמָה שֶׁנָּתַתָּ בִּי . . . , *My G-d, the soul you placed within me is pure. You created it. You fashioned it. You breathed it into me.*

In reciting this blessing, which follows the *Asher Yatzar* blessing, we are, in essence, saying:

"We thank You, Hashem, for returning our souls to us; for restoring our vitality in the morning with a soul of pure spiritual origin, and for maintaining us in life and in health."

clean, the Rabbis substituted the *Modeh Ani* which does not contain G-d's Name.

IV. Tefillin

מַחֲשָׁבָה, *thought,* is a very integral part of performing the *mitzvah* of *tefillin.*

The paragraph that is said before putting on the *tefillin* is very beautiful and directs our *thoughts* to the lofty purpose of this *mitzvah.* Recite it carefully, for it tells us that:

A. The *tefillin* on the arm is to recall the "outstretched arm" of Hashem, meaning, the might He displayed when He took us out of Egypt.

   (We might add that it also symbolizes that the work of our hands should be dedicated to serving Hashem throughout the day.)

B. The *tefillin* on the arm is placed opposite the heart to subjugate the desires and thoughts of our heart to G-d's service.

C. The *tefillin* are placed upon the head opposite the brain so that the *soul* in my brain, together with my other senses and potentials (all my spiritual aspirations and physical powers), may be subjugated to His Service.

Before putting on *tefillin* we *recite* a *berachah.* Then, we actually *put* the *tefillin* on our arm and head, fulfilling the aspect of *maaseh,* deed.

In all *mitzvos* where a *berachah* is involved, before reciting the *berachah,* one should give thought to what he is about to do. In this way, the *mitzvah* embodies דִּבּוּר, מַחֲשָׁבָה, and מַעֲשֶׂה.

V. Tefillah — Davening

Thought is a vital aspect of *tefillah.* When one *davens,* he must bear in mind that he is speaking directly to Hashem. It is also important that one do his best to *think* of the meaning of the prayers, and thus *daven* with greater *intensity,* greater *kavanah* (concentration).

Holding the *siddur,* following the words consciously with one's eyes, standing and perhaps swaying back and forth, will involve *maaseh,* action.

But, mainly, *davening* involves *dibur, speech.* One must *daven* clearly. One must enunciate each word carefully.

If you *daven* intently and with sincerity, bringing together all that we described above, an example will be set inspiring others to do the same.

Somebody watching you may say to himself:

"I will try to *daven* like the person in the third row."

Your stance and your actions while *davening* will have caught somebody's eye; he will take note of how you blended

thought, speech, and action in your *tefillah.*

Thus, you will have served as a role model.

VI. Shema

The most important part of the morning and evening prayers is the saying of *Shema.*

When we say *Shema Yisrael,* we accept upon ourselves עֹל מַלְכוּת שָׁמַיִם, *the yoke of the kingdom of Heaven,* by proclaiming G-d as our King. We are His subjects and are prepared to do His bidding.

The second *pasuk* in the first paragraph of *Shema* starts with the words:

וְאָהַבְתָּ אֵת ה' אֱלֹקֶיךָ

You shall love HASHEM, your G-d.

This sentence is immediately followed with a listing of *mitzvos* we should fulfill, and through them show our love for Hashem.

1. Thought

בְּכָל לְבָבְךָ וּבְכָל נַפְשְׁךָ וּבְכָל מְאֹדֶךָ. וְהָיוּ הַדְּבָרִים הָאֵלֶּה . . . עַל לְבָבֶךָ

Fill your *heart* and soul with the words and the spirit of the Torah. The Torah should constantly be in your heart and in your mind.

2. Speech

וְשִׁנַּנְתָּם לְבָנֶיךָ וְדִבַּרְתָּ בָּם . . .

Implant all these great ideals by teaching your children diligently. Talk to them about Torah constantly, *wherever* you are.

3. Action

וּקְשַׁרְתֶּם לְאוֹת עַל יָדֶךָ וְהָיוּ לְטֹטָפֹת בֵּין עֵינֶיךָ. וּכְתַבְתָּם עַל מְזֻזוֹת בֵּיתֶךָ וּבִשְׁעָרֶיךָ.

Put on *tefillin* every day, on your arm and on your head, and inscribe these words of Torah upon the *mezuzos* of your home and the gates of your cities.

Fulfill all these ideals
- in thought and feeling,
- in word and speech,
- in deed and in action.

VII. Shemoneh Esrei

In the fifth blessing of the *Shemoneh Esrei*, the blessing of *teshuvah*, we follow the same idea upon which our discussion has focused.

הֲשִׁיבֵנוּ אָבִינוּ לְתוֹרָתֶךָ וְקָרְבֵנוּ מַלְכֵּנוּ לַעֲבוֹדָתֶךָ

Cause us to return, our Father, to Your Torah. Bring us closer, our King, to Your service.

Machshavah: The word הֲשִׁיבֵנוּ, *Cause us to return,* is already in our thought before we actually enunciate it.

We are thinking of *teshuvah,* returning to G-d, and we call upon Hashem, our Father, to help us to return to Him.

How will we do *teshuvah?*

Dibur: Return us to Your Torah. By learning Torah, by delving into its words and discussing them, we will do *teshuvah* properly.

Maaseh: Bring us closer, our King, to Your service. Help us to serve You through performing Your *mitzvos.*

VIII. Rosh Hashanah, Yom Kippur, Succos

Each of the *yamim tovim* at the beginning of the year focuses on a different aspect of our service to Hashem:
- Rosh Hashanah — Thought
- Yom Kippur — Speech
- Succos — Action

Rosh Hashanah represents *machshavah,* thought. As this *yom tov* nears, we must turn our thoughts to Hashem. We must realize that a day of judgment is approaching. We must do *teshuvah.*

Before one can do so, one must *reflect* on the direction and the accomplishments of his life.

Yom Kippur then follows, representing *dibur,* the power of speech. We pour out our hearts before Hashem. We spend the entire day speaking to Him. We verbalize our thoughts; we put into words what we have been thinking about during the Ten Days of Repentance.

Succos is a *yom tov* of action, for thought and speech must be followed by action. We *build* a *succah* and then we *live* in it. We *buy* the four species and then hold them in our hands during the *yom tov.*

In our *davening* on Rosh Hashanah and Yom Kippur we exclaim with fervor:

וּצְדָקָה   וּתְפִלָּה   וּתְשׁוּבָה

Tzedakah   Tefillah   Teshuvah

can change any decree in Heaven that may not be to our benefit.

- *Teshuvah* is repentance through thought.
- *Tefillah* is speech.
- *Tzedakah* is action.

These three *mitzvos* will ensure that we will be inscribed for a good New Year.

IX. Shabbos

Shabbos was the climax of the Creation of the world. On Friday night, in our prayers, we say:

Shabbos may have been *last* in deed, but it was *first* in G-d's thoughts of Creation.

Shabbos was primary in Hashem's purpose for creating this world.

Whenever a great project is envisioned, a host of preparations must be made before the goal can be achieved.

Uppermost in Hashem's thought was that there would be a day of holiness. The entire universe had to be created first; yet סוֹף מַעֲשֶׂה בְּמַחֲשָׁבָה תְּחִלָּה, *last in deed was first in thought.* The actual creation of the world was preceded by Hashem's thought that there be a spiritual purpose to creation, and that the week conclude with a day devoted to the spiritual.

The *Midrash* states that the Torah was the architectural plan of Hashem.

אִסְתַּכֵּל בְּאוֹרַיְתָא וּבָרָא עָלְמָא

Hashem looked into the Torah and built His world.

- The purpose of all creation is *to know* that there is a G-d Who created everything.
- The purpose of Shabbos is to acknowledge that there is a G-d. No creation or work is permissible on Shabbos because Hashem did not create on Shabbos. By refraining from work, we demonstrate our belief in Hashem.
- The mission of *Bnei Yisrael* is to teach the world about G-d by example, by the way we speak and the way in which we conduct ourselves.
- The purpose of Torah is to have a guide through which *Bnei Yisrael* can study and learn and know how to conduct themselves.

קוּדְשָׁא בְּרִיךְ הוּא וְאוֹרַיְתָא וְיִשְׂרָאֵל חַד

Israel, Torah, and G-d are one and indivisible.
Israel, Torah, and G-d are unique and incomparable.

X. Tzedakah

When you give *tzedakah,* you have to *think* about the needs of an impoverished person and about the amount of *tzedakah* you will give him. This is *machshavah.*

The *maaseh* involves the actual act of giving.

Dibur: Although there is no *berachah* when giving charity, this *mitzvah can* involve speech.

> The *dibur* is the saying of something encouraging to the recipient of the *tzedakah.* This is called *piyus:* "I hope things will become better for you so that, one day, you will be able to give *tzedakah* to others."
>
> Speak to him, make him feel good. Certainly it is terribly wrong to give *tzedakah* while hurting the recipient's feelings.

I remember going to see a wealthy man, Fred Frankel of Flatbush, to ask him for a donation. He gave me a check for the yeshivah and I said: "Thank you."

He stopped me and said: "No, Rabbi Schwartz, *I must say,* 'Thank you.' "

"Why do you have to thank me?" I asked.

He replied: "You gave me the opportunity to do the *mitzvah* of giving *tzedakah.* If you had not come, perhaps I would not have given *tzedakah* today. Perhaps I would not have thought about it."

Mr. Frankel was fulfilling *machshavah* and *dibur* in his saying, "Thank you," to me. His writing a check and actually giving it to me was the involvement of *maaseh,* action.

In the vast majority of *mitzvos,* there is *machshavah, dibur,* and *maaseh* — if you look for it.

XI. Learning Torah

In the learning of Torah you are fulfilling *machshavah, dibur,* and *maaseh.* Let us suppose your *rebbi* asks a question. You think of an answer: This is *machshavah,* service to Hashem through thought.

> Who knows your answer while it is still in your thoughts, in your *machshavah? Machshavah* is a very fine and delicate aspect of learning. No one, besides Hashem and yourself, can know your thoughts before you express them. Your thoughts at that time are dedicated to Hashem and His Torah. You have dedicated the powers of your mind to G-d.
>
> Picture a *rosh yeshivah* sitting in front of a *Gemara.* No words are being said. The *rosh yeshivah* is merely swaying to and fro. He is thinking in depth about the *pshat,* the meaning, of the *Gemara* that he is learning at that moment.

My *Rebbi,* HaRav Shlomo Heiman, once described the great *Shaagas Aryeh*:

When the *Shaagas Aryeh* was looking out the window lost in deep thought he was thinking through all of *Shas,* the entire Talmud. עֶר טְרַאכְט דוּרְךְ גַאנְץ שַׁ"ס.

He was oblivious to anything else. He was thinking through various parts of the Talmud in a few short minutes.

This is true *machshavah*, dedicating one's thoughts to Hashem and to Torah. Thinking in learning is a very private *mitzvah*, one that is between Hashem and yourself.

In learning, when your *rebbi* poses a question, and you respond with an answer to the *rebbi* out loud, in class, you expand the *mitzvah* of learning Torah. Everyone who hears what you are saying becomes involved.

This is *speech service* to Hashem. *Dibur* expands the dimension of your Torah. It is a great privilege to share your Torah with as many people as possible.

Dibur goes further afield than *machshavah* alone.

Maaseh:

If the answer to your *rebbi's* question is written down, if Hashem helps you, and you write a *sefer*, you have involved *maaseh*, action, in fulfilling the great *mitzvah* of learning Torah.

Long after 120, you will be remembered.

We do not speak about *Rashi* in the past; and we do not say, "*Rashi*, zichrono livrachah, may his memory be blessed." We do not say of *Rambam*, zichrono livrachah. We do not say it because they are very much alive through their great writings, which are studied throughout the Torah world every day.

Everyone learning *Rashi* today feels as though *Rashi* is alive. *Rashi* has the *zechus*, the privilege, of teaching us today. This is the greatness and the strength of recording one's *divrei Torah* for future generations to learn from.

Rambam wrote his *sefarim* in the 12th century. He was born in 1135 and died in 1204. Whoever learns *Rambam* in this day and age adds merit to *Rambam* in Heaven above.

◆§ Thought and Expression

כִּי אִם בְּתוֹרַת ה׳ חֶפְצוֹ וּבְתוֹרָתוֹ יֶהְגֶּה יוֹמָם וָלָיְלָה
But his desire is in the Torah of HASHEM, and in His Torah he meditates day and night (Tehillim 1:2).

Rabbi Samson Raphael Hirsch explains:

Man's striving (what he seeks, what his goals are) lies in the teachings of Hashem's Torah;

and in His Torah he meditates [יֶהְגֶּה] day and night.

I heard this *pasuk* explained by my *Rebbi,* Rabbi Shraga Feivel Mendlowitz.

The term יֶהְגֶּה is used in *Tanach* to describe natural animal sounds. For example: כַּאֲשֶׁר יֶהְגֶּה הָאַרְיֵה וְהַכְּפִיר עַל טַרְפּוֹ, *As a lion or a lion cub roars over its prey* (*Yeshayahu* 31:4); and אֶהְגֶּה כַּיּוֹנָה, *I will chirp like a dove* (ibid. 38:14).

We also find this very term referring to the thoughtful expression of human speech. וּלְשׁוֹנִי תֶּהְגֶּה צִדְקֶךָ, *My tongue shall meditate upon the proclamation of Your righteousness* (*Tehillim* 35:28); לֹא יָמוּשׁ סֵפֶר הַתּוֹרָה הַזֶּה מִפִּיךָ וְהָגִיתָ בּוֹ יוֹמָם וָלַיְלָה, *This Book of the Torah shall not leave your mouth; you shall speak in it day and night* (*Yehoshua* 1:8; see *Radak*).

A lion or a dove does not possess the thought process of a human being; the sounds which such creatures emit are an expression of their very essence. Thus, explained Rabbi Mendlowitz, the human expression which the verses in *Tehillim* and *Yehoshua* refer to is a result of deep, active thinking and reflects the person's very essence.

> When a person immerses his mind in Torah study, this concentration produces rapturous melodies in praise of G-d. These melodies are even more beautiful than those of the harp. They flow from the person's essence.

XII. Mitzvos and Aveiros

In the event that you plan to do a *mitzvah,* and something occurs that prevents you from doing it, Hashem, in His generosity, credits you as if the *mitzvah* was actually done.

However, if one had a fleeting thought to commit a sin, but did not do it, he is not held accountable for the thought. Being human, a fleeting negative thought can enter a person's mind, but the immediate realization that it is a negative thought can erase it from his mind and from his record in Heaven.* However, if he did execute

---

* A Jew is not held responsible for negative thoughts except in the area of *avodah zarah,* idol worship. In this case, he would be held responsible for *machshavah* alone. Please note: There *is* one *mitzvah* in the Torah which does not involve these three facets of life:

שִׁכְחָה, *forgetting* the sheaves of the field.

If, in gathering the sheaves of grain in the field, one passed by one or two sheaves and forgot about them, he cannot go back and retrieve them. Rather, he must leave them for the poor.

This *mitzvah* does not involve intent. No *berachah* is said. No action is done.

his improper thought, then he is held accountable for the thought and for the action.

If one repeats or expresses a negative thought to a group of people, he has sinned through *dibur* and must do *teshuvah*.

If one writes an offensive word or expression on a wall in a public building, such as his yeshivah, thus desecrating it, this is a serious sin through *maaseh*, action. Whoever sees this writing, even years later, might be affected by it in a negative way and the writer will be held accountable for this as well.

This is true of all actions with long-term effects. With *maaseh*, one can be held responsible for the rest of his life and beyond. With this in mind, we realize how careful we must be regarding actions on both sides of the ledger, for wrongdoings as well as for good.

> Let us dedicate our lives to serve Hashem in every possible way. We can do it!

13

Do It —
Because Hashem Said So

Always remember:
- We must do what Hashem commands us to do.
- We need not know the *reason* for the *mitzvah*.
- We may not understand the scope
  and the depth of the *mitzvah*.
- We fulfill commandments because G-d *tells us* to.

◄§ Shabbos Observance

The *Mishnah* states:

לֹא יִקְרָא לְאוֹר הַנֵּר

One may not read by the light of the lamp on Shabbos
(*Shabbos* 11a).

The *Gemara* quotes a *baraisa* which offers a reason for the law: שֶׁמָּא יַטֶּה, "Lest one tilt the oil towards the wick" (*Shabbos* 12b). As *Rashi* explains, in those days, oil was commonly used as lamp fuel. Oil was poured into a receptacle with a wick at one end.

Frequently, the oil draws away from the wick, causing the light to grow dim. If one is engrossed in his activity and requires better light, he might, forgetting that it is Shabbos, tilt the lamp. This would cause the oil to run into the wick, thus causing the light to shine brighter. By doing this, he would have transgressed the prohibition against kindling a flame (or improving an existing one) on Shabbos.

The *Gemara* relates that Rabbi Yishmael ben Elisha reasoned:

"I will read by the light of the candle. I know that one is not permitted to touch the candle, nor to move the oil closer to the wick in order to have a brighter light. Were I to do so, I would be transgressing the law of Shabbos, but I will be careful not to do so." Rabbi Yishmael was confident that it would not be a problem.

One Friday night, Rabbi Yishmael was learning by the light of an oil lamp. He needed better light, so he stretched out his hand to tilt the lamp and move the oil closer to the wick. He was learning so intently that he forgot himself.

Someone stopped him before he transgressed the law, but he realized that he had almost done so.

He exclaimed: "How great are the words of our *chachamim.*"
The Rabbis in the *Mishnah gave no reason* for this law. The *baraisa* added the reason.

The *Mishnah* states:

> "One may not read by the candlelight on Shabbos." The law is written *as law. Do not* do this — without exception! Do not say that you know the reason and it does not apply to you!

Rabbi Yishmael made this error. He thought that he would be able to learn by the candlelight and not move it. So he thought.

But had the law been stated without a reason, he would simply have obeyed the law, without his own logic. Because of his rationalizing, he almost transgressed a Shabbos law.

The *Gemara* quotes another opinion, that he *did* tilt the lamp, and that he would have to bring a sin-offering on the Altar in the Temple, as soon as it is rebuilt (speedily, in our time).
I took a lesson from this.

Generally, I learn *Daf Yomi* every morning at home, before I go to the yeshivah to *daven*. Sometimes, I finish the *daf* after the yeshivah *minyan*. I become engrossed in my learning, so I asked my students to remind me if something is planned for the morning that I must take care of immediately after the *minyan*. When one is engrossed in learning, he tends to forget other responsibilities.

◆§ King Shaul

King Shaul was the first king of Israel. He was commanded to wage war against Amalek.
Shmuel told King Shaul to battle Amalek and to destroy the entire

nation; he should not have pity on this vicious, brutal people. He was told to destroy every person and all the cattle.

The war was over and Agag, the king of Amalek, had been captured. All the cattle had also been brought back (*I Shmuel* Chapter 15).

The *pasuk* states:

וַיָּרֶב בַּנָּחַל

"And he (King Shaul) fought in the valley" (ibid. v. 5).

The *Gemara* (*Yoma* 22:2) associates the word נָחַל, *valley,* with the same word found in *Devarim* 21:6 concerning the law of *Eglah Arufah*:

וְכָל זִקְנֵי הָעִיר . . . יִרְחֲצוּ אֶת יְדֵיהֶם עַל הָעֶגְלָה הָעֲרוּפָה בַנָּחַל (דברים
כא:ו).

If a wayfarer is found murdered outside a city, there is a formal ceremony to be done at a valley to show that the people of the city were not responsible for the death of this stranger.

וְאָמְרוּ יָדֵינוּ לֹא שָׁפְכוּ אֶת הַדָּם הַזֶּה

The elders of the city were required to proclaim: "We had no hand in the shedding of this person's blood" (ibid. v.7).

Shaul pondered this law and reasoned, "If the Torah considers it a calamity when one person is found dead and the city had to make atonement for his death, then surely he can allow King Agag to be left alive!" He also reasoned that since Agag was in captivity, he could be killed any time.

Shaul reasoned further that the *people* of Amalek had sinned, not the animals, and that the animals were taken alive not for personal gain, but to be offered as sacrifices to G-d.

But his reasoning was flawed, because he had been told to destroy everything and everyone from the nation of Amalek.

If the command is given to annihilate every last remnant of a totally vicious nation, then that nation should be destroyed completely.

Rashi explains that the animals had to be killed, because the Amalekites were magicians, masters of the powers of sorcery. They could turn themselves into sheep through this power. (During this particular era, many individuals knew how to harness the powers of sorcery. This ability has been lost. In any case, use of sorcery is prohibited by the Torah.)

The next day, the prophet Shmuel killed Agag. Agag was guilty of so many ugly and brutal deeds, and he had to be destroyed as the rest of

Amalek was. Shaul had not followed Hashem's command as he was supposed to. He *reasoned* over the command, and then followed his own logic. Because of this, he forfeited the right to be king of the Jewish people.

Shmuel's responses to Shaul's reasoning was:

הַחֵפֶץ לַה' בְּעֹלוֹת וּזְבָחִים כִּשְׁמֹעַ בְּקוֹל ה'

> "Does G-d have need of sacrifices? Are they as important as *listening* to the voice of G-d?
>
> Nothing is equal to fulfilling G-d's decree — totally and *without* personal evaluation or reasoning.
>
> Because you did not fulfill G-d's instructions as they were given to you, you have lost the monarchy"
>
> (see *I Shmuel* 15:23).

Chazal tell us that Shaul's "misplaced mercy" for Agag allowed him to live *one extra day*. Agag was killed the next day by Shmuel. But Agag had stayed with one of his wives on his final night and she conceived. From the child that was subsequently born descended Haman. Had Shaul killed Agag outright, as he was supposed to, there would never have been a Haman.

G-d *knows* what is right.

You must fulfill what G-d asks without rationalizing or questioning. Saul's rationalization brought forth Haman, who attempted to destroy all the Jews in the time of Esther and Mordechai.

- Do not rely on your own logic and reasoning.
- Fulfill G-d's commands *only* because G-d says so.

We must do whatever G-d commands us to do.

◄§ Shlomo HaMelech

Shlomo *HaMelech* (King Solomon) was the wisest of all men. Yet, in two laws concerning a king for which the Torah gives reasons, Shlomo erred.

רַק לֹא יַרְבֶּה לּוֹ סוּסִים וְלֹא יָשִׁיב אֶת הָעָם מִצְרַיְמָה

> *He* (a king) *should not acquire a multitude of horses, so that he will not return the people to Egypt* (which was the place where horses were commonly bought) (*Devarim* 17:16).

וְלֹא יַרְבֶּה לּוֹ נָשִׁים וְלֹא יָסוּר לְבָבוֹ . . .

And he should not have a multitude of wives, so that his heart not turn astray from serving Hashem properly (ibid. 17:17).

Rabbi Samson Raphael Hirsch comments:

The nation of Israel is commanded to grant the king considerable powers over them. This was necessary in order that the people should revere, fear, and respect him completely.

Verse 16 starts with the word *rak,* only, limiting the powers of the king in those areas where the virtue of rulers is often compromised and the happiness of their people shattered.

These are: the passion for military, glory and renown, women, and possessions.

The horse was the war animal in ancient times. Having an unlimited number of horses meant keeping a large military force. If the best horses were available from Egypt, the king and his people would become dependent on Egypt. The import of horses from the Egyptians would necessitate a relationship with them. The result of such a relationship would bring about an exchange of ideas and lifestyles. The general Egyptian outlook on life would filter into the way of life of all Israel.

A multitude of wives is not permitted to the king. Even without any other direct corrupting influences, his heart would become torn from the *spiritually* lofty service required of him, to fulfill his duty as king of Israel.

Yet Shlomo *HaMelech* did not obey this *mitzvah,* because he *relied on himself.*

Shlomo *HaMelech* said: "I will have many horses and I will not return to Egypt."

He said: "I will have many wives and they will not turn me away from serving Hashem" (*Sanhedrin* 21b). Yet in *Tanach* we see that Shlomo *HaMelech* erred in these decisions and his monarchy was almost entirely taken from his family because of this.

יַעַן . . . וְלֹא שָׁמַרְתָּ בְּרִיתִי וְחֻקֹּתַי . . . קָרֹעַ אֶקְרַע אֶת הַמַּמְלָכָה מֵעָלֶיךָ . . .
שֵׁבֶט אֶחָד אֶתֵּן לִבְנֶךָ לְמַעַן דָּוִד עַבְדִּי וּלְמַעַן יְרוּשָׁלַיִם אֲשֶׁר בָּחָרְתִּי

G-d said to Shlomo: ". . . because you did not observe my laws and decrees, your kingdom will be torn from you, and will remain a kingdom with only one tribe. . ." (*I Melachim* 11:11,13).

Shlomo felt that the reasons stated in the Torah for these prohibitions did not pertain to him. In spite of his wisdom, he fell prey to the rationalization. He felt that he was able to rise above the reasons given.

Rabbi Yitzchak said: "The Torah did not give reasons for *mitzvos* because in these two verses (concerning a king) the Torah gave reasons, and Shlomo *HaMelech* transgressed them both" (*Sanhedrin* 21b).

Again we see that we should fulfill *mitzvos only* because G-d commanded them, and not because we feel that the reason for a given *mitzvah* applies or does not apply to us.

⊷§ Chizkiyahu HaMelech

Chizkiyahu *HaMelech* became very ill. Yeshayahu *HaNavi* came to visit him and told him that he would die from this illness.

Chizkiyahu was a very righteous king, *unusually* so. He asked Yeshayahu why he deserved such a punishment. He wanted to know what he had done wrong.

Yeshayahu answered: "You transgressed a very important *mitzvah*, 'Be fruitful and multiply.' Why did you not marry?" (*Berachos* 10a).

Chizkiyahu defended himself.

He answered: "I saw through prophecy that I was going to have a son, but he would be very wicked." Chizkiyahu wanted to fulfill this *mitzvah*, but he reasoned to himself, "Rather than bring a *rasha* into this world, I would do better not to marry."

Chizkiyahu wanted to fulfill the *mitzvas asei*: "Be fruitful and multiply." But he had applied his own logic to it. He therefore reasoned that this *mitzvah* should not pertain to him.

Yeshayahu replied: "You must do your part in keeping all of the *mitzvos.* Let G-d take care of the result."

Chizkiyahu said to Yeshayahu: "You have a daughter. Give her to me in marriage. Perhaps, because of your *zechus* as a prophet, and my special position as king, we will be able to change this prophecy regarding my son."

Chizkiyahu then turned his face to the wall and proceeded to sincerely pray to Hashem, and he was forgiven.

Again we learn the catastrophic effects that one can bring upon himself when he applies his own reasoning to the fulfillment of G-d's *mitzvos*.

When doing a *mitzvah*, we must strive to perform that *mitzvah* the best way we can. We cannot ignore or tamper with a *mitzvah* because of our own reasoning.

Of course, we may and should learn the reasons for each *mitzvah*. But we must not do the *mitzvah* because the reasons appeal to us. The *mitzvah* must be done *only* because G-d commanded it.

◆§ Kashrus

Kashrus is a fundamental mitzvah of the Torah. There are numerous laws concerning kosher foods and the utensils used in their preparation. For example, we are not permitted to eat meat and dairy together. Therefore, we have separate sets of dishes.

> The laws pertaining to *kashrus* are essentially *chukim*, decrees of G-d whose reasons are not known to us.

Some people who have disregarded these laws have reasoned to themselves:

"In the desert we followed these laws since the facilities to clean utensils were not as perfected as they are today, in our modern kitchens.

"Automatic dishwashers today generate temperatures above 100 degrees. Our utensils are washed perfectly clean. Nothing remains on the dishes, and therefore it should be permissible to have only one set of dishes."

> When a person begins "learning *pshat*" in the *mitzvos*, when he begins reasoning about the purpose of the *mitzvah* and deciding for himself when the *mitzvah* applies and when it does not, then, G-d forbid, he is in danger of transgressing all of the Torah.

There are very few verses in the Torah concerning milk and meat, and kosher slaughtering. Yet, almost the entire *masechta Chullin* focuses on the topic of *kashrus*.

> • We do not know the reasons for these laws.
> • We follow these laws as a decree from G-d.

Of course, we can learn great lessons from these laws, but they are not the reasons for the *kashrus* laws.

For example, a three-year-old goes shopping with his mother. "Mommy, buy these crackers. They look delicious."

Mother says: "First let us see if they are kosher. Let us see what the ingredients are. Oh, no! We cannot buy these crackers. They contain glycerin, which is *treif*, non-kosher."

The three-year-old starts to cry. His mother sits down to explain it to him: "We cannot eat everything we see. We have Torah laws that we live by, and if Hashem says not to eat this, then we can be sure that we are better off without it."

That youngster grows up with the Torah as a way of life.

And he learns self-control:

- A person cannot have everything he wants.
- A person must have will power.
- He learns that we are different from
  the rest of the world.
- A Jew lives according to a Torah set
  of laws and customs.
- Without asking why, we follow Torah laws,
  because G-d has so decreed.

◈§ Adam and Chavah

G-d placed Adam and Chavah (Eve) in *Gan Eden*, לְעָבְדָהּ וּלְשָׁמְרָהּ, *to work it and to guard it* (*Bereishis* 2:15).

What manner of work was there in *Gan Eden* for Adam and Chavah to watch over and to guard?

Rabbi Samson Raphael Hirsch comments:
- G-d placed Adam in *Gan Eden*.
- G-d let him walk about as he pleased.
- G-d trusted Adam right away and gave him
  the garden to work and to guard.
- G-d positioned Adam in a garden of delight and
  happiness, to serve therein, and to *guard this happiness*.

"Work" and "guard" include not only the care of the garden, but also the *whole moral behavior of man*.

With the prohibition of *not* eating from the *Eitz HaDaas,* Tree of Knowledge, the education of man, for his moral and high calling, began.

1. It was a prohibition without a reason. It was the absolute will of G-d, a חוק, *a decree from G-d.*
2. Furthermore, it was a dietary law, like our laws of *kashrus.*
3. It was to be taught to others through oral communication. This law was given to Adam alone, and Chavah was to learn it from him and obey it.

Accordingly, this prohibition was a

1. מִצְוַת לֹא תַעֲשֶׂה, *negative commandment,*
2. a חוק, *an absolute decree.*
3. It involved a form of מַאֲכָלוֹת אֲסוּרוֹת, *forbidden foods;*
4. and it was to be taught as תּוֹרָה שֶׁבְּעַל פֶּה, *Torah that is transmitted orally*, from generation to generation, a tradition by which mankind was to live.

The command not to eat from the Tree of Knowledge was to teach a most basic lesson:

> Exercising self-control is the first obstacle to be overcome, and is the first problem to be learned, in human education and behavior.

At every demand of G-d's laws of morality, man has freedom of choice. He can decide whether he will follow his own judgment and sense; or, conscious of his higher calling, to follow the Voice of G-d.

Hashem gave Adam permission to eat of every tree in *Gan Eden.* Adam was given instructions to work in the garden and to guard it.

The only tree whose fruit was prohibited was the Tree of Knowledge.

Why did Adam transgress this one *mitzvah,* given to him directly from G-d? It is true that his wife, Chavah, gave him the fruit to eat. But the question remains: Why did he listen to Chavah and disobey G-d's command?

This episode reinforces the concepts introduced in this chapter. Adam made the same mistake as Shlomo *HaMelech.* He used his own mind and his own reasoning in deciding *how to fulfill* this one *mitzvah* that was given to him.

Adam reasoned as follows:

G-d had said: "And *from the Tree* of Knowledge, do not eat from it."

Adam may have reasoned that he would not eat of the fruit *while it was still on the tree.* But, once the fruit was already *detached from the tree,* it should be permissible to eat it. Therefore, when Chavah gave him the fruit, he ate it. Consequently, he transgressed G-d's law.

Had Adam adhered *exactly* to Hashem's command without analyzing and rationalizing, our world would be very different from what it is today.

◄§ *Avraham Avinu*

וַיֹּאמֶר ה׳ אֶל אַבְרָם לֶךְ לְךָ מֵאַרְצְךָ . . .

"G-d said to Avram: Go forth from your country, and from your birthplace, and from your father's house to the land that I will show you" (*Bereishis* 12:1).

This sentence is followed by *seven* different blessings that Avraham would be blessed with, amongst which were included:

1. He would be father to a great nation.
2. He would be blessed with wealth.
3. His fame would grow great.
4. He would have the power to bless others.

The Torah then continues:

וַיֵּלֶךְ אַבְרָם כַּאֲשֶׁר דִּבֶּר אֵלָיו ה׳

And Avram went as G-d had "told" him to (ibid. v. 4).

The question is raised:

What does this sentence add? If in the first sentence G-d told Avraham to go forth, then surely, when he went, he went as "G-d had told him to." These words seem superfluous. What do they add to the saga of Avraham's greatness?

One of the commentaries makes a very important observation:

We might think that Avraham went on his long journey because of the special seven blessings promised him. Perhaps this is what motivated Avraham to go.

Therefore, these words, כַּאֲשֶׁר דִּבֶּר אֵלָיו ה׳, "as G-d had told him to," are added. They teach a very important aspect of Avraham's greatness. He went because of only one reason: *because G-d had told him to.* He went *because of G-d's command,* not because of any personal reasonings.

Chapter 13: Do It — Because Hashem Said So / 153

Rabbi Samson Raphael Hirsch notes:

- In the first sentence, the word וַיֹּאמֶר,
  and G-d said, is used.
- In the fourth sentence, the word דִּבֶּר,
  G-d told him to, is used.

וַיֹּאמֶר refers to the entire prophecy, so full of benevolence and blessings. דִּבֶּר, however, means as G-d *told* him to — or, as G-d *ordered* him to.

> Avraham left for only one reason! Because it was G-d's wish that he do so. The word of G-d was enough to set Avraham on his wanderings. The blessings did not enter into his decision at all.

I would like to add another thought:

> Generally, if a *rebbi* tells you a word of instruction, or if you hear a profound thought (a good *vort*), in a *mussar* talk, you decide to become a little better in your service to Hashem.
>
> - You may *daven* with more *kavanah* (concentration).
> - You may do more *mitzvos.*
> - However, a week later, a month later, or half
>   a year later, you may forget your resolution.
> - You need another reminder.
> - You must be inspired and motivated once again.

This is one reason we observe Rosh Hashanah and Yom Kippur. We require a reminder of *Yom HaDin,* the Day of Judgment, each year, because one *does* forget. After Yom Kippur we start a new year with a clean slate, please G-d, with *renewed* inspiration.

Avraham *Avinu* never needed a reminder. Wherever he went, and whenever he went, it was as if

G-d had *just* spoken to him at that moment.

The inspiration of the moment when G-d spoke to him *never left him.* A month later, Avraham continued to serve Hashem with the same energy and devotion as he had when originally spoken to.

- Avraham did not need a reminder.
- Avraham followed the word of Hashem
  without question.
- G-d's command was always with Avraham.

There is a wonderful *Midrash* concerning Avraham's most demanding test:

When Hashem told Avraham to offer Yitzchak as a sacrifice, it seemed to run contrary to everything that Avraham stood for. It was a test that certainly was opposite of the *chesed* that permeated every act of Avraham's. Yet Avraham did not hesitate. He immediately followed G-d's wishes, G-d's command. He had complete faith in G-d.

Satan came to Avraham disguised as an old man. He said: "How can you do the act you are contemplating? Hashem promised you that your son, Yitzchak, would inherit the land and that he would continue your teachings of Torah and service to Hashem. Furthermore, you are an old man.

"What will happen to the continuity of your people, to the continuity of your way of life, if you sacrifice Yitzchak? You have no other child to follow in your footsteps!"

Avraham did not hesitate. He replied:

"I must serve G-d and do what G-d commands, even if I do not understand how it fits with all that God has told me previously."

The problem of continuation of the ways of G-d in this world is indeed a great one.

- I will let G-d find a solution.
- I will let G-d provide for the continuation of His Torah and His way of life.

I must fulfill G-d's command without questioning and without reasoning.

৵ Avraham Avinu's Matzah

Do you know why we eat *matzos* on Pesach?

Yes, the Torah explains the reason. When we left Egypt, we could not tarry; there was not time to bake bread. The dough was carried on the backs of the fleeing Jews. It was baked in the sun, and became *matzos.*

When the angels visited Avraham, in *Parashas Vayeira,* he served them *matzos.* This was an event which occurred *before* the redemption of the Jews from Egypt.

Why did Avraham serve the angels *matzos*?

My *Rebbi* and *Rosh Yeshivah*, Rabbi Shlomo Heiman, quoted his *Rebbi* and *Rosh Yeshivah*, Rabbi Boruch Ber Leibowitz of Kaminetz:

Had we asked Avraham why he served the angels *matzos*, he would have answered:

> "It is a חוֹק, a decree, of G-d. I do not know the reason for this *mitzvah*. I just do not feel that I can eat bread, or other *chametz*, at this time."

Avraham's answer can be explained as follows:

- There are 248 *mitzvos asei*, positive commandments.*
- There are 365 *mitzvos lo sa'aseh*, negative commandments.

  Together they add up to 613 *mitzvos*.

Chazal tell us:

- Man has 248 limbs in his body.
- Man has 365 *gidim*, sinews, in his body.

  Together they add up to 613.

Each limb of our body is attuned to a *mitzvas asei*.

Each sinew of our body is attuned to a *mitzvas lo sa'aseh*.

- A *lo sa'aseh* does not require a limb because it does not require an action.

  Do nothing and you are fulfilling the *mitzvas lo sa'aseh*.
- To fulfill a *mitzvas asei*, you require a corresponding limb, because action is demanded.

  - To put on *tefillin*, you need an arm and a head.
  - To *daven*, you need a mouth to say the words.

---

* When we say *Shema Yisrael*, morning and evening, we accept upon ourselves קַבָּלַת עוֹל מַלְכוּת שָׁמַיִם. We accept the command to serve Hashem;

- We accept and recognize G-d as our King.
- We accept G-d's demand that we fulfill and do all of the 248 *mitzvos asei*.

It is noteworthy that in the three paragraphs of *Shema*, there are 245 words. The *chazan* repeats the last three words, ה' אֱלֹהֵיכֶם אֱמֶת, *Hashem, Your G-d, is True*, thus making the words of *Shema* add up to 248. (When one *davens* alone at home, three words are added at the beginning of *Shema*: אֵ-ל מֶלֶךְ נֶאֱמָן, *Almighty Faithful King*. Again, the words of *Shema* add up to 248, corresponding to the 248 *mitzvohs asei*.

Thus, in saying *Shema* twice a day, morning and evening, with its 248 words, we are reminded to actually perform all the 248 *mitzvos asei*. This is the fulfillment of our accepting *to serve Hashem*.

Now, when you return to your classrooms, you do not have *to think* in order to raise your feet, to walk, to turn right or left. You go *naturally* to your rooms.

To Avraham, doing a given *mitzvah* was as natural as walking to our rooms is to us. He was so close to Hashem and his mind was so attuned to Hashem's will that the *mitzvos* came naturally to him.

When the Festival of Pesach arrived, the limb of Avraham's body that was attuned and corresponded to *matzah* caused him to bake *matzos.* Eating *matzos* at that particular time was *his natural* way of Torah life.

Of course, there had not been enslavement in Egypt as yet, and there had not been redemption. To Avraham, eating matzah was a חוק, a decree whose reason he did not know.

The most incomprehensible decree in the Torah is that of *Parah Adumah,* the preparation of the ashes of the Red Cow and its use in cleansing people of their *tumah* defilement.

There are many apparently conflicting laws in this *mitzvah.* How is it possible for some people to become spiritually cleansed through the application of the ashes of the Red Cow, while others, who assisted in the preparation of these ashes, became *tamei,* ritually defiled?

My *Rebbi* said that the *Geulah,* the Redemption of *Klal Yisrael* with the coming of *Mashiach,* will be done in such a manner that the law of the *Parah Adumah* will be understood by us.

My *Rebbi* said:

> "In the same way that we now understand the reason why we eat *matzos* on Pesach, and we understand the reason Avraham baked *matzos,* which was to him a *chok,* in the very same way, the eventual *geulah* will occur in such a way that the decree concerning the *Parah Adumah* will be understood and clarified."

◄§ The Vilna Gaon

I once heard a beautiful story about the Vilna *Gaon* which illustrates the best way to do a *mitzvah.*

One year there were no *esrogim* to be found in Vilna. Messengers were sent to all of the neighboring towns, searching for an *esrog* for the Vilna *Gaon.*

In a little *shtetl,* a certain Reb Yaakov had a visitor from *Eretz Yisrael* who had brought him an *esrog.* The messengers were overjoyed. Their *Rebbe* would have an *esrog* and would be able to fulfill this *mitzvah.*

However, when they approached Reb Yaakov, he said, "The *esrog* is not for sale." The messengers offered large amounts of money for this *esrog,* all to no avail.

Reb Yaakov said, "What is wrong with you people? Why are you willing to pay such a large sum for an *esrog?*"

They then explained that the *esrog* was for the Vilna *Gaon,* and Reb Yaakov's *esrog* was the only one in their area.

Reb Yaakov finally agreed but added:

> "I will give it to you on one condition. The Vilna *Gaon* must promise me his share in *Olam Haba* for this *mitzvah.* That is my price."

The messengers returned to the Vilna *Gaon.* As Succos approached, the *Gaon* saw that they were unhappy. Upon being questioned, they related to their *Rebbe* the conditions for purchasing the only *esrog* that they had found.

When the *Gaon* heard this, his face lit up with joy!

> "I will do this *mitzvah* without personal motivation.
>
> I will do this *mitzvah* without thought of reward from Hashem.
>
> I will do this *mitzvah only* because G-d has commanded it in His Torah.
>
> I will gladly give up my share in *Olam Haba* for the fulfillment of this *mitzvah!*
>
> This year I will *bentsh esrog* without any personal motivations. I will do it purely *leshem shamayim,* purely for Hashem."

✒ Emes and Yashar

The following *Dvar Torah* is a further explanation of how we are to perform and fulfill Hashem's *mitzvos.*

On the verse, עֲשׂוּיִם בֶּאֱמֶת וְיָשָׁר, *done in truth and uprightness (Tehillim* 111:8), Rabbi Samson Raphael Hirsch comments:

Torah and *mitzvos* are G-d's code of law for the entire world. They were turned over to the Jewish people, and through them, ultimately, to all peoples. In this way we can all become a harmonious part of G-d's world.

G-d's *mitzvos* find support forever until their ultimate purpose shall be attained

in *emes* and in *yashar,* in truth and in righteousness.

This depends upon the fulfillment of two essential conditions:

First, it must be done with *emes,* truth: Divine Law must be obeyed in a manner that is unadulterated and unabridged. It must be done truly in accordance with G-d's command.

Second, the individual fulfilling G-d's Laws must be *yashar,* must be straight and upright in character. He must have no ambition other than to satisfy G-d's demands *without any other ulterior motives* in doing the *mitzvah.* He must be an individual who fulfills G-d's precepts purely *for their own sake.*

אַשְׁרֵי אִישׁ יָרֵא אֶת ה' בְּמִצְוֹתָיו חָפֵץ מְאֹד...

Forward strides the man who fears the Lord, *whose greatest desire* is the fulfillment of *His commandments* (*Tehillim* 112:1).

It is his greatest desire and delight to practice and to fulfill G-d's *mitzvos* purely for the *mitzvah* itself.

The *Gemara* comments on this verse: וְלֹא בִּשְׂכַר מִצְוֹתָיו, He does not look for any reward that he might hope to gain by such obedience (*Avodah Zarah* 19a).

The verse states:

Fortunate is the man who is a *yirei shamayim,* who serves Hashem with full realization of obeying Him. He stands before G-d with full understanding of his awesome responsibility.

He wants to fulfill Hashem's *mitzvos* very much (מְאֹד). With his entire soul, with purest sincerity.

This sentence teaches:

Who is a *yirei shamayim*? One who *wants* to do G-d's *mitzvos.*

Chazal explain:

* He does not do the *mitzvah* with the expectation of a reward.

- He desires only to enjoy the feeling of
  having done a *mitzvah* in purity.

He is a person who serves Hashem מֵאַהֲבָה, because he loves Hashem. It is not because he fears Hashem. It is rather because he stands in complete awe of Hashem. His *yiras shamayim* is so great that he wants to do G-d's *mitzvos,*

> only because G-d proclaimed them; not because of any
> promised or expected rewards.

In reality, the Torah *does* explain reasons for many of the *mitzvos.*

Torah Temimah (*Devarim* 17:17) explains beautifully why and when the Torah does give us reasons for *mitzvos*:

(a) *Bris Milah*: as a sign of the covenant between G-d and Israel.
(b) Pesach: because G-d passed over the houses of *Bnei Yisrael* at the time of the tenth plague, the plague of the death of the first born in Egypt.
(c) Shabbos: because G-d rested (He did not create) on the seventh day.
(d) Gifts to the *Kohanim*: because G-d chose them to serve Him in the Temple.
(e) Gifts to the Levites: because they had no inheritance in the land of Israel.

⊷ *"We Will Do, We Will Listen"*

In this *shmuess*, we have stressed the importance of doing *mitzvos* not because we understand the reasons for them, but because G-d commanded us to do them. This does not mean that it is improper to delve into their reasons. To understand the reason for a *mitzvah* is part of Torah. Therefore, great commentators such as *Rambam* and *Sefer HaChinuch* teach us the reasons for many of the *mitzvos*. However, when we fulfill a *mitzvah,* we do so because *Hashem has decreed it.* And always remember: There may be many reasons for keeping a given *mitzvah.* Many of these reasons are beyond human understanding.

The reasons offered by the commentaries help make the *mitzvah* more understandable. However, there may be even more reasons, deeper reasons, than those stated by these luminaries. Whatever the case, the reasons stated for a given *mitzvah* do not affect our performance of the *mitzvah.*

Basically, we fulfill the *mitzvah* because G-d *decreed* it in His Torah.

At Mt. Sinai, Israel said, נַעֲשֶׂה וְנִשְׁמַע.

First, they said, "We will do."

Afterward, they said, "We will listen."

Our great leaders interpreted these words as follows:

- First we will do the *mitzvah.*
- First we will comply with G-d's commandments.
- First we will fulfill the *mitzvah* completely.
- After performing the *mitzvah,*
    only because G-d commanded it,
    then we will listen to reasons.

Rabbi Moshe Feinstein said:

"*Nishma* does not mean מִיר וֶועלֶן הֶערֶן, We will hear, or we will listen.

In Yiddish it means:

מִיר וֶועלֶן דֶערהֶערֶן, We will try to understand its meaning and purpose.

But,

- first, "we must be prepared to do."
    without questioning,
    without reasoning,
    and even without understanding,
- Only then, may we seek to understand.

14
Shleimus —
Striving for Perfection

⊷§ Become a Mushlam —
a Complete Torah Personality

Every yeshivah student should strive to be a *mushlam* — a complete personality in all facets of Judaism as expressed in the Torah.

This is why I have given you *mussar shmuessen* (talks) all my years as a *menahel* in the yeshivah. All my discourses were geared toward one purpose: to awaken you to *think* about the way Hashem wants you to live. It is a "higher way of life" we are trying to teach you.

- It is important to *daven* well.
  But this is not enough.
- One is also expected to learn well.
  One is not only expected to *daven* and learn well;
- one must also have *middos tovos* — good character.

This is what we mean by the word *mushlam.* The root letters form the word שָׁלֵם, *complete,* whole, a finished product.

Be a good-natured person, a *"baal derech eretz, a baal middos."* Show *respect* for others in your dealings with people.

Grow up to be
- a *talmid chacham,* a learned Jew;
- a *yirei shamayim,* a G-d-fearing Jew;
- as well as an exceptional *baal middos,*
  an individual of outstanding, sterling character.

All three go together. Nothing can be missing.

This idea also relates to a concept of which we often speak: *machshavah, dibur,* and *maaseh* — thought, speech, and deed.

- Your thoughts,
- your speech, and
- your actions

all belong to Hashem. Nothing can be missing.

ᴥ *Perfection in Mitzvos*

The *Kuzari* says something very profound. The *Kuzari* was written by Rabbi Yehudah Halevi in the 12th century (1085-1142), some 800 years ago. He explains very beautifully the importance of not omitting any detail when performing a *mitzvah,* so that its performance is שָׁלֵם, complete.

> If a person does a *mitzvah* but leaves out one detail out of ignorance, his performance of the *mitzvah* can still be considered basically "sound" (though he should study the relevant laws so that he will not repeat his mistake).

> If a person leaves out one detail because in *his mind* he decided that the *mitzvah* will be complete without it, that is almost like idol worship. It means that he is relying on his own mind, rather than faithfully adhering to G-d's decree. He considers his own thinking as superior to that which is expressed in our Torah, G-d forbid.

> > His mind decides how to live, how to do a *mitzvah.* His mind decides which part of the *mitzvah* should be done and which part should be discarded, because, to his mind, it is not important.

The *Kuzari* in his explanation of the Sin of the Golden Calf, says: "Surely the Children of Israel could not have believed that this golden calf was their G-d,

- Who had performed the miracles in Egypt,
- Who had split the Red Sea,
- and had led them to freedom?

Surely the Children of Israel could not have believed that this golden calf,

> that was formed from molten gold, was G-d Himself?"

In reality, says the *Kuzari,* the people recognized that Hashem was Master of the Universe.

> They made the golden calf solely to establish a place of congregation and worship. This would be the place where all Israel would come together. There, they would pray and serve the true G-d Above.

If so, asks the *Kuzari,* what was their wrongdoing?

The golden calf was a sign of idol worship, because it was conceived as a center point of Divine service, not by Hashem, but by a small group of individuals. Because they relied on their own ideas as to how to serve G-d, this action became a transgression in direct opposition to the will of G-d.

⮜ *Dangerous Medicine*

My *Rebbi,* Rabbi Shraga Feivel Mendlowitz, offered a beautiful example concerning this excerpt from the *Kuzari:*

When a person goes to a drugstore with a prescription, the pharmacist goes to his back room, takes a large bottle of medicine and pours the required amount into a little bottle. This is how many prescriptions are filled today. (In some cases, the required amount comes ready-packaged in a small bottle or tube.)

However, it was not like this years ago. Then, the pharmacist had to measure and weigh the chemical ingredients required. A very fine balance scale was used, which had a weight on one side. In preparing the medicine, the pharmacist had to be very careful to use the exact required measure of each ingredient; he could not be off by even a few milligrams. If, G-d forbid, he put in one "little pinch" more than was called for, the medicine could become dangerous or useless, depending on the error.

One day, continued *Rebbi,* a pharmacist left his store for a short while, leaving behind only an unlearned worker who would sweep the floor and keep the drugstore neat and clean. A man came in with a prescription. It was an emergency. The man was new in town and mistakenly assumed that the worker was the pharmacist. He asked him to fill the prescription.

> The worker thought: "I have watched the pharmacist do it many times. No problem."

In truth, however, he acted very recklessly in offering to fill the prescription. Had he omitted one ingredient from the mixture, it may not have had any curative effect. Had he added one extra milligram of ingredients, then use of the medicine could have proven fatal.

This, said Reb Shraga Feivel, is what the *Kuzari* means. When you intentionally omit *one* detail of a *mitzvah,* you have not completed the *mitzvah.*

"You are relying on your own mind."

When you do this, something is sorely lacking in the completeness, the true fulfillment of the *mitzvah*.

To be a complete Jew:
- Serve G-d completely.
  Strive for perfection, as much as is humanly possible.
- Serve G-d with your *mind,* your *speech,*
  and your *actions.*
  BUT
- Do not change a *mitzvah.*
- Do not leave anything out.
- Do not rely on your own mind.
- Rely only on instructions from Hashem,
  as detailed in the Torah.

In the Torah, we read:

וְאִם נֶפֶשׁ אַחַת תֶּחֱטָא בִשְׁגָגָה מֵעַם הָאָרֶץ בַּעֲשֹׂתָהּ אַחַת מִמִּצְוֹת ה' אֲשֶׁר לֹא תֵעָשֶׂינָה וְאָשֵׁם

If an individual from among the people of the land will sin unintentionally, by committing one of the commandments of Hashem [i.e. a transgression] that may not be done, and he becomes guilty (Vayikra 4:27).

The above translation represents the simple *p'shat* (plain meaning) of this verse. However, *sefer Iturei Torah* quotes *Zera Kodesh,* who, through a play on words, derives the lesson that we have been discussing from this very *pasuk*:

- וְאִם נֶפֶשׁ אַחַת תֶּחֱטָא . . . — *If an individual will sin . . .*
- בַּעֲשֹׂתָהּ אַחַת מִמִּצְוֹת ה' — *by doing a mitzvah of Hashem*
- אֲשֶׁר לֹא תֵעָשֶׂינָה — *in a way that it was not meant to be done . . .*
- וְאָשֵׁם — *and in so doing, he will have transgressed.*

Zera Kodesh illustrates his point with a story that is told about two followers of the *Maggid* of Mezeritch:

> One said, "What will happen to us? What will we do with all the transgressions that we have committed?"
>
> His friend responded: "I am not concerned about our sins. For this, we can do *teshuvah*. I worry about the *mitzvos* that we *have done*. How can we face Hashem with such *mitzvos*? Perhaps we *left out* important details or performed them without proper intent."

We can learn this same idea from the tragic episode of Nadav and Avihu, the two elder sons of Aharon *HaKohen*:

וַיַּקְרִיבוּ לִפְנֵי ה' אֵשׁ זָרָה אֲשֶׁר לֹא צִוָּה אֹתָם

> The sons of Aharon, Nadav and Avihu, each took his fire-pan, put fire in them, and placed incense upon it; and they brought *before Hashem a foreign fire* that *He had not commanded them.* A fire came forth from before Hashem and consumed them, and they died before Hashem (*Vayikra* 10:1-2).

נָדָב וַאֲבִיהוּא אָמְנָם עָשׂוּ אֶת הַמִּצְוָה בַּמִּדָּה הָרְאוּיָה שֶׁל הִשְׁתּוֹקְקוּת וּמְסִירַת נֶפֶשׁ, אֲבָל בֶּאֱמֶת לֹא הָיְתָה זוֹ מִצְוָה – שֶׁהֲרֵי עָשׂוּ ,,אֲשֶׁר לֹא צִוָּה אֹתָם ה' '' (שִׂפְתֵי צַדִּיק, בְּשֵׁם אָבִיו) ויקרא י:א

> *Sefer Sifsei Tzaddik,* quoting his father, comments:
>
> "In reality, Nadav and Avihu performed this service with proper yearning and self-sacrifice. *Nevertheless,* what they did was not a *mitzvah,* for [as the Torah states], they did what 'Hashem had not commanded them.'"

Not being expressly commanded by G-d, Nadav and Avihu had brought a *foreign offering.*

The *Chiddushei HaRim* learns a very important lesson from the words:

> "And they [Nadav and Avihu] brought a foreign fire that He [Hashem] had not commanded them."

He said:

"The most important aspect in fulfilling *mitzvos* lies in following 'the commandment of G-d.' This is more important than all other *kavanos* (spiritual thoughts and intentions) a person may have when doing a *mitzvah.*"

אֲשֶׁר צִוָּה ה׳, *As G-d commanded,* supersedes the holiest thoughts and sincerest intentions that a person may have when doing a *mitzvah.*

Nadav and Avihu were great *tzaddikim,* leaders of their generation. They had the finest and deepest thoughts and feelings when they brought their offering. But, because it was a foreign fire, *not commanded* by G-d,

they were punished.

The *Chiddushei HaRim* added:

„אֵשׁ זָרָה אֲשֶׁר לֹא צִוָּה אוֹתָם," עִיקַר עֲשִׂיַּית הַמִּצְווֹת הוּא בְּכֹחַ הַצִּוּוּי וְזֶה לְמַעְלָה מִכָּל הַכַּוָּנוֹת

If a person does a *mitzvah only because G-d commanded it,* then, even though he knows *nothing* of the depth of the *mitzvah,* he is credited as if he did the *mitzvah* in all its aspects, with full *kavanah* (intent) and sincerity.

When involved in performing a *mitzvah,* it is only strict adherence to what Hashem has commanded us to do that makes it a *mitzvah.* Any deviation from that which Hashem, in His Torah, has instructed us to do becomes a terrible transgression. At that moment, we are relying on our own mind to guide us in serving Hashem. In deviating from the word of Hashem, we are following the ways of "foreign ideologies."

Perhaps we can understand this even more clearly when we think of the mitzvah of *mikveh,* the immersion of a person who must cleanse himself from *tumah,* ritual impurity in a ritualarium. An ordinary person might think that the waters of the *mikveh* are the same as those found in any body of water, but this is not so.

When a *mikveh* is constructed and filled with water according to Torah law, then its waters have the power to lift a person from *tumah,* impurity, to *taharah,* purity. It is the law of the Torah that raises these waters from the status of plain liquid to the realm of a *mitzvah* object that has the power to sanctify. Without the word of G-d, without it being a *mitzvah,* these waters would be the same as any other.

This is true of all *mitzvos.* The Written and Oral Torah teach us "ingredients" for each *mitzvah.* No man has the right to say: "This part is not so important, I will leave it out. I will not do it."

Nadav and Avihu did not have the right to say that they would add this new fire-offering to the service of G-d in the *Mishkan*.

When we mix "the ingredients" according to our own thinking, it loses the power of Torah, for it is no longer "the word of G-d." It becomes a *foreign offering* as in the case of Nadav and Avihu.

"No deviation from the word of G-d" is a cardinal principle of the Torah Jew. To be a *yirei shamayim* is to follow implicitly every aspect of every commandment of Hashem.

The World of the Individual

15
You Must Do It Yourself

✑ *A Lesson from Avraham*

When Avraham welcomed three angels into his home, he invited them to refresh themselves.

וְרַחֲצוּ רַגְלֵיכֶם (בראשית יח:ד)

As he went about the *mitzvah* of *hachnasas orchim,* hospitality to guests and wayfarers, Avraham told his guests to wash their feet (*Bereishis* 18:4).

The *Gemara* explains that Avraham did this because he feared that they worshiped dust as their *avodah zarah,* and he did not want this dust to be brought into his house.

The question is asked: If Avraham *Avinu* served his guests personally, why did he tell them to wash their feet? Why couldn't he order his servants to do it for them?

We learn an important lesson:

- Nobody can rid you of idol worship or wrongdoing.
- You have to do it yourself.
- You must wash off this dust, yourself.

This is true of getting rid of anything that is preventing you from becoming a *talmid chacham* or a *tzaddik.*

To overcome the *yetzer hara,* Satan, so that you will be able to fulfill the Torah properly and do the *mitzvos* according to *halachah,*

you must fight the *yetzer hara yourself.*

Your parents and your *rebbi* will do their utmost to help in this daily, constant battle, but they cannot do it for you. The end result can be measured only by your own impetus.

- *You* must take charge!
- *You* must lead the battle!
- *You* must win this war!

When it comes to learning there is special help from G-d. Even a person that does not have a particularly "good head" can become a *talmid chacham* of renown. G-d actually helps each student to grasp and understand his Torah studies.

But in overcoming and battling your *yetzer hara,* it is basically up to you — and you alone.

⋅§ The Dust on Their Feet

What exactly was the dust on the feet of the wayfarers? Was the dust on their feet the actual *avodah zarah,* the object of worship?

One of the commentators says something very beautiful. We believe in *Hashgachah Pratis,* that G-d is watching over us constantly and guides our lives with exacting precision. We believe that everything we have comes from Him. However, the typical wayfarer thinks that he earns his living not with G-d's help, but rather by the dust of his feet.

He walks, he works, he buys and sells different items. He tends to forget about G-d's intervention. He forgets that there is a Master of the World and that everything belongs to Him. He thinks that his foot, *his own power,* is how he makes a living.

But he is wrong! It is not your feet — your own walking or working powers — that bring *parnasah,* that enable you to live comfortably.

Rather, remember that everything comes from Hashem.

We must have *bitachon,* trust in G-d. Yet, we must try to help ourselves. As the saying goes: "G-d helps those who help themselves." In order to serve G-d, we must do it ourselves. We must do our own cleansing.

⋅§ All Is from Hashem

Let us always remember: Everything comes from Hashem.
We can learn this same lesson from another source.

Reb Elchonon Wasserman was in the United States in 1939. I was privileged to be his secretary for one full day.

- I answered the phone.
- I went to *shul* with him.

- I slept overnight in an outer room of his suite
  at the Broadway Central Hotel
- and helped him with his appointments.

He spoke in Mesivta Torah Vodaath, and he described two incidents and two reactions to each:

I. People fail in business, and they blame the failure on others:

> "My partner told me to buy thousands of yards of material and we are stuck with it. Why did I listen to him? He is to blame for our losses this year. It is his fault."

When business goes well and profits are rolling in, then they take all the credit for themselves.

> "It is because of my business sense and acumen that I bought so much material. The merchandise is selling so rapidly that I could have manufactured and sold much more than I did."

II. The brothers of Yosef came to Egypt to buy food during the seven years of hunger. Unexpectedly, they were accused of being spies.
A natural reaction would have been:

> "What does this ruler want from us? We know we are not spies. We came, as others did, to buy food to bring back to our father and to our families in Canaan."

Reb Elchonon said:
The Torah demands a completely opposite reaction: Therefore, the brothers did not react this way when confronted by Yosef. Instead they said to each other:

> וַיֹּאמְרוּ אִישׁ אֶל אָחִיו אֲבָל אֲשֵׁמִים אֲנַחְנוּ עַל אָחִינוּ אֲשֶׁר רָאִינוּ צָרַת
> נַפְשׁוֹ . . . וְלֹא שָׁמָעְנוּ עַל כֵּן בָּאָה אֵלֵינוּ הַצָּרָה הַזֹּאת
>
> "Indeed we are guilty concerning our brother. We saw the anguish of his soul when he entreated us not to sell him, and we would not listen. Therefore, this anguish has now come upon us" (*Bereishis* 42:21).

The children of Yaakov were all *tzaddikim*. They understood that all that was transpiring was from Hashem. They realized that the accusation against them was a punishment for some wrong they had committed.

They had tried to convince Yosef that they were not spies. All their talking fell on deaf ears. Yosef refused to listen to them. In discussing this unfathomable crisis, they associated it with the time when their brother tearfully begged them not to harm him, not to sell him as a slave into a bleak future.

> They were being punished measure for measure. Since they did not listen to their brothers' entreaties, therefore, the Egyptian viceroy did not listen to them.

They immediately said, "We are guilty, we did something wrong."
This is the Torah approach.

When something unexpected and tragic happens, many people question G-d.

> Why are You doing this to us? Where is G-d?

But the Torah teaches us:

> "Blame yourself."

Ponder your own deeds. You may have brought this action upon yourself. This may be the result of something you have done in the past.

Reuvain said to his brothers:

> "Did I not say unto you, 'Do not sin against the child'? You would not hear. Therefore his blood is now being avenged" (*Bereishis* 42:22).

Rabbi Samson R. Hirsch explains:

Reuvain had looked upon Yosef as a mere child. Joseph's dreams and plans, of which they were so afraid, were mere childishness.

Reuvain said: "You are doing wrong in attacking the lad. It is no Divine fire that burns within you. Your pious indignation will only cause you to sin."

From this episode, we see that

- we ourselves are to blame if something goes wrong.
- We are to do *teshuvah*.
- We must have no complaints to G-d.

Reb Elchonon continued in the same vein in describing the first incident mentioned above:

If things go wrong in the business world, blame yourself. On the other hand, if things go well, do not take credit for yourself, but rather thank G-d for the good fortune He has showered upon you.

✑ The Danger of Arrogance

We find this same thought in *Devarim* 8:12-18: We are warned:

12. פֶּן תֹּאכַל וְשָׂבָעְתָּ וּבָתִּים טֹבִים תִּבְנֶה וְיָשָׁבְתָּ

Be careful. Lest you eat and be satiated, and you build goodly houses and settle.

13. וּבְקָרְךָ וְצֹאנְךָ יִרְבְּיֻן וְכֶסֶף וְזָהָב יִרְבֶּה לָךְ וְכֹל אֲשֶׁר לְךָ יִרְבֶּה

Your herds and flocks will multiply. You will increase gold and silver for yourselves, and everything that you have will increase.

14. וְרָם לְבָבֶךָ וְשָׁכַחְתָּ אֶת ה' אֱלֹהֶיךָ הַמּוֹצִיאֲךָ מֵאֶרֶץ מִצְרַיִם מִבֵּית עֲבָדִים

Do not let your heart become haughty and forget that G-d took you out of Egypt from the house of slavery.

15. הַמּוֹלִיכְךָ בַּמִּדְבָּר הַגָּדֹל וְהַנּוֹרָא נָחָשׁ שָׂרָף וְעַקְרָב וְצִמָּאוֹן אֲשֶׁר אֵין מָיִם הַמּוֹצִיא לְךָ מַיִם מִצּוּר הַחַלָּמִישׁ

Do not forget that G-d watched over you in your traveling through a great and terrible wilderness — of snake, fiery serpent, and scorpion, and thirst where there was no water — Who brought forth water for you from the rock of flint.

16. הַמַּאֲכִלְךָ מָן בַּמִּדְבָּר אֲשֶׁר לֹא יָדְעוּן אֲבֹתֶיךָ לְמַעַן עַנֹּתְךָ וּלְמַעַן נַסֹּתֶךָ לְהֵיטִבְךָ בְּאַחֲרִיתֶךָ

Do not forget that G-d fed you with manna in the Wilderness, which your forefathers knew not, in order to afflict you and test you, to do good for you in the end.

17. וְאָמַרְתָּ בִּלְבָבֶךָ כֹּחִי וְעֹצֶם יָדִי עָשָׂה לִי אֶת הַחַיִל הַזֶּה

And you might say in your heart: "My power and the might of my hand procured for me this wealth."

18. וְזָכַרְתָּ אֶת ה' אֱלֹקֶיךָ כִּי הוּא הַנֹּתֵן לְךָ כֹּחַ לַעֲשׂוֹת חָיִל לְמַעַן הָקִים אֶת בְּרִיתוֹ אֲשֶׁר נִשְׁבַּע לַאֲבֹתֶיךָ כַּיּוֹם הַזֶּה

Remember that Hashem, your G-d, endows you with this power to accumulate wealth, in order to establish His covenant that He swore to your forefathers, as this day.

Rabbi Hirsch comments:
- Arrogance is itself the beginning of forgetting Hashem.
- Where the thought of *G-d* lives,
    there is no place for pride and arrogance.

אָמַר הָרוּחַ גַּסּוּת בּוֹ שֶׁיֵּשׁ אָדָם כָּל עוּקְבָא מַר וְאִיתֵּימָא חִסְדָּא א״ר
(:ה סוטה) בָּעוֹלָם לָדוּר יְכוֹלִין וְהוּא אֲנִי אֵין הקב״ה

Of the proud and haughty person, G-d says, "I and he cannot live together in the world" (*Sotah* 5b).

It is solely G-d Whom you have to thank for your independence and present abundance. Everything that makes your creative personality and your capacity to earn,

> • your intelligence,
> • your skill,
> • your physical and mental health,
> • every factor of your existence
> > are given to you directly from G-d.

Reb Elchonon concluded:

> • When things go wrong, blame yourself.
> • When things go right, thank G-d.

16
Pride in Yourself

ৼ§ *The Spies' Report*

In *Parashas Shelach,* we learn about the *Meraglim* (Spies) (*Bamidbar* Chapters 13-14).

- What did the *Meraglim* want to accomplish on their tour of *Eretz Yisrael,* spying out the land?
- Were the *Meraglim* going to see if it was safe?
- Did the *Meraglim* go in order to find the easiest way to conquer the land?

When you learn this *parashah,* you will note the instructions which Moshe *Rabbeinu* gave the Spies. Moshe told them to see if the land was good, if the land was beautiful, if the land was habitable. He *did not* tell the Spies to see if the land was safe.

If Hashem tells you to go to *Eretz Yisrael,*

if Hashem tells you: "I am going to give you *Eretz Yisrael,*"

if Hashem says: "*Eretz Yisrael* is yours,"

we do not worry about enemies.

We do not fear war.

Hashem will take care of us.

In reality, the people wanted to know what kind of country it was. They wanted to know where each tribe would live. That is the reason Moshe *Rabbeinu* sent forth the Spies. Each tribe sent its own leader so as to satisfy its people that they would receive an accurate report. However, the Spies returned with a report of *Eretz Yisrael* that was filled with negativity.

One of the things that the Spies reported was that the land was inhabited by giants. They said that when they looked at these giants they felt very small and insignificant. If anyone were to look up at a giant he would feel very small; he would shrink into nothingness. When the Spies saw these giants, they developed a feeling of fear within themselves.

They said:

וַנְּהִי בְעֵינֵינוּ כַּחֲגָבִים

"We are nothing. In our eyes we were as small as grass-hoppers."

They also said:

וְכֵן הָיִינוּ בְּעֵינֵיהֶם

"And that is the way they looked at us. That is the way we appeared in the eyes of the giants as well" (*Bamidbar* 13:33).

The question is raised:

The Spies could have felt as small as an insect. This, we can understand. But how did they know what the giants thought of them?

How could they say:

"And that is the way we appeared in their eyes as well?"

Rashi answers this question by saying that they overheard the giants saying to one another, "We see ants crawling in the vineyards, resembling human beings."

⋞ Confidence and Pride

I would like to offer another reason for their statement: It is a psychological reason and requires close attention. It will make you *think about yourself.*

When an individual goes for a job interview, his whole future may depend on his getting that job. He must make a living. Of course, he cannot be sure of the interview's outcome. Sometimes, the impression he makes during the interview may be affected by the fact that

he is not sure of himself.

In answering questions, he may speak hesitantly; he may speak quietly and under his breath. This necessitates the interviewer to re-peat his questions again and again. The individual *sounds* like he is not too sure of himself; not quite happy with himself. He is not confident.

He does not get the job.

If you feel that you are *nothing,* that is the *impression* you will convey during the interview; this is what others will think of you.

The Spies felt small and afraid, and that is the way the giants perceived them. The impression they had of themselves was conveyed to the giants.

- If you are proud of who you are,
- if you are proud that you are going to a yeshivah,
- if you are proud that you are learning Torah,

then whoever talks to you says to himself:
"This person is a proud Jew. I would like to be like him."

When a new immigrant comes from Russia or another foreign country and he asks you what kind of yeshivah you attend, you must be positive in your answer. If you hesitate and say: "Well, it's all right, but there are many problems," the new immigrant will probably feel that there is something missing in your school. He will detect the doubts in your voice as you converse with him.

There are many yeshivos catering particularly to new Russian immigrants. Of course, there are problems. The Russian children face tremendous language barriers in English as well as in Hebrew. They lack understanding of what it means to be a Jew in the full sense of the word.

If you attend a school that caters to immigrants, such as:

- Sinai Academy
- Be'er Hagolah
- Shearith HaPleitah
- Nefesh Academy
- Mercaz Bnos
- Shalheves

please be positive in your attitude as you answer other new immigrants' questions.

One must develop a *pride* in what he does, how he does it, who he is, and what he represents.

If asked, be proud to say:

"I am learning *Chumash* and *Rashi,* something I never knew before.

We have a *minyan* every day and I have learned how to *daven* properly, with *kavanah.*"

If another person sees that you are proud of what you are doing and of *what you are,* he will have a different concept of what yeshivah is. He too will aspire to learn. The chances are good that he will enroll in your yeshivah. Wherever you are, the institution which teaches you often gets its reputation from *your* actions and words.

You are the *best ambassador* of good will for the yeshivah you attend.

⋖§ *Vacation Time*

Y ou are going on vacation soon, but, there is one thing you cannot *ever* have a vacation from.

- There is no vacation from Torah and *mitzvos*!
- There can never be a vacation from Hashem!

Even when one is away one must set aside a daily period for learning. He must make sure to *daven* with a *minyan* every day.

Whatever you do, do it *100 percent,* be it swimming, playing ball, or learning during your daily study period.

- This way you will get maximum pleasure
  and enjoyment during your vacation period.
- This way you will be serving Hashem
  100 percent.
- This way you will be creating the finest
  reputation for your school.

What about the youngster who stays at home and does not go away for a vacation?

- He should also go to a daily *minyan* and *daven* well.
- He should also set aside a *daily study* period
  to continue his learning. It is especially beneficial
  if you can find a *chavrusa* with whom to study.

This will certainly enhance his own standing as a *ben Torah* and will, at the same time, enhance the reputation of his yeshivah amongst people, both young and old.

Rabbi Shraga Feivel Mendlowitz of Torah Vodaath was *one of the first menahalim* (principals) of the yeshivah movement in the United States. He said:

"Our children were becoming destroyed by their vacation during July and August.

The entire year is devoted to teaching the children about the greatness, the pride, and the beauty of what it means to be a Torah Jew. Suddenly, in July and August, the children do not know what to do with themselves, nor where to go. They go swimming and play ball and they forget everything we have taught them. Their minds become ruined."

Rabbi Mendlowitz was one of the first to organize a *yeshivah camp* so that boys could enjoy their vacation, play ball, swim, have fun, and *still learn Torah.* Even in the summertime they are surrounded with an atmosphere of *serving Hashem.*

To me, July and August is a period of S.O.S.

Save Our Souls!

It is a danger signal because these two months can destroy everything that inspired the student during the entire year.

There is one other thought I want to leave you with, regarding summer camp.

There are many counselors in these yeshivah camps.

Who are these counselors?

They all come from yeshivos, *mesivtas,* and girls high schools.

They are all Torah-minded individuals.

The counselors are also coming to camp to *relax* a bit. They are coming to camp to earn some money during the summer. Many are *inspired* and *devoted* leaders.

- Perhaps they will inspire a boy or girl during the summer to be a better Jew.
- Perhaps they will influence a camper to be a more intensive Torah scholar.
- These counselors are in a position to help you.

Remember! וְכֵן הָיִינוּ בְּעֵינֵיהֶם .

Cooperate with your counselors and create a good impression of *yourself.* When you feel proud of *who you are,* others will be proud of you as well. You will then be a great example of what a yeshivah student should be,

both spiritually as well as *physically.*

This is the way you develop a reputation. You grow up being proud of *who* and *what* you are. You become proud of being a *ben Torah* or *bas Yisrael.*

People will say:

"Look how *proud* they are of their heritage, as Torah-true individuals.

Look how *thankful* they are to their *rebbeim* and *morahs* for everything they were taught throughout the year.

Look at their behavior in camp spiritually and physically.

Look at the way they speak about their Torah schools."

- *Think* this way and you *will grow* this way.
- *Believe* in this and you will *believe in yourself.*

Come back in September to a new term with one major thought:

To be a better and a greater Jew than you are today.

Your slogan should be:

A year *older* means *a year better.*

17

"And G-d Saw that It Was Good"

The Torah opens with: בְּרֵאשִׁית בָּרָא אֱלֹקִים אֵת הַשָּׁמַיִם וְאֵת הָאָרֶץ, "In the beginning G-d created heaven and earth." It is a most important statement, for it lays the foundation for our lives in this world and the next.

- We must know that the world belongs to Hashem and so do we.
- G-d created the world for a purpose.
  WE ARE THE PURPOSE!
- We are to bring G-dliness into this world in which we live.
- We are to endow everything we do with a spirit of G-dliness.
- We are to bring a spiritual element into the material world that surrounds us.

But why must we have a detailed account of *each day* of Creation? Why is it important to know what was created on each particular day?

There are two expressions constantly repeated throughout the first chapter of *Bereishis*. They are:

- וַיַּרְא אֱלֹקִים כִּי טוֹב, *And G-d saw that it was good.*
- וַיְהִי כֵן, *And it was so.*

In some places, both expressions are used when speaking about the same day; at other times one is omitted. Let us examine the order of Creation and see how these two expressions are used.

First Day:

On the first day G-d created light. "G-d saw that it was good" is stated; "and it was so" is omitted.

Second Day:

On the second day, G-d made the *rakia,* firmament. This was a division between the waters above the *rakia* and the waters below the *rakia.* Nothing could be seen because the waters filled the entire universe. This seems to be an *unfinished* process. We find the expression "and it was so," but "G-d saw that it was good" is omitted.

Third Day:

On the third day, G-d completed what was begun on the second day. The waters below the *rakia* receded and formed oceans, rivers, seas, and lakes. Dry land was seen for the first time. This, in reality, was the purpose of the division on the second day.

Both expressions — "it was so" and "it was good" — are used for this day (vs. 9,10).

Once dry land appeared, G-d created everything that grows from the earth: grass, trees, flowers, etc. Once again we find both expressions used (vs. 11,12).

Thus, on the third day, we find two elements of creation:

1. Dry land (completing the second day's creation).

2. All natural growth from the earth. Therefore, the expressions "and G-d saw that it was good" and "it was so" are used twice.

> (I remember my mother saying, "It is *mazeldik* to move on a Tuesday because G-d blessed that day with two expressions of good.")

Fourth Day:

On the fourth day, G-d created the sun, moon and stars. Both expressions are used.

Fifth Day:

On the fifth day, G-d created marine life and birds. The expression "and it was so" is omitted.

Sixth Day:

On the sixth day, G-d created the animal kingdom and man. In the verses which speak of animals (vs. 24, 25), both expressions are used.

When G-d created man, the words "and G-d saw that it was good" are omitted.

Man is the most important part of Creation. Man is the very purpose of Creation. Man is to be imbued with a G-dly spirit. Yet on man there is no "stamp of approval by Hashem" as is found with the rest of Creation. Why?

Read this chart for clarification of the two expressions and see clearly the many differences. One check in the column indicates that the phrase is used. A double check indicates that the expression is used twice.

	וַיַּרְא אֱלֹקִים כִּי טוֹב	וַיְהִי כֵן
FIRST DAY	✔	
SECOND DAY		✔
THIRD DAY	✔ ✔	✔ ✔
FOURTH DAY	✔	✔
FIFTH DAY	✔	
SIXTH DAY animals man	✔	✔ ✔

Let us try to understand all these varied differences:

"And It Was So"

The second expression "and it was so" is missing only in the first and fifth days. This expression indicates that this particular aspect of Creation would remain that way forever.

Once G-d had imprinted His words "and it was so," that part of Creation would never change.

These words were omitted on the first day, because the special, radiant light of the first day was stored away for the future world. It is therefore known as the אוֹר הַגָּנוּז, *hidden light.* The light of the first day was "too good" for our world. It could not stay with us forever. We must strive to be worthy of it. That light was taken away from our world, but it will be returned in the future. The lights for *our* world are the sun and the moon, which were created on the fourth day.

On the fifth day, G-d created the תַּנִינִים, huge sea creatures. These creatures could destroy our world, and so G-d took away one of them so that they could not multiply. Thus, this part of Creation could not be forever and could not be stamped with the words "and it was so."

Now let us understand why only one expression is used on the second and sixth days.

"And G-d Saw that It Was Good"

On the second day, the act of Creation was not yet completed (as stated above) so it could not be stamped with the words "and G-d saw that it was good."

> We can learn from this that *division* is not always good. Unity and togetherness is generally better. This is particularly true when the same "element" (in this case, water) is divided.

אֵין מַיִם אֶלָּא תּוֹרָה

Chazal tell us:

> Torah is compared to water. If there is a division in the Torah world between various groups, this can never be "good." Let Torah views, ideals, and goals speak with one strong powerful voice. I am sure that G-d will stamp this with His words "and G-d saw that it was *good.*"

We may also learn that when you start something and do not finish it, it *cannot* be good.

In *Parashas Eikev* (*Devarim* 8:1), *Rashi* tells us that a *mitzvah* is considered done, is counted, and credit is given only when the *mitzvah* is fully completed (learn this *Rashi* at the source). There are many *"starter-uppers"* in the world but they leave the completion for others to accomplish.

On the sixth day, marking the creation of man, the words "and G-d saw that it was good" are omitted.

> Man is different from all other creations.

Trees are the same today as when they first appeared on this world. Animals, fish, fowl, and birds are the *same today* as when they *were first created.*

"And G-d saw that it was good" stamped all of them with their characteristics forever and gave His approval of them as well in their present form.

However, explains the *Meshech Chochmah,* G-d could not give man His approval of "goodness." Had G-d said "and it was good," then man could *never* do wrong.

> Man would not have *bechirah,* the power of choice.

Without *bechirah,* man could not possibly fulfill his purpose on this world.

Man could not exercise restraint in not violating a *mitzvah* of the Torah. He therefore could not be worthy of *Gan Eden* and reward.

- *We* must strive to be good, to do *mitzvos,*
  to serve Hashem properly and spiritually
  because *we decide to do so.*
- *We,* the Jewish people, must weather the
  storms of problems that beset us as we grow.
- *We* must elevate ourselves to be what G-d wants
  us to be. This is why G-d gave us the Torah.
- *We* must put the stamp of approval upon ourselves.
- We are starting Torah all over again.
- We start at *Bereishis,* the beginning.
  Start **now!**
Not only will our beginning of the year be good;
our end of the year will also be good.

When we fulfill all the *mitzvos* of the Torah, when we learn Torah regularly, daily and intently, then, subconsciously, we will hear G-d's voice whispering to us.

וַיַּרְא אֱלֹקִים כִּי טוֹב

And G-d saw that it was good.

We will have earned *G-d's stamp of approval.*

18

Let Greatness
Leave Lasting Impressions

✑§ Spreading Hashem's Name

Avraham *Avinu* acted as an emissary of Hashem in spreading His Name amongst the people of his generation. This was his mission in the world.

How did Avraham proclaim Hashem's Name? How did he convince people to serve Hashem?

עוֹלָם חֶסֶד יִבָּנֶה

"A world can only be created through and with *chesed*, kindness" (*Tehillim* 89:3).

If you want to create a new world, a new Jew, you can only do so by making people aware that there is a Hashem. This can only be accomplished by doing *chesed*, kindness and favors for others.

Every Jew is a world unto himself. By teaching others of the greatness of Judaism, you are creating new worlds.

How did Avraham get to know people? How did he act with *chesed* towards them?

In the desert he built an *aishel*, a lodging place, an oasis in a barren land. When weary travelers saw a tree growing, they knew there must be water nearby. They sat in the shade, quenched their thirst, ate a meal, and rested from their long journey.

אֵשֶׁל = אֲכִילָה ˗ שְׁתִיָּה ˗ לִינָה

The three letters of the Hebrew word *aishel* stand for three words which indicate what it was:

- The first letter *aleph*, א, stands for *achilah* =
food, eating.
- The second letter, *shin*, ש, stands for *sh'siah* =
drinking, quenching one's thirst.
- The third letter, *lamed,* ל, stands for *leenah* =
sleep, a place to stay overnight — to rest
from the weary travels through a desert.

The next morning, when a traveler thanked Avraham *Avinu* profusely for reviving and refreshing him, Avraham said: "Do not thank me. All this does not belong to me. I did not create this tree; nor did I create this body of water. Thank Hashem. All this comes from Him."

Avraham did not just stand in the desert and lecture to the people that everything comes from Hashem. He first acted towards them with an abundance of *chesed.* Then he requested that they thank Hashem, Who is the Owner of everything in the world. It was his personal approach that brought people to an understanding and appreciation of G-d.

≈§ The Art of Listening

Avraham's father Terach was an idol worshiper. But Avraham smashed all the idols. We learn all this from the *Midrash,* not from the *Chumash.*

To the naked eye, to one *who did not learn* the *Midrash,* and therefore did not realize the greatness of Avraham, the following may seem strange. At the end of *Parashas Noach,* we read that Terach had several children: Avraham, Nachor, and Haran.

In the first sentence of the next *parashah, Lech Lecha,* G-d spoke to Avram.

וַיֹּאמֶר ה׳ אֶל אַבְרָם לֶךְ לְךָ מֵאַרְצְךָ וּמִמּוֹלַדְתְּךָ וּמִבֵּית אָבִיךָ אֶל הָאָרֶץ אֲשֶׁר אַרְאֶךָּ

Hashem said to Avram: "Go forth from your country, from your birthplace, and from your parents' home to the land that I will show you" (*Bereishis* 12:1).

Why did G-d speak only to Avraham? Why didn't G-d speak to Terach, to Lot, to others?

Sfas Emes comments on this and explains:

> Hashem, in essence, spoke to everyone. Hashem spoke to the entire world, to Terach, to Lot, and all the others. Hashem told everybody, "Go forth. . ."
>
> The difference is that Avraham *Avinu* was LISTENING.

He wanted to do something for the sake of Hashem's Name.

The others were busy worshiping their idols.

Avraham was searching for the Lord and Master of the entire world. He was waiting for an indication of approval from G-d.

This can be compared to a *rebbi* teaching a class. He is teaching all the students. Some students are playing, some may be daydreaming, but others are *listening* attentively. They hear what the *rebbi* is saying.

Avraham did not feel that the world evolved from itself. He was searching for a Creator. His mind was attuned to listen to what G-d would say.

◆§ *A Trained Ear*

When G-d said "Go forth . . .," Avraham heard G-d's voice talking to him.

Rabbi Mendlowitz explained this with a *mashal.*

There were two brothers in an orphanage. One day, two different families came to adopt the boys. One was a wealthy banker while the other was a farmer.

One boy would visit his father in the bank. He grew up attuned to the sound of the jingling of coins. The brother on the farm would arise in the morning to the melodious tunes of the birds singing outside his window.

The two brothers kept in touch with each other by phone and by mail. Many years later, they decided to meet in a big city. They met on a busy, noisy street that was bustling with life. As they were walking along and talking to each other, the farmer stopped suddenly. When his brother, the banker, asked him why he did so, he explained that he had just heard the beautiful singing of a bird and he wanted to listen.

The banker could not comprehend. With all the honking, with all the hustling and bustling that was taking place on the street, his brother had actually heard a bird singing. The banker said that he had heard nothing.

The farmer did not respond. But as they continued walking, he took two coins out of his pocket and dropped them onto the sidewalk. They jingled as they rolled away. The banker stopped suddenly and said, "I heard the jingling of coins!"

Each one heard what he was accustomed to hearing.

We see from this that the sounds you grow up hearing are the ones that will be familiar to you. You will be attuned to hearing them.

Growing up in a yeshivah has attuned your mind and heart to listen and react to Torah teachings. Listening to your parents and *rebbeim* has finely tuned your power of hearing into listening.

- You may hear words spoken.
- You may hear sounds coming forth, but,
  are you listening?

Listening has a far greater effect on a person than just hearing.

Listening implies that the words have penetrated into your mind and heart. They have literally entered your bloodstream. They have transformed you into a Torah individual.

Avraham *Avinu* grew up hearing the voice of Hashem because his mind was attuned to listening, to searching for Hashem.

- If we will take upon ourselves the responsibility to accustom ourselves to be attuned to good thoughts, that will definitely be beneficial to character building and to developing excellent *middos*.
- If we will perk up when we hear a *dvar Torah* we will become greater *talmidei chachamim* and better Jews.
- If we listen when we hear a sound piece of advice or a *mussar* thought, we will become finer, better people, with superior qualities.

◆§ *A Lasting Impression*

וַיַּקְהֵל מֹשֶׁה אֶת כָּל עֲדַת בְּנֵי יִשְׂרָאֵל וַיֹּאמֶר אֲלֵהֶם (שמות לה:א) . . .

וַיֵּצְאוּ כָּל עֲדַת בְּנֵי יִשְׂרָאֵל מִלִּפְנֵי מֹשֶׁה (לה:כ)

We find the same idea in *Parashas Vayakhel:* "Moshe assembled the entire community of the Children of Israel and spoke to them . . ." (*Shemos* 35:1).

When Moshe finished speaking to them, we read:

"All the congregation of the Children of Israel departed

from the assembly, *from before Moshe"* (ibid. v. 20).
(They departed from being in the presence of Moshe.)

Moshe had prayed that Hashem should forgive Israel for making the Golden Calf.

Finally, G-d had said, וַיֹּאמֶר ה' סָלַחְתִּי כִּדְבָרֶךָ, "I have forgiven Israel as you have requested" (*Bamidbar* 14:20) (see *Rashi, Shemos* 33:11).

Moshe had gone up once again to Heaven and had brought down another set of Tablets upon which were inscribed the Ten Commandments. This had taken place on the tenth of Tishrei, the date of Yom Kippur.

The very next day, Moshe gathered all Israel together to tell them about the building of the *Mishkan,* the Sanctuary in the desert (*Shemos* 35:1).

The Torah relates that when Moshe finished speaking to Israel, all Israel departed from the assembly "from before Moshe" (from before his presence) (v. 20).

Since the Torah does not use any extra words, the above is rather puzzling. Why does the Torah write that *Bnei Yisrael* went away "from before Moshe"? Obviously if he gathered them and spoke to them, then after Moshe finished speaking to them, they left "from before him," they departed from being in his presence.

The Torah imparts a very important message.

When you spend time listening to a Moshe *Rabbeinu,* the effect on you when you leave him is inevitable.

> Israel walked away from before Moshe, properly and with *derech eretz.* His speech had left an impression on them. They could feel Moshe's greatness as they left from before Moshe. His words continued to ring in their ears. He had a profound effect upon all Israel.

Towards the latter years of Reb Moshe Feinstein's life, I was privileged to *daven* with his *minyan* in his home. Only 10 people were invited and you had to call for permission to be one of the 10.

I watched Reb Moshe *daven.* I was inspired with his concentration, his *kavanah,* and the clarity of his words.

When we finished *davening,* we left from
> before Reb Moshe.

He left his impression of greatness upon all of us.

L'havdil, * when you see a drunk coming out of a bar, he cannot walk properly. He sways as he walks; he stumbles and falls. You can readily see where he came from. You can readily see the effect of the liquor upon his entire being.

L'havdil, have you ever been on a train at about 2:30 p.m. when children are dismissed from a public school?

- They scream.
- They push.
- They shove people aside as they enter the train.
- They use vile language.

People on the subway are frightened as they tensely watch the "goings-on."

You can readily feel and see where these youngsters are coming from. Character training, morality, and respect for others are not part of their schooling.

These youngsters do not think of anybody else. They think only of themselves.

L'havdil, when our yeshivah students were dismissed at the end of a day, I would always tell them to create a *Kiddush Hashem,* a sanctification of G-d's Name, to elevate the name of our people, *Bnei Yisrael,* in the eyes of all.

- Let people see that you quietly take your seats.
- Let people see that you will offer your seat to an older person.
- Let people see that when you leave the yeshivah, the lessons of Torah are written on your face and in your actions.
- Let people see that you are leaving the yeshivah from *before Moshe,* from *before a place of Torah.*
- Let the greatness and the purity of your Torah learning rub off on you!

---

* To create a division and difference between two examples.

19

Inspired Forever

۶§ City of Unity

In 1973, my wife, Marcia, ע״ה, and I were in Israel. It was at that time
we merited to stand at the *Kosel HaMaaravi* (the Western Wall) from
where the *Shechinah* has never departed. It was there, as we prayed
alongside Jews of all shades and stripes, that we experienced the
unifying power of Jerusalem.

יְרוּשָׁלַיִם הַבְּנוּיָה כְּעִיר שֶׁחֻבְּרָה לָהּ יַחְדָּו

> The built-up Jerusalem is like a city that is united
> together (*Tehillim* 122:3).

Sforno comments:

While the *Beis HaMikdash* stood, the Jews would ascend to
Jerusalem in honor of the *yamim tovim*. As time went on, the throngs
swelled to such large numbers that it became necessary to expand the
city in order to accommodate everyone. The newer additions to the
city blended perfectly with the original sections. Thus, Jerusalem's
areas formed a city *united together*.

Talmud Yerushalmi (*Chagigah* 3:6) offers another explanation:

Jerusalem serves as a unifying force. During the time of the *Beis
HaMikdash,* a wide variety of people would converge upon Jerusalem
for the Festivals, from different tribes and from various places.

> There were old and young, rich and poor, learned and
> ignorant, from all stations and walks of life.

Other times of the year, these groups were divided by social and
other barriers, but on the Festivals, Jerusalem transformed and
unified them.

- The city brought everyone together.
- It made all Jews comrades.

- They embraced one another as part
  of *one indivisible nation.*

The *Gemara* (*Bava Kamma* 82b and *Yoma* 13a) teaches that though the Land of Israel was divided among the 12 tribes, the city of Jerusalem, according to one opinion, remained the property of the entire nation. Thus, the city was unified in a very literal sense.

In our times, we literally saw the city *become one.*

ᴔ *A Modern-Day Miracle*

As a result of the War of Liberation in 1948, Jerusalem became two cities; one under the banner of Israel, and another under Jordan. From 1948 until 1967, Jews were not permitted to enter the Old City and could not approach the *Kosel.*

A miracle happened in our time.

In 1967, Israel beseeched Jordan not to join the Egyptian forces who had mobilized on the borders of Israel. The night before the Six Day War erupted, Jordan joined Egypt, hoping to gain new territory and to annihilate the State of Israel. *Baruch Hashem,* their evil plans backfired.

- This was *Hashgachah Pratis* (careful watchfulness by Hashem over His beloved people)!
- This was Divine intervention!
- This was the Hand of G-d at work, the outstretched mighty arm of Hashem fighting the battle, so that the two parts of Jerusalem became
  One, Once Again.

ᴔ *Inspiration that Lasts*

During one of our visits to the *Kosel,* the entire student body from Yeshivah Shalavim, which is outside of Yerushalayim, came there as well. The *Rosh Yeshivah,* Rabbi Schlesinger, expressed a very inspiring idea concerning the Splitting of the Sea at the time of the Exodus from Egypt.

At that time, says the *Midrash,* "All the heavens opened up, and Hashem, sitting on His Throne of Glory, could be seen."

The moment of the revelation of the *Shechinah* was awesome and breathtaking.

Bnei Yisrael, crossing the Red Sea, were ecstatic at that great moment in history.

It was the greatest miracle of all time.

Even a simple servant girl was lifted up to such great heights of spirituality that she, too, could gaze at the open Heavens and perceive Hashem's Presence.

In the opening chapter of the Book of *Yechezkel*, Yechezkel *HaNavi* begins with a prophetic description of G-d sitting upon His Throne, surrounded by various angels. This prophecy is known as *Maaseh Merkavah*, the Workings of the Heavenly Chariot.

Few people in the history of the Jewish people were great enough to understand Yechezkel's awesome vision of Heaven. Yet, *Chazal* teach:

מַה שֶּׁרָאֲתָה שִׁפְחָה עַל הַיָּם לֹא רָאָה יְחֶזְקֵאל בְּמַעֲשֵׂה הַמֶּרְכָּבָה שֶּׁלוֹ

What a maidservant saw at the [Red] Sea, Yechezkel did not see in his Maaseh Merkavah (Mechilta, Shemos 15:2).

Was the servant girl at the Splitting of the Sea greater than Yechezkel *HaNavi*?

Absolutely not!

There is a vast difference between Yechezkel and the maidservant.

After the great miracles at the Sea, the maidservant remained a maidservant.

Though she was inspired for the moment, we do not know who she was; we do not know her name. We know nothing further about her, for her momentary inspiration did not have a lasting effect. She remained a maidservant and no remembrance remains of her.

However, when Yechezkel *HaNavi* saw *Maaseh Merkavah*, this was a שְׁלִיחוּת, a message from Hashem. This revelation penetrated to the depths of his soul. He recorded it as a prophecy from Hashem. It became part of *kisvei kodesh*, the holy *Tanach*. Yechezkel became a *navi* because when he experienced the light of Torah and *kedushah* (sanctity), he took that momentary inspiration and continued his prophecies to climb another rung on the ladder of spreading G-d's messages.

Sometimes, one becomes inspired by a good thought that he hears. One may be inspired with what his *rebbi* told him. He may be inspired to the extent that he wants to learn a little more.

But what happens to the inspiration?

Does he utilize it to try and become a better Jew, a better person?

If not, then he is no better than the maidservant.

True, he was inspired; but only for the moment. He said, "Yes, I am going to do this and that," but the next day he forgot about his lofty plans.

The person that becomes truly inspired uses his inspiration to improve himself. He will reach a higher level of spiritual closeness to Hashem. And he will utilize his inspiration to inspire others as well.

Yechezkel *HaNavi* said other prophecies as well. This is why Yechezkel *HaNavi* is far greater than the maidservant. There is no comparison.

He spent his lifetime inspiring other people, admonishing and exhorting *Klal Yisrael* to become better Jews in spite of the fact that after the destruction of the First *Beis HaMikdash* they were in exile in *Bavel.*

He lifted the spirits of our people by prophesying about the Third *Beis HaMikdash.* He was telling us not to be downcast over being exiled to *Bavel.*

We are not to lose hope through the long exile we are *now* in, since the destruction of the Second Temple.

Yechezkel *HaNavi* even spells out the dimensions of the size of the Third *Beis HaMikdash.* He tells us what changes should be made in its construction.

We will yet come back to *Eretz Yisrael. Mashiach* will lead us back to the greatest heights of our people.

Rabbi Schlesinger continued to speak about the difference of the servant girl and Yechezkel *HaNavi,* and made a very apt observation concerning our time.

⋙ The Six Day War

In 1967, Israel defeated the Arab nations in the Six Day War. Miracles were manifest before our very eyes. All Israel was uplifted to heights of euphoria never before felt in modern times.

We were vastly outnumbered by the Arab armies. Because of the fear of many deaths, ר״ח, graves were prepared in all major cities. Who knew how long the war would last? Who knew how many casualties would result?

As the war unfolded, everyone felt that Hashem was fighting our war. Miraculously, we bombed and destroyed the airfields and the air force of Egypt on the first day of the war. Then we turned around and did the same to Syria.

The night before the war started, Jordan had joined Egypt and Syria so that she, too, could gain additional territory from a "defeated" Israel (G-d forbid).

> Instead, and miraculously, Yerushalayim became a unified city and became the capital of Israel *for all time,* please G-d.

Rabbi Schlesinger spoke in 1973, just six years after the Six Day War. He said that when the war ended, many people, in Israel, even among the non-religious, felt that only the presence of G-d had helped us win the war so speedily.

- We were all feeling the ecstasy of a closeness to G-d, rarely experienced by such a large segment of the population.
- We should have held on to the inspiration of that great moment of victory.
- We could have inspired so many of our people to a greater and deeper belief in Hashem. Torah and *Yiddishkeit* could have been strengthened beyond our imagination.
- We could have had a mass movement of *teshuvah,* a mass return to G-d.

But, we lost the moment of that spiritual ascension. We were like the maidservant at the Splitting of the Sea. We did not take advantage of a golden spiritual opportunity.

Rabbi Schlesinger concluded: Now, as we look back to 1967, we must do our utmost to go forward in 1973. We cannot recapture the glorious moments of Revelation of G-d in our midst in 1967. Yet we yeshivah students must live inspirational lives of Torah.

> We must feel a sense of responsibility for all *Klal Yisrael*: to inspire others, through being inspired ourselves.

This is what I hope and pray for, from all yeshivah *talmidim* and *talmidos.*

I have often told my students:

There are times when you are inspired with a "good *vort*" (a Torah thought) from your *rebbi,* or possibly from me. You are inspired and you decide to learn better, to listen better. But what happens? You go to sleep and you forget about your moment of spiritual inspiration and growth. The next day, you get up late, you miss the *minyan,* and you get into trouble.

> When this happens, you are following the path of the maidservant. You saw or heard something beautiful and you let its effect upon you wear off in no time at all.

Students of all yeshivos, continue to hear words of encouragement. We expect a great deal from you. We want you to learn well and improve in performance of *mitzvos.* We want you to have respect for your parents, your *rebbi,* and for anyone older than yourself.

> Good character and behavior will set you aside
> from the children of the secular world.

When *you* are looked up to by others, as a fine upstanding individual, *you* will influence others by your example. Your moment of inspiration will have changed yourself and changed others as well — now, and forever.

20

Lead the Way —
The Right Way!

⊷§ Introduction

In March 1984, we celebrated the *siyum* (completion) of *Mesechta Shekalim* in the *Daf Yomi* cycle of Talmud study. This was followed by *Shabbos Shekalim*. During the preceding weeks, we read the *parshiyos* in the Book of *Shemos* which discussed the building of the *Mishkan* and the Sin of the Golden Calf (עֵגֶל הַזָּהָב).

A passage in *Yerushalmi Shekalim* (2b and quoted in *Torah Temimah)* focuses on these topics:

"R' Yehudah ben Pazi said in the name of Rebbi (Rabbi Yehudah Hanasi): הֵן נִקְרָא וְלֹא נִבָּעֵת, *Can we read [these verses] and not be shaken?*

"There are several verses in the Torah that are read by us, and every time we read them, we are embarrassed, ashamed, and even horrified. They are so difficult for us to even read the words *to ourselves* because they pinpoint some of our worst failings."

R' Yehudah goes on to contrast three sets of verses from the Torah. Each set contains one verse that speaks of the good of *Bnei Yisrael* and one that speaks of its errors.

> In each set, we see that when something good, something positive, was taking place, there had to be some special motivation for it to occur.
>
> When something bad, something negative, was taking place, there was spontaneous reaction; people were ready to participate in whatever was happening without any external motivation.

Chapter 20: Lead the Way — The Right Way / 199

The commentary *Taklin Chadetin* comments that from this we learn how great is the power of the *yetzer hara* (evil inclination).

Let us examine R' Yehudah's three contrasts.

I. The Mishkan and the Golden Calf

לְטוֹבָה: כֹּל נְדִיב לֵב (שמות לה:כב)

לְרָעָה: וַיִּתְפָּרְקוּ כָּל הָעָם (לב:ג)

Regarding the *Mishkan* (Tabernacle) which was to be built in the Wilderness, we find two statements concerning those who contributed:

> *Everyone whose* **spirit** *prompted him to contribute* (*Shemos* 35:21), and the *men alongside of the women came to give, all urged on by their* **hearts** (ibid. v. 22).

Rabbi Samson Raphael Hirsch differentiates between *heart* and *spirit:*

- *Lev,* the heart, is the organ of thought and will in man.
- *Ruach,* spirit, is the *whole* Inner Man, the *whole* source of action. The gifts flowed from the hearts and spirits of gracious individuals.

At the building of the *Mishkan,* כֹּל נְדִיב לֵב, every individual who was possessed by a generous heart and lofty spirit, brought contributions.

Others held back and did not contribute at all.

Verse 22 quoted above indicates that when it came time to contribute for the *Mishkan,* the women were in the forefront as they came forth to contribute their jewelry. However, at the time of the sin of the Golden Calf, they refused to give their jewelry.

The men, unfortunately, were not of this pure faith and spirit.

When Aharon addressed the people prior to the making of the Calf, he told them, "Bring me the gold and silver from your wives and children."

Aharon was, in actuality, stalling for time. He was sure that this would provoke family differences, that the wives would surely refuse to surrender their jewelry for the making of the Calf.

However, the Torah states (*Shemos* 32:3), וַיִּתְפָּרְקוּ כָּל הָעָם, that all the people (except for the women and the tribe of Levi) spontaneously brought their gold, ornaments, rings, and bracelets, to facilitate the making of the Golden Calf as soon as possible, early in the day, as soon as they awakened.

אָכֵן הִשְׁכִּימוּ הִשְׁחִיתוּ (צְפַנְיָה ג:ז) אָמַר ר' חִיָּיא בַּר אַבָּא: כָּל הַשְׁחָתָה . . .
בְּהַשְׁכָּמָה הָיוּ עוֹשִׂין.

בָּעֵגֶל כְּתִיב וַיַּשְׁכִּימוּ מִמָּחֲרַת מִיָּד . . . הֵבִיאוּ בַּבֹּקֶר וּבְנִדְבַת הַמִּשְׁכָּן כְּתִיב
וְהֵם הֵבִיאוּ אֵלָיו עוֹד נְדָבָה בַּבֹּקֶר בַּבֹּקֶר – וְלֹא בְּהַשְׁכָּמָה מַמָּשׁ (קרבן
העדה)

The prophet Tzefaniah (3:7) decries the fact that the
people arose early in the morning to fulfill their wicked
intentions.

Gemara Shekalim quotes R' Chiya bar Abba:

"Every evil occurrence was acted upon in the morning."
Korban HaEidah comments:

"It was taken care of immediately upon arising. They
immediately brought their contributions for the Golden
Calf."

Yet, for the building of the Mishkan, they brought their
contributions בַּבֹּקֶר בַּבֹּקֶר, every morning, day after day, but
not necessarily בְּהַשְׁכָּמָה, in the early morning as soon as
they arose.

At the time of the Mishkan, only those individuals of generous heart
responded.

At the time of the Golden Calf, all the people responded.

Thus we see, as Taklin Chadetin states, how great is the power of the
yetzer hara!

In the words of one great tzaddik, "Der yetzer hara brent,
der yetzer tov brent nisht."

The yetzer hara burns within a person and often causes him to run
without thinking into the web of sin. The yetzer tov, on the other hand,
does not "burn." To do the right thing, a person has to awaken his own
spirit, and overcome natural laziness and other factors that seek to pull
him in the wrong direction.

II. Receiving the Torah and the Sin of the Spies

לְטוֹבָה: וַיּוֹצֵא מֹשֶׁה אֶת הָעָם (שמות יט:יז)
לְרָעָה: וַתִּקְרְבוּן אֵלַי כֻּלְּכֶם (דברים א:כב)

In the narrative of the receiving of the Torah at Mount Sinai, the
Torah states, And Moshe "led" the people towards G-d (Shemos 19:17).
No one moved on his own until he was led by Moshe Rabbeinu.

However, when Moshe chastised the people for their part in the sin of the *Meraglim* (Spies), he said, *"And all of you approached me* — all of *you* demanded that I send spies to scout out the Land of Israel, to see if *Eretz Yisrael* was good for us or not."

We must understand! Was it necessary for the Jews to find out whether or not *Eretz Yisrael* was good, whether the land was fit for them or not? Did we have to send spies? If G-d was granting them the Land, then surely it was good! That should have been sufficient.

It is most interesting to note *Rashi's* explanation of *Devarim* 1:22 concerning how the request for the Spies was put forth by the people. בְּעִרְבּוּבְיָא, *with confusion.*

They approached Moshe from all sides, in a disorganized and confused state. Youngsters were pushing aside the elders, and the elders were pushing aside the leaders of the people.*

It became, in essence, an instance of mob activity. Everybody joined in this demand. It was a tumultuous multitude of people pushing forward to have their voices heard.

Rashi (*Devarim* 1:22) refers to the way in which the people came to Mount Sinai to receive the Torah.

Rashi quotes *Devarim* 5:20:

You approached me properly; children honored the elders and

---

* Rabbi Samson Raphael Hirsch (*Bamidbar* 13:2) comments: The request for spies was not the problem.

Israel had already journeyed through the wilderness of Paran, described as "the great and awesome desert" (*Devarim* 1:19). They had reached the border of the land that was to be conquered. The first request was וַיַּחְפְּרוּ, which means to excavate, to uncover hidden faults. They wanted to reconnoiter the land; to convert the knowledge of it from the darkness of the unknown to the clarity of daylight, to the known. The express purpose of this was to find the best way to enter the land. They wanted to locate the weak spots which would enable them to conquer the land more easily.

This was לְרָעָה, for bad and evil intent.

G-d changed the direction of the Spies. G-d used the word *v'yasuru* (וְיָתֻרוּ), which means "searching out the good points, suitable for some intended purpose."

The word *v'yasuru* changes the mission. No longer was it to spy out the land for the most suitable way to conquer the land. The task now became one of knowing the land itself with the express purpose of the *natural development* of the people of the land. The ultimate purpose was that it would lead to the further and future spiritual greatness of *Bnei Yisrael.*

What made this request a denigrating one was the way it had been proposed. The mob psychology had brought all Israel together to demand that this be done, and for different purposes.

The pushing and the yelling, the lack of respect for elders and leaders, were totally inappropriate.

allowed them to go ahead of them. The elders honored their leaders and allowed them to go ahead of them.

It is interesting to note that *Kli Yakar* (*Devarim* 1:22) disagrees with *Rashi's* understanding of this latter situation. He contends that at the Giving of the Torah, there was something wrong in the way the people approached Moshe and that, too, was part of the *mussar* offered by Moshe in the beginning of *Chumash Devarim*.

At Sinai, when the time came to hear the voice of Hashem as He uttered the commandments and presented them with the Torah, the people did not surge forward; rather, *Kli Yakar* interprets both of these events in the same vein:

In the matter of the Spies, the people wanted to know what their future life in the Land of Israel would be like. They were *all* interested in the physical and the material advantages of the new land. They wanted to know how they themselves would be affected materially. Therefore, the youth pushed themselves to the head of the group to ensure that their voice would be heard.

After all, settling in a new country would affect the young generation the most, especially if they were primarily concerned with their material well-being.

At the Giving of the Torah, says the *Kli Yakar,* the young people were preoccupied with the same wrong intentions, but this was reflected in an opposite manner.

The youth held back.

Torah and *mitzvos* were primarily for the elders, they felt. Those who were advanced in years and no longer had the energy or desire to indulge in physical pleasures could devote themselves totally to learning Torah and doing *mitzvos*. The youth, in this instance, let the older people go first, to show their lack of interest in the demands of the Torah. "We are young yet, and we want to 'live,' " were their thoughts.

Thus, according to the *Kli Yakar,* both the receiving of the Torah and the sending of the Spies were events where the people's thoughts were dominated by wrong intentions.

III. A Song and a Cry

לְטוֹבָה: אָז יָשִׁיר מֹשֶׁה וּבְנֵי יִשְׂרָאֵל (שמות טו:א)

לְרָעָה: וַתִּשָּׂא כָּל הָעֵדָה (במדבר יד:א)

When the Israelites crossed the *Yam Suf* (Sea of Reeds), Moshe and the Jewish people sang a song of praise to G-d.

The song that the Children of Israel sang, *Az Yashir*, was one which declares the glory and power of the Almighty G-d. The people declared, אָשִׁירָה לַה', *I will sing to Hashem*. Overwhelmed by the miracles they had witnessed, they expressed with great excitement the recognition of Hashem which they had now experienced so clearly.*

But, when did the Children of Israel sing?

Only after Moshe led them.

It was not a spontaneous song of gratitude for the greatest miracle of all time. The sea had split and all Israel made their way through it while the Egyptians drowned behind them — a miracle of miracles. Yet, they did not sing on their own. Moshe began the song and then, the nation joined in.

Moshe led them in the song.

The reaction of the people was quite different after the Spies returned from the Land of Canaan with their slanderous report.

Then, the entire congregation raised its voice in distress and the people wept through that night.

(*That night* was the Ninth of Av; the day on which, in the future, the saddest and most tragic catastrophes in our nation's history would later occur.)

No one led Israel in its collective weeping. This was a spontaneous action on the part of the people.

- To sing to Hashem in thanksgiving and praise, they waited until Moshe led them.
- To cry out and weep in rejection of Hashem's goodness, no prompting was needed. All cried out and wept in unison.

Should *we* not cry each time we read these sentences in the Torah?

Should we not be ashamed and embarrassed that this could happen to our great nation?

In each place where the above verses are related in the Torah, *Torah Temimah* repeats the expression found in *Talmud Yerushalmi*.

הַנִּקְרָא וְלֹא נִבְעָת

Can we read [these verses] without being shaken?

Should we not be troubled by the various actions described above?

---

* Rabbi Samson Raphael Hirsch comments:

A song is used to express thoughts and feelings that are called into existence *within* oneself. Generally, it would be an inspired, rapturous expression of some external event that has become revealed to the inner self.

The lesson is a crucial one.

- When it comes to doing "good," only chosen individuals respond.
- When it comes to doing wrong, everybody jumps on the bandwagon, everyone responds.

◈§ *Yosef and the Brothers*

וַיּאמֶר יוֹסֵף אֶל אֶחָיו אֲנִי יוֹסֵף . . . וְלֹא יָכְלוּ אֶחָיו לַעֲנוֹת אתוֹ כִּי נִבְהֲלוּ מִפָּנָיו (בראשית מה:ג)

Let us examine another verse in the Torah (not mentioned in *Yerushalmi Shekalim*), where our reaction should, once again, be: הַנִּקְרָא וְלֹא נִבְעַת, *Can we read this without being shaken*?

When Yosef finally revealed himself to his brothers, he said two simple words: אֲנִי יוֹסֵף, *I am Yosef* (*Bereishis* 45:3).

His brothers were unable to answer him as they were frightened and confused by this confrontation.

Rashi comments that the fear experienced by the brothers was very intense because of the shame that they felt concerning their own conduct.

Torah Temimah quotes *Chagigah* 4b:

Rabbi Elazar, when he read this verse, wept and said:

> If, when rebuked by a man of flesh and blood, the brothers were unable to respond and instead, were left bewildered and shaken, then how much more so will be our response when the time comes to stand in judgment before Hashem.

Yalkut Shimoni quotes R' Shimon Ben Elazar:

אוֹי לָנוּ מִיּוֹם הַדִּין. אוֹי לָנוּ מִיּוֹם הַתּוֹכָחָה.
Woe to us on the Day of Judgment. Woe to us on the Day of Rebuke.

Our every deed, action, and thought will be presented to us after 120 twenty years. We will be asked to render a verdict concerning certain transgressions without realizing that we will actually be judging ourselves. We will literally render a verdict regarding our very own errors.

In *Avos* (3:20) our Sages teach:

נִפְרָעִין מִן הָאָדָם מִדַּעְתּוֹ וְשֶׁלֹּא מִדַּעְתּוֹ

Man is punished with his knowledge, and without his knowledge.

What does this mean?

Rabbi Shraga Feivel Mendlowitz's explanation is as follows:

As mentioned above, Hashem presents a case study of a person's deeds to the person himself, for him to pass judgment on.

One's transgressions, therefore, are judged according to one's own thinking and knowledge, one's own evaluation and understanding.

This is done without the person realizing that this case study concerns himself, and that his very own actions are being judged.

The person renders his decision without the knowledge (i.e. realization) that he is actually judging himself.

Each person is reproved after he has issued his own verdict. Because he himself has passed judgment on himself, he can no longer justify his behavior. No longer can he offer any excuses.

This is what occurred during Yosef's meeting with his brothers. The brothers felt that whatever they had done to Yosef had been correct.

The brothers of Yosef had acted as a *beis din* to judge Yosef and his dreams.

Their great-grandfather Avraham's legacy was carried on by only one son, by Yitzchak, and not by Yishmael.

In turn, Yitzchak's legacy was carried on by only one son, Yaakov, and not by Eisav.

Was this trend of events to continue on, into the future?

Was Yosef, alone, going to carry on the heritage and legacy of our three Patriarchs, of Avraham, Yitzchak, and Yaakov?

Were the brothers to be shunted aside and only one son bear the standard as in the previous generations?

The brothers were convinced that Yosef wanted to claim the right to mold the future of *Bnei Yisrael* as its leader. They were sure that it was this feeling which caused Yosef to dream of being a king over them. Yosef's dreams of grandeur convinced the brothers that he deserved to be eliminated, for he was wrongfully claiming to be the primary inheritor of the legacy of Avraham, Yitzchak, and Yaakov. They ruled that it was correct to kill him or, at least, to sell him into slavery.

When Yosef uttered the words, "I am Yosef," the brothers realized that Yosef's dreams *had come true*.

This proved that his dreams were messages from Heaven, not the result of fantasies of grandeur, as they had thought. They now realized that when they had judged Yosef as guilty, it was actually *they* who were guilty — guilty of wrongly accusing their own brother.

The brothers had been terribly wrong in their reckoning. They were frightened and shaken by Yosef's revelation. הַנִּקְרָא וְלֹא נִבָּעֵת, *Can we read this and not be shaken?*

This is why Rabbi Shimon ben Elazar declared,

Woe to us on the Day of Judgment, when we will judge ourselves. When that happens, there will be no excuses.

Therefore, woe to us on the Day of Rebuke because we will have decided the verdict ourselves. There can be no greater rebuke than that.

◄§ *Important Lessons*

The following will summarize our discussion.

We should learn a *mussar haskel,* an important, thought-provoking lesson from the passage in *Yerushalmi Shekalim.*

We should learn to think before we act. One should not "jump on the bandwagon" before he has clearly thought out and judged what should be done. He must have a clear, rational perception of right and wrong in order to make a proper evaluation of his deeds. This should determine his role and position in any controversy.

In that passage in *Shekalim,* it was those of noble character that made the right decision in all three instances where the people acted for the good.

- The נְדִיבֵי לֵב, the good hearted and generous, were the leaders in contributing toward the building of the *Mishkan.*
- Moshe brought *Klal Yisrael* to the foot of Sinai to receive the Torah.
- Moshe led the people in song after they passed through the Sea of Reeds.

The decision may seem simple. Yet, one must always look to see who the leaders are. If the leadership is composed of the finest individuals, then you cannot possibly go wrong.

Let us turn now to the three negative instances cited in *Shekalim*.

Not all of *Klal Yisrael* partook in the making of the Golden Calf. There was a small group that instigated this act.

Not all of *Klal Yisrael* cried when the Spies returned from spying out the land. Again, the crying was instigated by a small group.

> The problem arose when something wrong was being proposed and the people allowed the idea to gain momentum. They did not stop to think.

Rabbi Samson R. Hirsch (*Bamidbar* 14:1) states:

Bnei Yisrael first broke out in a cry at the bad news, and then let their voices go on wailing and complaining.

> Remember: Do not jump on the bandwagon when matters are not clearly heading in the right direction. Do not make snap judgments.

As a *ben Torah*:

- You must think.
- You must evaluate.
- You must choose.
- You must *know yourself*.
- You must not be carried away by mob reaction.

If you decide that something is wrong, become a leader to stop the movement.

Let your voice be heard *loud and clear*.

Stop others from joining the rabble-rousers.

- Become a leader for good.
- Become a leader for stopping anything bad or evil.

The one word that I always stress to all my students is
> *responsibility*.

Develop a sense of responsibility for your own actions, and particularly for your actions when they concern *Klal Yisrael*. And remember: The way you behave in public affects all of *Klal Yisrael*.

The following article appeared in the newspaper one day:

> A 12-year-old child lit matches in the stairwell of his school and started a fire by burning some paper.
>
> There were two older boys who saw this youngster light the matches and they *did not try to stop him*.

Some first graders smelled the odor of smoke and immediately ran to tell their teacher.

Imagine! This was a school building. There were over 500 children, teachers, and others in the building.

Is it possible that this youngster did not realize what he was doing? Surely he should have realized the danger of fire in a school building. And why did the two older students do nothing to stop him?

This bothers me. The purpose of this *mussar shmuess* is to ensure that this should never happen in our community.

- You must become a leader for good.
- You must become a leader for stopping and preventing evil.
- If there is no leadership, *you* must become the leader. Stop! Think! Accept responsibility!
- If you train yourself to think matters through, you will prevent many wrongdoings.

The trouble with the current generation is that the media — newspapers, radio, and television — all headline the wrongs being done. We start our day reading and hearing about murder, drugs, gang wars, fires, etc. Things that are good and positive are seldom headlined.

This approach is the very opposite of the Torah's approach, as we shall see.

◆§ Signposts

In the Torah, we are taught the laws of the עָרֵי מִקְלָט, *cities of refuge,* to which a Jew fled if he killed בְּשׁוֹגֵג, *inadvertently.* As long as he remained in the עִיר מִקְלָט, he was safe. However, outside the city, he was liable to be killed by the גּוֹאֵל הַדָּם, *avenger of blood,* a relative of the man he had murdered. It was, therefore, crucial that the murderer reach the עִיר מִקְלָט as quickly as possible.

תַּנְיָא ר׳ אֱלִיעֶזֶר בֶּן יַעֲקֹב אוֹמֵר: מִקְלָט הָיָה כָּתוּב עַל פָּרָשַׁת דְּרָכִים כְּדֵי
שֶׁיַּכִּיר הָרוֹצֵחַ וְיִפְנֶה לְשָׁם (מכות י:א-ב)

The *Gemara* (*Makkos* 10a,b) states that at every cross-roads, signs were posted: "This way to the city of refuge." The murderer did not need to stop to ask directions.

However, at these same crossroads there were no signs pointing the way to Jerusalem for the עוֹלֵי רֶגֶל, those who made their way to the Holy City for the Festivals of Pesach, Shavuos, and Succos.

At least three times a year, hundreds of thousands of families went up to Jerusalem to bring sacrifices and to stand in the Presence of the *Shechinah* at the *Beis HaMikdash*.

Why were there no signs at every crossroads in *Eretz Yisrael* pointing the way for these many good people to the holy city of Yerushalayim?

How many people killed inadvertently and needed to run to cities of refuge? Very few, only a very, very minute number compared to the hundreds of thousands, if not millions, of Jews who visited the *Beis HaMikdash* annually.

The reason for the signposts pointing toward the cities of refuge was to help the murderer to hurry on his way. This was for his protection. as explained above. Because there were signposts, he did not have to stop and inquire about directions, but could travel to his destination as speedily as possible.

Perhaps there was also a psychological reason for these signposts — and for the absence of signposts pointing toward Jerusalem.

The Torah does not want people to speak about murderers. If a person were to arrive at a crossroads and stop to ask directions from a passer-by to the city of refuge, he would be announcing terrible news. The passer-by would have gone home, and quite possibly, would have spread the news to others:

"Today I met a murderer running for his life."

In no time at all, the entire town would have been buzzing with the news of this terrible event.

But, if there were clear directions, the murderer would not have needed to stop and ask the way. In this way, no one would have even known that a murderer had been in the vicinity.

Now, let us see what happened when people asked directions to Jerusalem, since there were no signposts.

Suppose Yaakov, living in Beer Sheva, had decided as a particular *Yom Tov* approached, that he would not be going to Jerusalem to fulfill the *mitzvah* of *aliyah l'regel*. Then, at a crossroads, he met a caravan from Eilat. They stopped and asked him directions.

Yaakov then came home and related this meeting to his wife: "I met a whole caravan going to Jerusalem and they live much further away than we do. I've changed my mind. If they can go to Jerusalem for *Yom Tov,* so can we."

The Torah wants us to talk about good things, about performing *mitzvos.*

This represents the opposite of what today's media is accomplishing.

Let us always try to help create a mood for good, positive action.

- Be a leader against evil.
- Be a leader for good.

Hashkafah

21
Kedushah — Holiness: The Essence of the Jew

ᴇ§ Sanctified and Separate

I f we look for one word to describe the greatness of Israel, if there is one word which sums up exactly how a Jew should live,

that word is — *kedushah,* holiness.

Let us examine carefully what the term *kedushah* represents.

Let us examine carefully how this one concept can be applied to all the activities in which we are involved all day long.

The Torah states:

דַּבֵּר אֶל כָּל עֲדַת בְּנֵי יִשְׂרָאֵל וְאָמַרְתָּ אֲלֵהֶם קְדֹשִׁים תִּהְיוּ כִּי קָדוֹשׁ אֲנִי ה׳ אֱלֹהֵיכֶם. . .

> *Speak to the entire assembly of the Children of Israel and say to them: You shall be holy, for holy am I, Hashem, your G-d (Vayikra 19:2).* *

Rashi explains the most elementary approach to *kedushah* is to separate oneself from immorality. We must stay away from anything immoral. To be *kadosh,* holy, means to be different from all other nations of the world in the moral way we live. *Rashi* adds that wherever one finds a protective fence against immorality, he finds *kedushah,* holiness.

Immorality generally deals with marriage laws, whom we may marry and whom we may not. At the end of *Parshiyos Acharei Mos* and

---

* For further elucidation and clarity of the word *kedushah,* see addendum at end of chapter.

Kedoshim (*Vayikra* Chs. 18,20) we are taught the laws of the forbidden unions.

Doing things that are immoral is a contradiction to the *kedushah* of Hashem, His Torah, and *Klal Yisrael.*

We live in a world filled with incidents of immorality. The laws of our Torah seem far removed from the conscience of today's average man in the street.

There must be a clear *havdalah,* separation, between ourselves and the nations of the world.

After stating the command to be קְדֹשִׁים, *holy people,* the Torah then teaches us how to capture this *kedushah* and infuse our daily lives with it.

◈§ Fundamental Mitzvos

אִישׁ אִמּוֹ וְאָבִיו תִּירָאוּ וְאֶת שַׁבְּתֹתַי תִּשְׁמֹרוּ, אֲנִי ה׳ אֱלֹהֵיכֶם

Every man shall revere his mother and his father and you shall observe My Sabbaths — I am Hashem, your G-d (Vayikra 19:3).

Keeping Shabbos is a *mitzvah* between G-d and man. Shabbos is a day that reminds us of the Creation of the world. Shabbos reminds us that there is a Creator to this world.

G-d created the world in six days and rested on the seventh.

Was G-d tired?

Did He need a rest, a vacation?

Of course not!

Yet, on Shabbos, G-d *did not create.* This is why we keep the Shabbos. We emulate what G-d did.

- He did not create.
- We do not create.

When I observe the laws of Shabbos, it shows that I believe in Hashem. It shows that I believe He created the world, and I try to emulate Him. It is my way of declaring that the entire world belongs to Hashem.

The Chofetz Chaim said that one who keeps the Shabbos, who will be a true Sabbath observer, will also put on *tefillin,* will eat only kosher food, and will do all the other *mitzvos* of Hashem. For Shabbos is the אות, *sign,* that one is a faithful, observant Jew.

> But how will I know about the beauty of Shabbos?
> How will I know about the laws of Shabbos?

In order to do, understand, and fulfill all the *mitzvos* of the Torah, we need teachers to influence and inspire us. Our primary teachers of Torah-true Judaism are our very own parents. Therefore, in the same verse which begins with the *mitzvah* of Shabbos, we are commanded to respect our parents. They will teach us exactly how to live. They will take care of our education. They will send us to a yeshivah whose *rebbeim* will inspire and influence us to grow up properly in the Torah way of life.

Your parents will teach you about the Shabbos and other *mitzvos.* If you stand in awe of them, you will listen to them and follow their way of life.

- Your mother will teach you to say *Modeh Ani* every morning when you wake up (and other prayers as well).
- Your mother will teach you to recite a *berachah* before you eat anything.
- Your mother will teach you to recite the *Shema* before going to sleep (and other prayers as well).

Thus, your mother will be teaching you to acknowledge Hashem's Presence throughout the day.

- Your father will teach you Torah.
- Your father will take you to *shul.*
- Your father will review your studies with you whenever possible.
- Your father will sit and learn Torah by himself or attend a *shiur* (lecture). He will teach through example the importance of learning Torah, any time of day or night, wherever and whenever possible.

The above is indeed a description of the ideal transmission of Torah and its way of life, from generation to generation.*

---

* Unfortunately there are many instances when this is not possible.

A *baal teshuvah* is one who was not given a Torah education but through his own courageous efforts found his way back to Hashem and His Torah.

Thousands of *baalei teshuvah* have found alternate ways to learn about and become connected to Torah and *mitzvos.*

Indeed, we stand in awe of them and their dedication.

◄§ Sound Advice

In 1961, my dear wife, Marcia, and I enjoyed our first visit to *Eretz Yisrael.* It was inspiring and spiritually elevating, never to be forgotten.

We went with a private group and we were told that the Gerrer *Rebbe,* Rabbi Yisrael Alter, would be in Jerusalem for just one Sunday during his vacation month, and that hundreds of people would line up to receive his blessing.

My group decided that we would *daven* with the *netz,* sunrise, the earliest *minyan* of the day. In this way, we felt certain that we would be first on line to receive a *berachah* from the *Rebbe.*

By 8:30 A.M., the line stretched for several blocks. Luckily we were near the front of the line.

Joe, a wealthy man from my group, was in front of me. He asked the *Rebbe* for a blessing that his children should grow up to be learned Jews, *talmidei chachamim.*

The *Rebbe* looked at him and said:

"Sit and learn."

Joe said: "*Rebbe,* I am not asking for a *berachah* for myself. I want my children to know how to learn well. I want them to be *bnei Torah.*"

"*Nu, Nu,*" the *Rebbe* said. "I already answered you. Sit and learn."

The *gabbai* (attendant) came in and said: "Next," and Joe was ushered out of the *Rebbe's* presence. Joe felt that the *Rebbe* had not blessed him at all.

"Eli," he said, "what is going on here? They did not even give me a chance to explain my request. They just pushed me out."

"Joe," I said, "take it easy. The *Rebbe* fully understood you. He gave you the best advice.

"If you want your children to sit and learn, then you must set an example. He told you that *you must sit and learn.*

"Let your children see *your* desire for learning. If you will be their role model, they too will sit and learn.

"In this way, *you* will be a greater *talmid chacham* and your children will follow your commitment to Torah study.

"The *Rebbe* gave you a beautiful *berachah.* The *Rebbe* taught you that you must become personally involved in learning if you want the blessing of sons who are *bnei Torah* to come true."

You should and must become involved in Torah learning, *yourself*. Learn Torah *yourself* and your wishes that your children should become *bnei Torah* will come true.

Thus, I tell my students: How will you know the details of the מִצְוַת עֲשֵׂה, the positive *mitzvos* which must be observed and fulfilled? Your parents will teach them to you through their own actions and through the teachings of the yeshivah to which they send you. Your parents will teach you *all* the *mitzvos* of the Torah through a variety of ways. Just observe their deeds, follow their actions, and listen to their words.

- Respect and honor your parents.
- They will lead you to Hashem.

Thus, two *mitzvos* literally open the doors to all other *mitzvos*.

1. Shabbos is a weekly reminder that Hashem is the Creator of all.
2. Fulfilling the *mitzvah* of morah av v'eim, respect for one's parents, will enable you to be aware of all the *mitzvos*.

The next verse in *Parashas Kedoshim* states:

אַל תִּפְנוּ אֶל הָאֱלִילִם וֵאלֹהֵי מַסֵּכָה לֹא תַעֲשׂוּ לָכֶם אֲנִי ה׳ אֱלֹהֵיכֶם

Do not turn to the idols, and molten gods you shall not make for yourselves — I am Hashem, your G-d (*Vayikra* 19:4).

In the second paragraph of the *Shema*, we find:

הִשָּׁמְרוּ לָכֶם פֶּן יִפְתֶּה לְבַבְכֶם וְסַרְתֶּם וַעֲבַדְתֶּם אֱלֹהִים אֲחֵרִים וְהִשְׁתַּחֲוִיתֶם לָהֶם

Beware lest your heart be seduced and you turn astray and serve gods of others (i.e. idol worship) *and bow to them* (*Devarim* 11:16).

Rashi explains:

An imperceptible, seemingly innocent surrender to temptation can be the beginning of a course that will end in idolatry. If one separates himself from Torah, we do not know how far he will stray. One temptation can lead to another temptation resulting in the end with idol worship.

Rabbi Samson Raphael Hirsch comments:

Take care of yourselves. Be on your guard to remain solely under the influence of Torah and *mitzvos*. Beware of every influence that might estrange you from what you were meant to be. The slightest deviation can lead to a second and third deviation culminating with idol worship.

The second, third and fourth verses of *Parashas Kedoshim* all close with אֲנִי ה׳ אֱלֹהֵיכֶם, *I am Hashem, your G-d.* These three sentences call us to *kedushah.* They show us how to bring *kedushah* into our daily lives and how to avoid that which can, G-d forbid, lead us away from *kedushah.*

- Be holy because G-d is Holy.
- Respect your parents.
- Keep Shabbos.
- Avoid sin, for it can ultimately lead to the very worst — idol worship.

⋐ *Havdalah — Separation*

The essence of the term *kedushah* is intimately connected with the term *havdalah,* separation.

- *Kedushah* reminds us to serve Hashem properly.
- *Havdalah* reminds us that our way of life is completely different from that of all other nations.
- *Havdalah* means that there must be a very clear distinction between a *ben* or *bas Yisrael* and all other people.
- *Havdalah* is a most elementary and crucial aspect of *kedushah.*

In every Jewish home on Friday night *Kiddush* is recited in honor of Shabbos. Shabbos is enhanced with the singing of *zemiros* (Shabbos songs) and *divrei Torah* (Torah thoughts) at the Shabbos meal.

The recitation of *Havdalah* is also an important *mitzvah.* It is a way of ushering out the wonderful day of Shabbos. *Havdalah,* too, should be accompanied with songs for a *"gut voch"* (good week).

At the conclusion of *Havdalah* (and in many homes at the *Melaveh Malkah* meal on *Motzaei Shabbos*), we sing about Eliyahu *HaNavi,* and express the hope that he should appear to inform us of the arrival of *Mashiach* (speedily, in our time).

We sing *Ani Maamin,* "I believe with complete faith in the coming of *Mashiach,* and even though he may delay, nevertheless, I anticipate every day that he will come."

In my home we always danced together as we sang these songs.

✍ *Three Distinctions*

It is most interesting to note that in the blessing of *Havdalah,* we make mention of three distinct *havdalos,* separations:

הַמַּבְדִּיל בֵּין קֹדֶשׁ לְחוֹל בֵּין אוֹר לְחֹשֶׁךְ בֵּין יִשְׂרָאֵל לָעַמִּים. . .

[Blessed are You, Hashem. . .] Who separates between holy and secular, between light and darkness, between Israel and the nations of the world. . .

The order of these varying separations needs clarification.

The clearest *havdalah,* separation, is between light and darkness. When it is light, it is still Shabbos. When it is dark, it is no longer Shabbos.

Of course, we usher in the Shabbos before sunset, to start this day of *kedushah* somewhat earlier, while it is still daytime.

We also observe the Shabbos at its conclusion well past sunset, when it is *already* dark.*

Can a person confuse between light and darkness? Hardly. This is the clearest *havdalah* possible. It would seem, then, that this distinction should have been mentioned *first;* yet, it is mentioned second.

What about the difference "between holy and secular"? Can a mistake be made in this category? Yes, it can.

For example, a person may want to do an action for a holy purpose. Yet, the action he is planning may, in fact, be a transgression of Torah law.

An illustration:

On Rosh Hashanah, there is a very important *mitzvah,* to hear the blowing of the *shofar.* We look forward to hearing the *shofar* being blown. What if there is a question concerning the synagogue in your neighborhood? What if men and women sit together; if there is no *mechitzah* (partition between men and women)?

---

* There are different opinions as to how many minutes after sunset one is permitted to do labor that is forbidden on Shabbos.

The law is very clear. It is better not to hear the *shofar* blowing, better not to fulfill this important *mitzvah,* than go to a synagogue that does not act according to *Halachah* (Jewish law).

There are many other examples.

Thus, in the separation of holy from secular, mistakes can often be made. This distinction, then, is not always clear. Yet it is placed first in the *Havdalah* blessing, before that of "light and darkness," which is centered between the *havdalah* of "holy and secular" and the *havdalah* of "Israel and the nations."

This was done for a very important reason. Our Rabbis wanted to make sure that we realize what is holy in all instances. In the very same way that we cannot confuse light and darkness, so we must never confuse holy and secular, or holy and profane.

Not everything is *kadosh,* holy, simply because it appears so. Before you label a given act as "holy," this has to be as clear to you as the difference between light and darkness.

Now, we will understand the third *havdalah* separation in this blessing and why *Chazal* (our Sages) placed light and darkness immediately before the distinction between Israel and the nations.

Just as there is a major difference between light and darkness, and this difference is clearly understood and recognized, so too there must be a clear distinction between "us" and "them," between Yisrael and the other nations of the world.

- We are human beings and so are they.
- We wear suits and ties, and so do they.

What is the difference between us and the rest of the world?

- The way we behave.
- The way we talk.
- The way we walk.

We have Torah and *mitzvos.*

We *must* act accordingly.

Chazal tell us that in the same way we cannot confuse light and darkness, for there is a clear distinction between the two,

we cannot blur the distinction between ourselves and the other nations. We are a nation of Torah, and this must be clearly recognized in the way we act

at home • at school • in the street • on a bus • in a park • in public • in the privacy of our rooms.

Everyone must see the *kedushah* of a Jew as clearly as he differentiates between light and darkness.

⊷§ *A Message for All*

Parashas Kedoshim begins with Hashem instructing Moshe: דַּבֵּר אֶל כָּל עֲדַת בְּנֵי יִשְׂרָאֵל, *Speak to the entire assembly of the Children of Israel* (*Vayikra* 19:2).

Rashi comments:

This *parashah* was taught בְּהַקְהֵל, at a gathering of all men, women, and children of Israel.

Why? "Because the majority of the essentials of the Torah depend on it."

Rabbi Moshe Feinstein, at a Torah Umesorah convention, noted:

True, there are many *mitzvos* in this *parashah,* a total of 51; 13 are positive (מִצְוֹת עֲשֵׂה), while the other 38 are negative (לֹא תַעֲשֶׂה) [13 + 38 = 51]. But this is far less than a majority of the 613 *mitzvos.* Why, then, does *Rashi* state that a majority of the Torah's essentials depend on this *parashah*?

Reb Moshe answered:

"The term תְּלוּיִן בָּה, *depend on it,* used by *Rashi* does not refer to *Parashas Kedoshim.* It refers to the commandment קְדֹשִׁים תִּהְיוּ, *You shall be holy.*"

This *parashah* was taught to all Israel, in one huge gathering of men, women, and children, because the majority of all the essentials of the Torah are *dependent* on *kedushah,* holiness.

Go about your life with this message uppermost in mind. Then, you will infuse your every act with *kedushah,* an act which every Jew should strive to attain.

⊷§ *Addendum:*

Rabbi Samson R. Hirsch remarks that this *mitzvah* of *Kedushah* is one of two *mitzvos* that were given to the entire community of all Israel; men, women, and children.

This admonition to the highest degree of moral human perfection was addressed expressly to each and every individual of the nation.

There are two words which need clarification:

- קָדוֹשׁ — *Kadosh*, in the singular, is written *with* the *vuv* after the *daled*. This word, *Kadosh*, refers to G-d alone.

- קְדֹשִׁים — *Kedoshim*, in plural, is written *without* the letter *vuv*; the dot, alone, to the left of the letter *daled* signifies the sound of *OH*. This word refers to all the Children of Israel.

Kedoshim 19:3. This sentence spells out for us that we shall be holy "because I (G-d) am Holy, Kadosh."

G-d is the true essence of Holiness, of Spiritual Perfection. There can be nothing missing in the Holiness of G-d.

The word *Kadosh* referring to Hashem is written with the *vuv*; the word *Kadosh* is written in its completeness.

This word *Kadosh* referring to Hashem teaches us that the fullness of Holiness, its completeness, its essence in its entirety, can only be found in G-d. We mortal humans cannot imagine or understand G-d's *Kedushah*.

The word *kedoshim* is directed to all Israel. You, Israel, shall be holy because I, G-d, am Holy. The word *kedoshim*, you should be holy, is written defectively. It is not fully written, as the *vuv* is omitted.

We mortal human beings can never reach the ultimate heights of *Kedushah*, for they can be found only in G-d. Therefore, when *we* are commanded to be holy, the word *kedoshim* referring to the people of Israel is written *incompletely* with the letter *vuv* missing.

אַתָּה קָדוֹשׁ וְשִׁמְךָ קָדוֹשׁ וּקְדוֹשִׁים בְּכָל יוֹם יְהַלְלוּךָ סֶּלָה

In the third blessing of *Shemoneh Esrei*, we say these words. They refer to and are directed to G-d.

You are Holy, Your name is Holy, and Holy ones (the angels) praise and extol You every day, forever.

Every word of *Kedushah* in the blessing is written in its *fullness, with* the letter *vuv*.

- Only G-d and His angels can be termed *Kadosh*, *with* the *vuv*.

- Only G-d's name can be completely *Kadosh* *with* the *vuv*.

- Only angels can be full, complete *kedoshim*, written *with* the *vuv*.

- G-d and His angels can be and are the epitome of *Kedushah*.

22

Faith — True Emunah:
Everything Comes from Hashem

◆§ *Times of Morning, Times of Night*

The word בֹּקֶר, literally, *morning,* often refers, both in *Tanach* and in the writings of *Chazal,* to happy times. In the morning the world looks bright.

- The sun is shining.
- The world looks rosy and beautiful.
- There is a buoyancy in the air.

Similarly, when times are good,

- There are happy tidings.
- Everything and everyone is well.
- Prosperity is in abundance.
- Everyone is in good spirits.
- Everything seems to be going right.
- There is a mood of optimism.

The word לַיְלָה, literally *night,* often refers to dark, difficult times, times when there are

- bad tidings,
- problems with health, children, etc.;
- times when business is not good, and perhaps,
  when there is an economic depression in the world.
- Times when nations are at the brink of war and
  worried citizens walk around with heavy hearts.
  The mood of the people is a gloomy one.
  They do not know what to expect tomorrow.
- Nothing is going right. There is an aura of pessimism.

Each day of the week at the conclusion of *Shacharis,* we recite a שִׁיר, a song for the day. This is a psalm from *Tehillim* which was sung by the *Leviim* during the Temple service in the *Beis HaMikdash.*

In the Song for the Day of Shabbos, we say:

מִזְמוֹר שִׁיר לְיוֹם הַשַּׁבָּת. טוֹב לְהֹדוֹת לַה׳ וּלְזַמֵּר לְשִׁמְךָ עֶלְיוֹן. לְהַגִּיד בַּבֹּקֶר חַסְדֶּךָ. וֶאֱמוּנָתְךָ בַּלֵּילוֹת (תהילם צב:א-ג)

*A psalm, a song for the Shabbos day. It is good to thank HASHEM, and to sing praise to Your Name, O Exalted One; to proclaim Your kindness in the **dawn** and Your faith in the **nights** (Tehillim 92:1-3)*

Rabbi Samson Raphael Hirsch comments:

Regardless of our situation, as Shabbos enters into our midst,
> whether it finds us at the dawn of a better time, or
> in utter darkness, reeling night after night, seemingly without hope of a morning,

our song will sound forth with the same joy *each and every Shabbos.*
The beautiful uplifting day of Shabbos reminds us

- of Hashem's lovingkindness in the "morning,"
- and of His faithfulness in the "nights."

◈ *Kindness and Faith*

The third *pasuk* we quoted contains two phrases.

The first phrase refers to בֹּקֶר, *morning,* and speaks of *chesed,* the boundless kindness of Hashem.

The second phrase refers to לַיְלָה, *night,* and speaks of *emunah,* faith.

When everything is going smoothly and happily, we are *not to say:*
"We are deserving of G-d's blessings."

We are *not to think* that we are such good people that Hashem is granting us our just reward for the good deeds *we* do.

Rather, when everything seems to be going *"our way,"* we talk about Hashem's *chesed,* His kindness.

- We thank only G-d alone for *His* goodness *to* us;
  not that we are being rewarded for
  our goodness towards *Him.*
- It is purely G-d's kindness *to us* which permits
  us to enjoy the sunshine of בֹּקֶר, *morning.*

We are the recipients of his *chesed,* whether or not it is deserved.

The second phrase of this same *pasuk* carries another very important message:

> When it is לַיְלָה, *night,* when darkness surrounds us, when nothing seems to be going right, then we call forth our *emunah,* our faith in Hashem.

> When nothing seems to be right, when we seem to be surrounded by insurmountable problems to which there apparently are no solutions, it is at such times that we turn to Hashem with complete faith in Him, in His judgment, and in His compassion and kindness which is without limit.

> - *We have no complaints.*
> - We pray for better times.
> - We place our future completely and unequivocally in His hands.

◌§ *Faith in His Kindness*

The above explanation takes the *pasuk* and divides it into two parts. The first speaks of *morning,* the second speaks of *darkness* and *night*.

Rabbi Mordechai Pogromansky offered another interpretation:

The entire sentence has *one subject.*

> *Chesed,* Hashem's graciousness and kindness.

The first phrase is exactly as above. We speak about G-d's *chesed* in the morning when everything is clear and bright.

In the second phrase, we also speak about His *chesed*;

> We speak about G-d's *chesed* with complete faith in Him, *even* when darkness appears.

> Suddenly, without warning, darkness has enveloped us.

Though we *do not* understand why whatever has happened had to occur, nevertheless, even at night, in darkness, we still have *emunah* that this too is *chesed* from Hashem.

Our faith remains strong and unwavering and we declare confidently,

> "Hashem knows what He is doing."

It is with the strongest *feeling* of *faith* that we accept G-d's *judgment* as *chesed,*

> that whatever Hashem does is correct, and ultimately is for the best.

With this explanation, we call forth the strongest, deepest faith to which we mortal human beings can aspire. We must grasp this faith and retain it forever.

In our daily prayers, we reiterate this same thought:

After saying the *Shema* in the morning we say: אֱמֶת וְיַצִיב, *true and certain.* We attach the word *emes,* true, to the end of *Shema,* but the message is clear.

In the morning we declare:

> "It is *true* and *certain."* It is all clear.
> - No problems.
> - No questions.
> - No doubts.

From generation to generation G-d endures.

His sovereignty endures *forever.*

After saying the *Shema* at night, we say: אֱמֶת וֶאֱמוּנָה, *True and faithful.*

"True and certain" recited in the morning concentrates on G-d's kindness in having redeemed us from Egypt.

> *"True and faithful"* recited at night symbolizes our exile. It stresses our faith in Hashem.

G-d will redeem us from this exile, from this long night of darkness, just as He did at the time of the Exodus.

◂§ *A Play on Words*

We find the same idea in the very first *mishnah* in Shas.

מֵאֵימָתַי קוֹרִין אֶת שְׁמַע בְּעַרְבִית (ברכות ב.)

From when are we permitted to recite Shema in the evening? (Berachos 2a).

The second *mishnah* asks the same question concerning the morning *Shema.*

מֵאֵימָתַי קוֹרִין אֶת שְׁמַע בְּשַׁחֲרִית (ברכות ט:)

*From when are we permitted to recite Shema in the morn-
ing? (Berachos 9b).*

The *Gemara* asks:

Why does the *Mishnah* teach first about *Shema* of the evening and
then of the morning?

The *Gemara* answers:

In the *Parashah* of *Shema* it says:

בְּשָׁכְבְּךָ וּבְקוּמֶךָ (דברים ו:ז)

"[You should speak about the Torah] when you go to
sleep and when you wake up" *(Devarim 6:7).*

The Torah speaks of the night first, and then of the morning. The
Mishnah follows this same pattern.

The *Gemara* offers another explanation of the *Mishnah's* order.
Concerning the Creation of the world, we find the words:

וַיְהִי עֶרֶב וַיְהִי בֹקֶר (בראשית א:ה)

*And there was evening and there was morning (Bereishis
1:5).*

Here, too, morning follows evening.

The *Vilna Gaon* offers a brilliant answer to the *Gemara's* question:

When a boy becomes *bar mitzvah,* he is obligated to fulfill all the
mitzvos. As we know, according to Jewish law, night belongs to the
next day, just as Shabbos and all of our holidays begin at night.

Thus, the first *mitzvah* of a *bar mitzvah* is the recitation of
the evening *Shema.* Therefore, the *Mishnah* opens with
the very first *mitzvah* that a Jewish male is obligated to
perform, the *mitzvah* of *Krias Shema* at night.

The three answers quoted above are basic explanations to the
question raised by the *Gemara.*

In a play on words I would like to offer another answer, one which is
derush, a homiletic interpretation as opposed to *p'shat,* the plain meaning of the words. As mentioned above, the first *mishnah* opens with a
question מֵאֵימָתַי קוֹרִין אֶת שְׁמַע בְּעַרְבִית, which in its plain meaning means,
"From when are we permitted to recite *Shema* in the evening?" In our
explanation, in the way of *derush,* the question encompasses only the
first four words, "When should one read the *Shema*?" The *answer* to the
question is the *fifth* word, בְּעַרְבִית, *in the evening,* in times of darkness.

When it is dark, when there is oppression, when there are things happening that we cannot fathom, that we cannot understand, then we cry out with faith in Hashem!

שְׁמַע יִשְׂרָאֵל ה' אֱלֹקֵינוּ ה' אֶחָד

Hear, O Israel, HASHEM is Our G-d, HASHEM, the One and Only.

- When a person is in despair,
- when a person has a heavy heart,
- when a person is despondent or dejected,

he must cry out: *Shema*! I believe in Hashem and I have faith that He cares for me as a father cares for a child.

In essence, the declaration of the *Shema* is one of *emunah*, faith in Hashem.

- There is One G-d Who created this world.
- There is One G-d Who is directing the affairs of this world.
- We believe in Him alone, and therefore, we place our complete faith in Him.

◆§ *Two Names*

This message of faith is hinted to in the *pasuk* of *Shema Yisrael,* where two of God's Names appear.

- יְ־הֹ־וָ־ה represents HASHEM as a G-d of mercy, kindness, and compassion.
- אֱלֹקִים represents Hashem as G-d of justice, of strict adherence to the law, as One Who administers punishment which fits the sin that was committed.

In the first *pasuk* of *Shema,* we recite both of these names of G-d. שְׁמַע יִשְׂרָאֵל ה' אֱלֹקֵינוּ ה' אֶחָד.
The full understanding of this sentence is:

- Whether we see G-d as יְ־הֹ־וָ־ה, when He judges us with mercy and compassion, or
- whether we see Him as אֱלֹקֵינוּ, when He treats us with strict justice and painful judgment, we know that everything emanates from ה' אֶחָד, the One and Only G-d.

We accept the harshness of Hashem's judgment as part of His mercy and goodness to us.

Whatever Hashem does is for our good, for our benefit.

We find this same message hinted to in a *pasuk* in *Tehillim*:

וַאֲנִי תְפִלָּתִי לְךָ ה׳ עֵת רָצוֹן, אֱלֹקִים בְּרָב חַסְדֶּךָ עֲנֵנִי בֶּאֱמֶת יִשְׁעֶךָ (תהלים

סט:יד) .

The meaning of David's words is:

"As I present my *tefillah,* my prayer to You, יְ-ה-וּ-ה, let this moment be

- a time of acceptance,
- a time of favor,
- an opportune time.

"May the timing of my prayer be favorable to You, Hashem. Let it be a time of forgiveness of my mistakes.

"And if my prayer comes before You, אֱלֹקִים, at a time when I must face judgment, please judge me with an abundance of Your kindness and graciousness. Please answer me with the truth of Your salvation" (*Tehillim* 69:14).

As the great Rabbi Akiva was being tortured to death by the wicked Romans, his lips uttered the sacred words of *Shema*. He might not have understood why he had to die this way, but he accepted his fate. Rabbi Akiva had complete, unquestioning faith in G-d.

As Rabbi Akiva said the words: ה׳ אֶחָד, his *neshamah* departed,

- in absolute holiness,
- in absolute purity,
- with unshakable faith.

Perhaps we can understand why *Shema Yisrael* is said by a Jew in his dying moments (G-d forbid). A person may be suffering on his deathbed. He may be heavy of heart and in the throes of physical pain. Nevertheless, he recites *Shema*, proclaiming his faith in Hashem. Though he does not know why he is leaving the world at this particular time, nevertheless he declares,

- G-d knows what He is doing.
- G-d knows why it is being done in this manner.

His declaration of *Shema* also means:

- "My fate is in Your hands, Hashem,
- "Thank You, Hashem, for everything."

ᴥ§ The Darkness of Galus

It is especially appropriate that the very first *mishnah* in *Shas* opens with *Shema*.

The *Mishnah* was arranged in its present order by Rabbi Yehudah HaNasi (the Prince) some two thousand years ago. This occurred soon after the destruction of the Second *Beis HaMikdash*. The Romans had already killed Rabbi Akiva and many other great sages. The Bar Kochba uprising had already been crushed by the Romans, who had also taken oxen and plowed the Temple Mount, destroying everything except for the *Kosel HaMaaravi*, the Western Wall. This was a very dark hour in the history of *Klal Yisrael*.

- It was nighttime.
- It was *galus*.
- Persecution and destruction reigned.
- The people were despondent, confused, and pessimistic concerning the future of our nation.

The first *mishnah* is a response to this situation: When must a Jew show his *emunah* in Hashem? When must he cry out: *Shema Yisrael*?

The answer is:

בְּעַרְבִית, *in nighttime.*

Let us not think for one moment that, since there is no *Beis HaMikdash,* since Jerusalem is destroyed and *Bnei Yisrael* are in *galus,* that this is the end of *Klal Yisrael* and *Eretz Yisrael.*

Absolutely not!

When it is dark and life is exceedingly difficult, when things seem to be going wrong,

we recite the *Shema,* our declaration of faith in Hashem.

- Hashem will never forget us.
- He will always watch over us.

Now, particularly, in our own difficult times after the Holocaust, the world is still against the Jew.

The United Nations is only united when there is a decree against *Eretz Yisrael.*

Russia and China were fighting with each other before Soviet Russia fell apart. Russia and the United States were enemies particularly during the '70s and the '80s during the era of the cold war. The African countries do not agree with each other. The Arabian countries have the same problem. Many of them are constantly at war with each other.

It is only when all of these nations are against the nation of Israel that they become united.

Nevertheless we must, at all times, be hopeful. We must place our trust in G-d's kindness and compassion as He watches
- over *Klal Yisrael,* over all Israel,
  wherever we are;
- and particularly, our beloved *Eretz Yisrael.*

There is a special *tefillah* found in the morning prayers after the Torah reading on Monday and Thursday. This brief plea for G-d to shower mercy upon all suffering Jews is often recited communally, when prayers are offered for Jews who are in danger:

אַחֵינוּ כָּל בֵּית יִשְׂרָאֵל הַנְּתוּנִים בְּצָרָה וּבְשִׁבְיָה . . . הַמָּקוֹם יְרַחֵם עֲלֵיהֶם וְיוֹצִיאֵם מִצָּרָה לִרְוָחָה וּמֵאֲפֵלָה לְאוֹרָה וּמִשִּׁעְבּוּד לִגְאֻלָּה, הַשְׁתָּא בַּעֲגָלָא וּבִזְמַן קָרִיב וְנֹאמַר אָמֵן

Our brothers, the entire family of Israel, who are delivered into distress and captivity. . . — may Hashem have mercy on them, and remove them from distress to relief, from darkness to light, from subjugation to redemption, now, speedily and soon — and let us say, Amen.

We refer to our nation as *Beis Yisrael. Beis* means a household. We are all members of one large family. If one part of a household is in pain, the entire family hurts.

We must have complete *emunah* in Hashem, both in the morning and in the evening.

The more we are endowed with faith, the more Hashem will be with us.

Whatever happens to us through the course of our lives is all from Hashem.
- Let us face the future with hope and faith.
- Let us always look for the bright side of things.

Remember:
- We must remain optimistic about tomorrow.
- G-d is always with us.

May *Mashiach* come speedily in our time!

23
Chillul Hashem and Kiddush Hashem

৺ Gravest of Sins

Rabbi Elazar ben Azaryah quotes and explains (*Yoma* 86:1) what Rabbi Yishmael said in a lecture concerning four kinds of sins.

"There are three ways whereby one is forgiven and receives *kaparah* (atonement) for a transgression;

> *teshuvah* (repentance) must be part of the *kaparah* process *at all times.*

The three variations are:

1. If one transgresses a *mitzvas asei,* a positive commandment (i.e. he *did not fulfill it*), and did *teshuvah,* the individual is *immediately* forgiven (נִמְחַל מִיָּד).

2. If one transgresses a *mitzvas lo saaseh,* a negative commandment, *teshuvah* is needed but one must wait for the primary day of forgiveness — Yom Kippur — before one is completely exonerated.

> תְּשׁוּבָה תּוֹלָה וְיוֹם כִּפּוּר מְכַפֵּר
> "Repentance suspends the punishment, and Yom Kippur provides atonement."

3. There are certain transgressions that are so severe that they are punished with *kareis* (death by Heaven), or death by *beis din* (court of Jewish law).

> The requirement to achieve atonement for these are
> (a) *teshuvah,*
> (b) the primary day of Yom Kippur, and

(c) some aspect of suffering (*yisurim*) before one is completely forgiven.

יִסּוּרִין מְמָרְקִין

Repentance and Yom Kippur suspend the punishment and the suffering completes the atonement process.

But there is a fourth sin for which even the above is not sufficient —

4. The sin of *Chillul Hashem,* desecration of G-d's Name.

If one commits a *Chillul Hashem,* then *teshuvah,* Yom Kippur, and *yisurim* (suffering) allow the judgment to be suspended — but complete forgiveness is attained only through death, יוֹם הַמִּיתָה מְמָרֶקֶת.

Four verses from *Tanach* are brought in support of Rabbi Yishmael:

שׁוּבוּ בָּנִים שׁוֹבָבִים אֶרְפָּה מְשׁוּבֹתֵיכֶם (ירמיה ג:כב): תְּשׁוּבָה מְכַפֶּרֶת

"Return, you rebellious children, and you will be forgiven" (*Yirmiyahu* 3:22).

This refers to *mitzvos asei. Teshuvah* alone is enough to be forgiven.

כִּי בַיּוֹם הַזֶּה יְכַפֵּר עֲלֵיכֶם . . . (ויקרא טז:ל): יוֹם כִּפּוּר מְכַפֵּר

"For on this day (Yom Kippur), you will be forgiven" (*Vayikra* 16:30).

This refers to *mitzvos lo saaseh.* The Yom Kippur day shall effect atonement for *you.*

וּפָקַדְתִּי בְשֵׁבֶט פִּשְׁעָם וּבִנְגָעִים עֲוֹנָם (תהלים פט:לג): יִסּוּרִין מְכַפְּרִים

"I will punish them for their sins. . ." (*Tehillim* 89:33).

This refers to transgressions punishable by *kareis* or death by *beis din.*

In these two areas, *yisurim* must be experienced to effect atonement.

אִם יְכֻפַּר הֶעָוֹן הַזֶּה לָכֶם עַד תְּמֻתוּן (ישעיה כב:יד): מִיתָה מְכַפֶּרֶת

"Ultimate atonement will not be completed until the day of death" (*Yeshayahu* 22:14).

This refers to a *Chillul Hashem*:

There is no power in repentance to suspend judgment,
nor can Yom Kippur atone,
nor can affliction purge.

Only death can purge the individual completely.

All four categories of *teshuvah* are necessary.

Maimonides (*Hilchos Teshuvah* 1:4) discusses these different types of sins and the corresponding forms of *teshuvah*. *Torah Temimah* (*Vayikra* 16:30) quotes *Avos D'R' Nassan* (*Perek* 29), who follows this same line of thought.

✎ *Understanding the Term*

What does *Chillul Hashem* mean?

חוֹטֵא וּמַחֲטִיא אֲחֵרִים

Rashi (ibid.) explains: *Chillul Hashem* means one who sins and influences others to sin.

In fact, to be guilty of *Chillul Hashem* can mean:
- to profane Hashem's Name,
- to disgrace and desecrate Hashem's Name,
- to cause others to have less belief in Hashem,
- to cause others to lose their closeness to Hashem because of some action that one did.

These ideas are reflected through the Hebrew term חִלּוּל הַשֵּׁם, *Chillul Hashem.*

We all know that

Hashem is everywhere. There is no place where Hashem cannot be found.

The word חָלָל, *challal,* means a vast emptiness. When one is guilty of *Chillul Hashem,* he has created a spiritual emptiness where the presence of Hashem is not found or felt, and he has diminished the grandeur of *Hashem Yisbarach* in the eyes of others.

Through his action, *the individual,* so to speak, has prevented the Presence of Hashem from entering that place. This is the utmost degradation of G-d's Name. There is nothing worse than *Chillul Hashem.* When one commits a *Chillul Hashem,* he creates a vacuum, where G-dliness and *kedushah* are not present. Worse, others who observe him learn to act the same way. This is the utmost degradation of G-d's Name.

Thus, only the severest punishment (death) can enable the person to be completely forgiven.

⋑ Classic Illustrations

The *Gemara* cites a few examples:

1. Rav lived around the year 235. Who was Rav? He is considered the first of the group called *Amoraim,* whose opinions and teaching comprise what we call the *Gemara,* the Talmud. An *Amora* cannot debate with a *Tanna,* a member of the earlier generations whose opinions form the basis of Oral Law called the *Mishnah.* Rav was so great that he is referred to as the last of the *Tannaim* and the first of the *Amoraim.* Thus, Rav possessed the authority to debate, at times, with a *mishnah.*

   Virtually every *Tanna* or *Amora* was blessed with *Ruach HaKodesh* (Divine Inspiration). He possessed a spirit of G-dliness and holiness far beyond that of ordinary men.

   Rav said: "I might possibly create a *Chillul Hashem* if I were to buy meat from a butcher and not pay him right away."

   Rashi explains that Rav said:

   "If I do not pay right away, the butcher might worry that I will be preoccupied with my *shiurim* (lectures) and that I will forget to pay him."

   Rav feared that the butcher might say: "If Rav won't pay me, then he is almost like a thief."

   Rav feared that the butcher would learn from him, and perhaps he would not be as careful as he should be when dealing with other people.

   The butcher might reason that if the great Rav was not careful about paying his debts on time, then surely he, the butcher, did not have to be careful in such matters.

   Rav reasoned:

   "Imagine the great *Chillul Hashem* I would cause! The butcher would learn from my bad example to handle debts carelessly by delaying and ultimately ignoring their payment."

   Rav, because of his esteemed reputation, worried about his *every act.* Rav felt that he must be more careful than others lest he create a *Chillul Hashem.*

2. Abbaye, a renowned *Amora,* said that when he bought meat from two partners, he made sure to pay one partner half the price, and

the second partner the other half. In this way, the partners would confer and see that he had paid his bill.

See how careful our leaders were in ensuring that they did not create a *Chillul Hashem*!

◌ৡ *Kiddush Hashem*

Abbaye quotes a *baraisa* to explain how we can create a *Kiddush Hashem,* glorifying the Name of Hashem.

In the *Shema* we read:

"You should love Hashem, your G-d" (*Devarim* 6:5).

How do you show love of G-d?

"Make G-d's Name beloved through you" (*Yoma* 86a).

As the *baraisa* continues, by dealing honestly with people and speaking in a refined manner, you will influence other people to love G-d. People will say, "Look how wonderful this student of Torah is."

If a student behaves properly, people will praise his yeshivah and it will encourage others to send their children to that yeshivah.

As the *baraisa* puts it:

‏,,וְאָהַבְתָּ אֵת ה' אֱלֹקֶיךָ" שֶׁיְּהֵא שֵׁם שָׁמַיִם מִתְאַהֵב עַל יָדֶךָ (יומא פו:א)

"You shall love Hashem, your G-d" means the Name of Heaven (Hashem) shall be beloved *because of you* (*Yoma* 86a).

"If someone studies Torah and Mishnah, serves *talmidei chachamim,* is honest in business and speaks pleasantly to others, what do people say of him?

Fortunate and praiseworthy are the *parents* who taught him Torah. Happy is the *rebbi* who taught him Torah.

This man who has studied Torah practices it and lives it.

Look how fine are his ways.

Look how righteous are his deeds.

"Of him the prophet Yeshayahu says (47:3),

And G-d said unto me: 'You are My servant, Israel, in whom I will be glorified.' "

Such a person is forever bringing about a *Kiddush Hashem* — the very opposite of a *Chillul Hashem*. Through him, the Name of Hashem is glorified, elevated, and sanctified.

⋙ *In Every Action*

A *Kiddush Hashem* can be brought about in many ways. Some of these ways may seem insignificant but in truth involve important individual actions:

- the way one *walks* down the stairway,
- the way one *eats* lunch,
- the way one *bentshes,*
- the way one *plays ball* during recess.
- the way one shows *derech eretz*, proper *middos,*
  to his *rebbeim* as well as to the *English* staff.
- the way one *behaves* in public.

An out-of-towner, a resident student, was leaving for home. I approached him and told him that people back home would notice that his character had changed.
I said to him:

"They will see that your stay in yeshivah had quite an affect on your life. They will see the following changes:

- You do not *daven* as you did previously.
- You are much better.
- You do not learn the same way.
- You are much better.
- You learn with more intensity.
- You are much better.
- You do not act the same as before.
- You are much better.
- You have become a new person.
- You make G-d's Name beloved and praised.
- You are causing a *Kiddush Hashem*!"

People generally consider it is a *Chillul Hashem* when a Jew living amongst gentiles does not act properly, but this is also true when acting improperly
> *amongst Jewish* people.

When a *Chillul Hashem* occurs, onlookers speak against "the G-d of Israel and His people."

One must be *ever careful* of his actions and speech, whether in front of gentiles or in front of Jews.

> *Kiddush Hashem transcends time, place, and people.*
> This is what we must strive for every day of our lives.

ᴥ§ *To Love Hashem*

"You should love G-d, your G-d" (*Devarim* 6:8).

The first *parashah* of *Shema* tells us how to fulfill this commandment. Read the entire first paragraph of *Shema* carefully.

After all, the question is raised:

Love is an emotional and abstract feeling. We can be commanded to wear *tefillin*, to keep Shabbos, etc. We are commanded to *DO* many *mitzvos*. This we can and must fulfill.

- But how can LOVE *be commanded?*
- How can there be a *mitzvah* to love somebody?
- How can there be a *mitzvah* to love Hashem?

Love must come from within you, from your heart, from an emotional tug.

How can the Torah mandate:

"Love Hashem your G-d with your whole heart"?

The answer is beautiful:

The *Shema* continues and tells us *how* to display our love for Hashem.

וְשִׁנַּנְתָּם לְבָנֶיךָ וְדִבַּרְתָּ בָּם . . . וּקְשַׁרְתָּם לְאוֹת . . . וּכְתַבְתָּם עַל מְזֻזוֹת בֵּיתֶךָ (דברים ו:ז,ח,ט)

> Teach Torah to your children. Speak words of Torah wherever you are. Bind them for a sign on your hand and head (the *tefillin*). Write them on the doorposts of your house (*mezuzos*) (*Devarim* 6:7-9).

Let the words of Torah be in, and on, your heart.

- Let the words of Torah be part of you —
  part of your daily living.
- Let the words of Torah be part of your bloodstream.

- Let the words of Torah flow through your veins
  and arteries, to every part of your spiritual body,
  in the very same way the heart pumps blood
  to every part of your physical body.
- Learn Torah constantly.
- Follow through by translating your learning into action.
- Do everything Hashem tells you to do.
  Follow all of G-d's commandments.
- Reinforce your Torah learning by
  discussing it constantly.
- Repeat a good thought to your parents.
- Review and repeat a *d'var* Torah when you meet friends.

This will bring you closer and closer to Hashem.

You will come to the realization that whatever you are and whatever you have,

> *comes only from Him.*

This closeness and understanding will bring you to the height of the emotional feeling of

> "Love Hashem, Your G-d."

You love your parents because you feel a constant closeness to them. You see how they are concerned about you. You see how devoted they are to your welfare. You realize how their hopes and their *nachas* are centered around you.

This close bond evokes the love between parents and children.

The close bond that you will create between G-d and yourself will evoke the love between G-d and yourself. Thus, you will fulfill the *mitzvah* of:

> You shall love Hashem, Your G-d.

P.S. Rabbi Avraham Pam, the *Rosh Yeshivah* of Mesivta Torah Vodaath, once said:

The only way to be forgiven for having caused a *Chillul Hashem* is to look for ways and means of creating a *Kiddush Hashem*.

> *Wipe away* the desecration of G-d's Name that you may
> have caused in the past, by *glorifying* the Name of G-d at
> all times.

24

Wherever You Are, Be a Steadfast Jew

◆§ "Yosef Is Still Alive!"

וַיַּגִּדוּ לוֹ לֵאמֹר עוֹד יוֹסֵף חַי וְכִי הוּא מֹשֵׁל בְּכָל אֶרֶץ מִצְרָיִם וַיָּפָג לִבּוֹ כִּי
לֹא הֶאֱמִין לָהֶם (בראשית מה:כו)

The brothers of Yosef came to their father Yaakov, and exclaimed the good news: "*Od Yosef chai,* Yosef is still alive and he is the ruler of the entire land." But Yaakov's heart rejected this earth-shattering report (*Bereishis* 45:26).

Yaakov *did not believe them*! Why?

Yaakov had not seen Yosef for 22 years, but he did not know for certain what had happened to Yosef. His children had come back from Egypt, and told him that Yosef was still alive. We would imagine that a person in such a situation would react by exclaiming, "Hurry up. Drink a *l'chaim!* Let's celebrate! Give a *kiddush!* Let us rejoice!"

Yaakov did not believe them. His spirit was still not revived. The next *pasuk* reads:

וַיְדַבְּרוּ אֵלָיו אֵת כָּל דִּבְרֵי יוֹסֵף אֲשֶׁר דִּבֶּר אֲלֵהֶם וַיַּרְא אֶת הָעֲגָלוֹת . . .
וַתְּחִי רוּחַ יַעֲקֹב אֲבִיהֶם (שם כז)

The brothers repeated *all the words* of Yosef's message and Yaakov also saw the עֲגָלוֹת, *wagons.* Then the spirit of Yaakov their father was revived and uplifted (ibid. v. 27). He believed them.

The significance of the wagons is explained by *Chazal*. When Yaakov had told Yosef to go to Shechem to look for his brothers, Yaakov taught him the laws of *eglah arufah* which deal with the case of a Jew who was found murdered outside of a city in *Eretz Yisrael* (see *Devarim* 21:1-9). The words *agalah,* wagon, and *eglah* (*arufah*) sound alike. Yaakov understood that the wagons sent by Yosef were a sign that Yosef remembered his father's final teaching to him. This we can readily understand.

But what were כָּל דִּבְרֵי יוֹסֵף, *all the words of Yosef,* which made such a difference that they revived Yaakov's spirit?

◆§ *"Your Son"*

L et us examine the exact words of Yosef in his message to his father.

כֹּה אָמַר בִּנְךָ יוֹסֵף שָׂמַנִי אֱלֹקִים לְאָדוֹן לְכָל מִצְרָיִם (בראשית מה:ט)

So said your son, Yosef: "God has made me master of all Egypt" (*Bereishis* 45:9).

However, the brothers, in relaying this message to their father, omitted the word בִּנְךָ, *your son.* All they said was עוֹד יוֹסֵף חַי, *Yosef is still alive* (also that *he is ruler over the land of Egypt,* ibid. v. 26).

The major difference here is that Yaakov was not only interested in the fact that Yosef was alive. Yaakov did not care that Yosef was a ruler, that everyone knew of him and acclaimed his greatness. Yaakov wanted to know if he was *still his son*! Is he still Yosef, the *tzaddik,* or did he become assimilated in Egypt? Until he knew the answer to this, his spirit could not be revived.

When the brothers then repeated *all the words of Yosef,* they imparted a *clear* and *meaningful* message.

"I am still *your* son. No matter where I was, even though I was all alone in Egypt, I did not change."

What does the word בִּנְךָ, *your son,* imply? It implies that Yosef did not become assimilated; he did not forget his *Yiddishkeit* even though he was all alone in a foreign country.

Yosef also said: *"G-d has made me* a master over all the land of Egypt." The full message was:

"Tell my father that *I am still his son* and that this was the *hashgachah pratis* of Hashem; this was G-d's way of personally watching over me and His way of bringing about the fulfillment of my prophetic dream" (see ibid. 37:5-11).

Upon hearing this, Yaakov believed his sons and his spirit became revived and joyous again.

A Jew must speak about himself in the same way Yosef *HaTzaddik* spoke. Yosef was sent to Egypt by Hashem. "Do not worry! Whatever Hashem demanded of me, I did. G-d *made* me a ruler. G-d *took care* of me and I am *still* your son."

Yosef's message was beautiful:

> "I know that the entire world belongs to Hashem. I know that I was sent to Egypt by Hashem.
>
> G-d watched over me. He made the prophetic dreams of my 'being a ruler' come true.
>
> G-d *took care* of me all the years that I was in Egypt. I am *still* your son. I *did not* change."

Yosef was speaking to us as well.

✿§ Yosef's Message to Us

No matter where one is living, no matter what one does in life, one can be, and should be, a G-d-fearing Jew. An individual must know that Hashem is watching over him his entire life.

Even if you live in a neighborhood where you are the only Jew, you cannot and must not say, "If I lived in Boro Park, I would be a better and more observant Jew." Yosef was the only Jew in Egypt and remained בִּנְךָ, *your son*, the son of Yaakov *Avinu.*

I often speak to my students about their future hopes. The answers vary considerably. Some say that they want to be a *rebbi* in a yeshivah, a *rosh yeshivah*, or a rabbi in a community. Some wanted to become professionals: a doctor, a lawyer, an engineer, or an architect, etc.

I tell them:

> But,
> - "First be a *talmid chacham*, then a doctor.
> - First be a *talmid chacham*, then a lawyer.
> - First be a *talmid chacham*, then a professional.

"I will be satisfied with whatever your choice in life will be, but I do want you to be

- a *talmid chacham,* learning Torah all your life;
- a *yirei shamayim,* a practicing Jew,
  doing and fulfilling all the *mitzvos*; and
- a *baal middos,* displaying a beautiful character
  in your relationships with your fellow men."

"Realize that Hashem is always with you and watching over you. Remain true to Hashem and to all Israel.

"In this manner of living, you will be an inspirational force and bring others closer to Hashem.

25

Always Remember —
G-d Is with You

৵§ The Case of the Borrower

In *Parashas Mishpatim,* we learn the law of the שׁוֹאֵל, *borrower*:
If a man *borrows* something from his neighbor, he is held
responsible should anything happen to the borrowed object. He must
pay full damages, even if the damage occurs through an unavoidable
accident (*Shemos* 22:13).

There are two exceptions to the above rule, both of which are stated
in the Torah.

A borrower is not obligated to pay should the animal die of natural
causes while he was using it for work. There is an obvious reasoning
for this law. The man did not borrow the animal so that it would remain
in its stall; he borrowed it for the purpose of work. Therefore, when the
animal dies naturally while "on the job," the borrower is exempt from
payment.

אִם בְּעָלָיו עִמּוֹ לֹא יְשַׁלֵּם (שמות כב:יד)

If its owner is with him, he shall not make restitution (ibid.
v. 14).

The other case in which the borrower is exonerated is when the
animal's owner was employed by the borrower at the time of the
borrowing. In such a case, the borrower is also exempt from payment.

This is a *gezeiras hakasuv,* a decree of the Torah, whose reason was
not revealed to us.

In a play on words, the Chassidic sage, Rabbi Simchah Bunim of P'shische, said:

> "Every person is a שׁוֹאֵל, *borrower,* from Hashem. Everyone has a *neshamah* (soul) which comes directly from Hashem. We are all responsible to care for our *neshamah,* by using it in the way that Hashem intended, so that we can return it after 120 years as pure as when we received it."

Like a שׁוֹאֵל, we are responsible even when we transgress "by accident." It is not enough to say, "Hashem, I'm sorry. I didn't mean it." We are responsible for our actions. We are supposed to be careful with everything we do, with every action, and with the kind of impression we convey to others. The more aware we are of our responsibilities as Jews and *bnei Torah,* the less likely we are to make mistakes.

The Talmud tells us that if a *talmid chacham* commits a transgression, he cannot say it was an accident. Since he is learning Torah, he should know better. He should know what the *dinim* (laws) are.

The *Rebbe* of P'shische continued, "When is a person *not* liable for inadvertent acts? אִם בְּעָלָיו עִמּוֹ, *if His Owner is with him* — if he is the type of Jew who is forever aware of G-d's Presence."

If Hashem is always before you, you will generally avoid committing sins.

However, if something does go wrong, Hashem will forgive you, since you are always striving to live by the Torah and do the right thing.

- If you always do your best to please Hashem,
- if you always try to keep your *neshamah* pure because בְּעָלָיו עִמּוֹ, *Hashem is always with you,* then Hashem will forgive you if something goes wrong.

If only you will feel that Hashem is with you, then surely you will be a better person and a more observant Jew.

The opening chapter of *Shulchan Aruch,* the *sefer* wherein are detailed all the laws that we must observe, quotes the very meaningful words of David *HaMelech:*

שִׁוִּיתִי ה' לְנֶגְדִּי תָמִיד (תהילם טז:ח)

I always set Hashem before me (*Tehillim* 17:8).

- I always feel His presence.
- He is constantly with me.

With those words in your mind at all times, you will become greater and better in every possible way.

With Hashem always at your side, you will be given the privilege of being pardoned through the exemption of בְּעָלָיו עִמּוֹ.

> G-d has loaned us our soul, our life, for the time we spend on earth.

> We will be exonerated for an occasional inadvertent mistake if we truly live with the knowledge that Hashem is always with us.

26
When Is Mashiach Coming?
It's up to You!

⚜ *Mashiach's Response*

A s I entered the *beis hamidrash* for a *mussar* talk, my students were singing a song about *Mashiach*:

אֲחַכֶּה לּוֹ, אֲחַכֶּה לּוֹ, אֲחַכֶּה לוֹ בְּכָל יוֹם שֶׁיָּבוֹא. וְאַף עַל פִּי שֶׁיִּתְמַהְמֵהַּ עִם
כָּל זֶה אֲחַכֶּה לּוֹ בְּכָל יוֹם שֶׁיָּבוֹא.

I await him, I await him, I await him every day that he should come. And even though he may delay, I await him every day that he should come.

This is a very important song. I heartily encourage your singing it; we all want *Mashiach* to come very, very soon.

The following story was told to me when I was a youngster. This story took place about 150 years ago.

In Europe, pogroms occurred very often. A pogrom was a situation where gentiles would come and beat up Jews for no reason other than hatred, the burning hatred of anti-Semitism. They took the Jews' money and possessions, persecuted them, and killed them. They tried to destroy every last Jew, literally.

The Russian Cossacks who carried out these pogroms were unruly wild peasants, uneducated and lowly. They were mob oriented. They would get drunk and roam the countryside on their horses in search of victims of their hatred and drunkenness. A pogrom often lasted several days.

When Jews would learn that Cossacks were coming to a particular town, they would run to warn the Jews to flee the town or hide.

The Cossacks would come in a drunken stupor and destroy everything in sight. No one should ever know of a pogrom or experience the fear or the pain of seeing people killed, slaughtered, or maimed. The Cossacks started fires, looted, and stole anything they could lay their hands on.

Once, a certain Jewish community learned that a pogrom was being planned against them. The entire town started to run to the forest. They heard the yells and the screams of the Cossacks on the outskirts of the town.

As one of the men was running away, he saw a cave in the forest. He directed everyone to follow him. They all ran into the cave, covering the entrance with brush. At the end of this cave, they saw a light burning and they ran towards it. They saw an old man sitting at a table with a lit candle and learning.

"Who are you?" they asked

"I am *Mashiach,*" the old man answered.

One of the leaders started to shout:

"We are saved!

Mashiach is here!

We have nothing to worry about!"

But, *Mashiach* remained seated and continued to learn!

The leader ran over to *Mashiach* and said: "I do not understand you. There is a pogrom in our town. The Cossacks are looting, burning, and destroying. They want to kill us. *Mashiach*, you must save us!

We are waiting for you."

Mashiach stopped his learning and said:

"My son, you are making one big mistake.

You are not waiting for me.

I am waiting for you."

This may be a legend but its impact is powerful. We keep on saying: "We want *Mashiach* to come now. We cannot wait any more. We are suffering through a long *galus* (exile). We wait for *Mashiach* longingly and hopefully."

Mashiach, where are you?

Mashiach's answer to us is:

"You are not waiting for me.

I am waiting for you."

We must prove to *Mashiach* that we are ready.

We have it in our power to bring *Mashiach*.

Let us do more *mitzvos* each day. Let us devote more hours to Torah every day.

Then, we will deserve *Mashiach's* coming, and he *will* come. It is really up to us. *Mashiach* is truly waiting for us.

⊷§ *Awaiting Faithfully*

In a Torah scroll, there is only a space of one letter between *Parashas Vayigash* and *Parashas Vayechi,* unlike all other *parshiyos* in the Torah, where there is a space of nine letters.

The first *Rashi* in *Vayechi* asks: Why is this a *parashah s'tumah* (a closed *parashah*)? Why is there just one space between these two portions?

Rashi answers:

Because Yaakov *Avinu* wanted to tell his sons when *Mashiach* was going to come, but Hashem took away ("closed") his power of prophecy.

This *Rashi* teaches us that it is Hashem's desire that the date of *Mashiach's* arrival remain hidden from us. We are supposed to wait for *Mashiach* to come, faithfully and hopefully, from day to day. We *are* waiting for *Mashiach* to come *every* day.

One of the commentaries says something very beautiful to explain why the power of prophecy was taken away from Yaakov *Avinu,* so that he could not reveal when *Mashiach* will come. If we would know when *Mashiach* will come, and it were not to be for another 100 years or so, and not in our own lifetime, perhaps some people would be downcast and give up hope.

⊷§ *"I Will not Hasten It"*

Another reason why the date of *Mashiach's* arrival is hidden from us is because his arrival can actually come about in two possible ways, and each way has a date of its own.

There is a *pasuk* about the future Redemption which says, בְּעִתָּה אֲחִישֶׁנָה, *in its time I will hasten it* (Isaiah 60:22). *Rashi* explains: זָכוּ אֲחִישֶׁנָה לֹא זָכוּ בְּעִתָּה.

This seems to be a paradox.

- "In its time" means a stipulated definite period in time.
- "I will hasten it" (*Mashiach's* coming) means that *Mashiach* can come before the stipulated time.

The answer to this paradox is that *in its time* does not convey a fixed time prior to which *Mashiach* cannot come. Rather, it means there is a certain limit — a time by which Hashem has decreed that *Mashiach must come*, whether or not we have earned it. This time is known only to Hashem.

"I will hasten it" (*Mashiach's* coming) means:

- If everyone would learn like he never learned before,
- would *daven* like he never *davened* before,
- would do more *mitzvos* than ever before,

then we could bring about *Mashiach's* coming sooner.

- If the Jewish people would set an example for the rest of the world,
- if an act of supreme *kedushah* would be brought about, and every one of us would be an outstanding Jew, a model for others to emulate
  in our attitudes,
  in our responsibility,
  in our listening,
  in our learning,
  and in our respect to others,
- if we, collectively, would be doing thousands of extra *mitzvos,*

then *Mashiach* would come earlier.
We would deserve G-d's redemption.

This is what the story told above means when *Mashiach* said, "You are not waiting for me, I am waiting for you." Doing *teshuvah* properly will bring *Mashiach* closer, speedily and in our time.

There is another reason given as to why Yaakov lost his power of prophecy at that time.

The only date which Yaakov would have been permitted to reveal to his children would have been the definite final date by when *Mashiach* must come, the time which the prophet refers to as בְּעִתָּה.

Had Yaakov revealed that date alone, it would have seemed as if he was casting aspersions upon *Bnei Yisrael,* as if he was implying that they could never merit to bring *Mashiach* any sooner.

Rather than permit Yaakov to convey such an impression, Hashem caused him to lose his power of prophecy so that he could not predict any time at all as to when *Mashiach* will come.

- It is up to *Klal Yisrael.*
- We can bring *Mashiach* sooner.
- It is up to you and me.

27
Life Commitments:
The Goals of a Yeshivah

᥍ What a Talmid Should Become

What should the goals of a yeshivah be?
Our yeshivah strives to produce a *talmid* who will be:
- a *talmid chacham,*
- a *yirei shamayim,*
- and a *baal middos.*

Let us understand what this means.

1. A *talmid chacham* is someone who knows *how* to learn Torah, who has amassed a significant amount of Torah knowledge, and indeed, someone who, all his life, *continues to study Torah* to the best of his ability.

> But even this is not everything, for after one has studied Torah and acquired much knowledge, he must ask himself: "Am I teaching anyone else Torah or am I learning only for myself?"
>
> Becoming a *talmid chacham* is only the first step. When you learn Torah, you have to translate your learning into action, and this includes sharing your knowledge with others.

2. To be a *yirei shamayim* means to think before you act; to ask yourself, "Will Hashem be pleased with what I am about to do? Will it be considered a *mitzvah* or, G-d forbid, the opposite?" To be a *yirei shamayim* also means to do *mitzvos* with *kavanah* (concentration) and with feeling.

In Yeshivah Toras Emes, we celebrate the day that a boy puts on *tefillin* for the first time (generally about a month before he becomes a *bar mitzvah*, so that he will be fully accustomed to putting them on correctly at the time the *mitzvah* becomes incumbent upon him).

I bless each student that the *tefillin* which he wraps around his arm close to his heart, and the *tefillin* which he places on his head,

should penetrate to the depths of his *neshamah*.

I tell my *talmid*:

"May the *kedushah* (sanctity) of this *mitzvah* enter your bloodstream and permeate every organ of your body. May you live up to the *holiness* of this great moment, so that every day of your life will be infused with *kedushah* as you dedicate it to serving Hashem."

To be a *yirei shamayim*, one must develop an attitude that:

- He cannot live without doing a *mitzvah*.
- He cannot live without keeping Shabbos.
- He cannot live without learning Torah.
- He cannot live without *davening* three times a day.

But even these two goals, to become a *talmid chacham* and *yirei shamayim*, are still not enough. They pertain primarily to your relationship with Hashem. The Torah demands of us that we also perfect our relationship with our fellow man, to the best of our ability.

3. This means to become a *baal middos*, a person of good character. If you are a *baal middos*, people will love and respect you as a person who is kind, good, and polite. You will inspire others to refine their own behavior as well.

   The good *middos* of a yeshivah student make an impression on everyone with whom he comes in contact.

   Often, I would receive telephone calls after a *bar mitzvah* celebration which I could not attend personally. The caller would say that I should be proud of my students.

   - "They sang beautifully.
   - They danced beautifully.
   - They sat quietly and respectfully during the speeches.
   - They stood up when a *rav* was called upon to speak."

Their behavior was so exemplary that everyone was talking about it.

Caterers and hotel managers would call to say, "Your students are so well behaved. You can be proud of your yeshivah."

These should be the goals of every yeshivah — and such should be the goal of every Jew.

In addition to these goals, there are four major *life commitments* I ask of my students. To some, these commitments may seem very basic and obvious. Please bear in mind that in my half a century of dealing with yeshivah boys, I have dealt with, literally, thousands of boys from all types of backgrounds and various levels of *mitzvah* observance.

❧ Life Commitments

The first *life commitment* is:

> To *daven* and put on *tefillin* every day for the rest of one's life. Every Jew must *daven,* and every Jewish male must *daven* three times a day with a *minyan.*

No one should ever say that the work he is occupied with at any given time is more important than *davening* with a *minyan.* Rabbi Moshe Feinstein used every available second for the most important work of all — studying Torah. Yet, he always interrupted his learning in order to *daven* with a *minyan.*

The second *life commitment* I ask is:

> That the student remain a *shomer Shabbos* (one who keeps Shabbos) for the rest of his life.

At the beginning of the 20th century when our people came to America in large numbers, they were unable to find well-paying jobs because most employers refused to hire workers who kept Shabbos. Yet, many avoided work on Shabbos even though this meant making do with less. They lived with the faith that by keeping Shabbos, one of the foundations of Judaism, they would earn Hashem's favor and assistance. Today, one can be a *shomer Shabbos* without concern that this will interfere with his livelihood.

But being a *shomer Shabbos* does not only mean not going to work.

It means going to *shul* on Shabbos, *davening* with a *minyan,* and paying careful attention to the weekly Torah reading. It means learning Torah on this very special day.

Shabbos must add a spiritual dimension to your life.
Too many people think of Shabbos as a multitude of
> *Don'ts*: "Do not do this"; and "Do not do that," etc.
In reality, Shabbos must be a series of *Do's*:
Do everything possible that will capture the beauty of Shabbos.

- Eat together with the entire family.
- Sing *zemiros* and rejoice together.
- Recite a *dvar Torah* (Torah thought)
  at your Shabbos meals.
- See that your young children attend an
  Oneg Shabbos (Shabbos party) so that they
  can feel the joy of Shabbos on their level.
     If there is none in your area,
       prepare one for your children.
- Show your children how good and pleasant it is
  for the family to be together in a relaxed and
  spiritual atmosphere.
- Attend a lecture or class on a Torah theme.

Shabbos is much more than a day of rest.

- It is a day of joy.
- It is a day of sanctity.
- One should be so elevated and so inspired
  with the holiness of the day that it should
  remain with him for the entire week.

The third *commitment* I ask is:
> that the student eat kosher. This is easier in our time with so many good and reliable kosher symbols to look for.

The fourth *life commitment* I ask is:
> that when the student grows up, he will marry a fine religious Jewish girl. If you marry such a girl, your home will be a religious home, and your children will become *talmidei chachamim.*

This is basic as far as one's future as a religious Jew is concerned. This is what I hope for, and ask of, every one of my yeshivah students.

These four objectives are the basic goals to which every Jew must be committed.

However, I worry about one major problem. I speak so much to my students about their becoming *talmidei chachamim.* But what if one cannot or does not learn well? What if he is not up to par with the rest of the class?

There are children who are unable to learn Torah well. There are some children who go to a special school because their minds are unable to learn in depth. They go to a "P'tach" program, a program for those who have learning disabilities. Not everyone is able to become a *talmid chacham.*

Does that exclude him from being a good Jew?

Does a child say to himself, "I cannot learn *Gemara.* It is too hard for me. Therefore, I cannot be a good Jew. I am not part of *Klal Yisrael!*"

Chas v'shalom — G-d forbid!!

- Every Jew is important to *Klal Yisrael.*
- Every Jew can observe the basics of *davening* and put on *tefillin* each day.
- Every Jew can keep Shabbos.
- Every Jew can keep *kashrus.*
- Every Jew can marry a fine religious Jewish girl.

Every Jew can fulfill all the other *mitzvos* as well. And even a Jew who does not have the abilities to become a *talmid chacham* can fulfill the greatest of all *mitzvos* — by studying on his own or attending a class on his level, all his life.

Every Jew can, should, and must fulfill all of these life commitments. Hashem does not demand that every Jew be as great as the Vilna Gaon; He wants us to do our best.

There are those who do not know *Chumash* or cannot learn *Rashi.* Others may not understand *Mishnah.* Many can only read about Jewish law in English because they do not understand Hebrew.

Is such a person a good Jew? Absolutely! He can be a 100-percent good Jew! He is as important to Hashem, and perhaps more important, than someone born with a brilliant mind. A person who *davens* every day, keeps Shabbos and *kashrus* is as important to G-d as any other Jew. He is an important member of *Klal Yisrael.*

He adds to the *shleimus,* completeness, of the Jewish people.

ᵃ Torah and the Jewish People

The Torah says, תָּמִים תִּהְיֶה עִם ה׳ אֱלֹקֶיךָ, "You shall be complete (i.e. wholehearted) with Hashem, your G-d" (*Devarim* 18:13).

And in *Tehillim* (19:8) we read, תּוֹרַת ה׳ תְּמִימָה, "Hashem's Torah is perfect."

These sentences, one referring to each Jew, the other referring to the Torah, use words of the same root: תָּמִים (male) and תְּמִימָה (female), both of which mean *complete* and *perfect*.

R' Yitzchok Elchanan Spektor, the great Kovno *Rav,* explained: *Klal Yisrael* and Torah are one. They are also similar in essence.

If there is a letter missing in a *sefer Torah,* a Torah scroll, the scroll is *pasul,* invalid; it cannot be used for the Torah reading in the synagogue.

Which letter has to be missing for the scroll to be rendered *pasul*? It makes no difference; *any* letter that is missing invalidates the entire *sefer Torah.*

There is an incident recorded in the Torah of a מְקֹשֵׁשׁ עֵצִים, a person who desecrated the Shabbos by gathering wood on that holy day (see *Bamidbar* 15:32-36).

What if the first letter of the word מְקֹשֵׁשׁ was missing in a *sefer Torah*? The scroll cannot be used. The מְקֹשֵׁשׁ עֵצִים was a person who committed a terrible sin.

Yet, if the letter מ is missing from the word used to describe him, it invalidates the entire Torah.

What if the מ of the name of Moshe *Rabbeinu* is missing in a *sefer Torah*? Again, the scroll is *pasul* and cannot be used.

The מ of מְקֹשֵׁשׁ and the מ of מֹשֶׁה are both equal in the Torah. If one letter, any letter, is missing, the Torah is flawed and cannot be used, for there is something missing in the *shleimus,* the completeness of the Torah.

Rav Yitzchok Elchanan said: It is the same way with *Klal Yisrael.* If there is a person who commits sins, and he is lost to our people, there is something missing in the completeness of our people. His lack of observance is as tragic in the eyes of Hashem as if, G-d forbid, an active Torah Jew had suddenly become lost to us.

In the very same way that *any* missing letter renders a *sefer Torah* incomplete, the lack of *shmiras hamitzvos* (observance of *mitzvos*) of any Jew ruins the completeness of our people. Whenever a Jew strays from *Yiddishkeit,* all of us are affected, for all Jews are like a single body, a *united Torah scroll.*

There are many Russian immigrants in the United States.

They are almost lost to *Klal Yisrael.*

- We must reach out to them.
- We must befriend them.
- We must teach them.

If one Russian or American Jew is lost to our people, the completeness of our nation is shattered, and the chain of our continuity is disrupted.

- In *Klal Yisrael,* not everyone is a *Rosh Yeshivah.*
- Not everyone is a *gadol hador* (leader of his generation).

Klal Yisrael is guided by our great and learned leaders, our *Roshei Yeshivah* and Chassidic *Rebbeim.*

Klal Yisrael would *not be* a complete nation without every single Jew.

- Every Jew is most important to Hashem.
- Every single Jew must strive to find his niche,
  his place, as an active member of our people.
- Each individual must accept the responsibility of his
  own actions, to learn the ways and laws of our people
- Every individual should strive to become learned
  in Torah; even though he may not grasp the
  difficulties of math or science, or he may not
  be well versed in English.

Many educators think that if you cannot learn math, then perhaps, you do not have a *"head"* for Torah either. The admission exams given in many yeshivos follow this idea as a measuring rod for admittance to the yeshivah.

But this is not correct. When it comes to Torah, our Rabbis tell us that there is סִיַעְתָּא דִשְׁמַיָּא, *special help from Hashem.* If a student is sincere and prays to Hashem for help, then Hashem literally "opens his head" to learn Torah. If you persevere in your efforts to learn Torah, your mind will develop and you can reach the heights of Torah learning. With this special help from Hashem Himself, you *can* become a *talmid chacham* in the full sense of the word.

These are the basic goals for *all* children who are given a yeshivah education.

- We dare not lose even one youngster.
- We must not fracture the *shleimus,* the completeness of our people.

28

Miracles: Performed by Hashem with Our Involvement

◆§ *Why Eight and not Seven?*

The very *essence* of the festival of Chanukah is not clear. The only Talmudic source in which there is a discussion regarding Chanukah is in *Mesechta Shabbos* 21b, where the Sages ask: "מַאי חֲנוּכָּה, *What is the essence of Chanukah?*"

The following passage is the Sages' brief answer: "When the Syrian-Greek armies entered the Temple, they defiled all the oils. When the *Chashmonaim* prevailed and conquered the Syrian-Greeks, they sought and found but one jug of oil which remained with the *seal* of the *Kohen Gadol* (High Priest). There was only enough oil to burn for one day, but a miracle occurred and it burned for eight days. The following year, they established [these days] as a *yom tov* with *hallel* and *hoda'ah*, praise. This passage seems to imply that the primary reason for establishing the Chanukah festival was the miracle of the tiny cruse of oil as opposed to the miracle of the *Chashmonaim's* military victory.

The question is raised: If there was sufficient oil for one day, then the first day's lighting of the *Menorah* was not a miracle. It should follow, then, that if we are celebrating the *miracle*, then Chanukah should be a *seven-day* festival!

Scores of answers to this question have been suggested. Among them are:

1. Discovering the jug of oil was itself a miracle; it is this miracle which the first day commemorates.

2. The *Kohanim,* realizing that it would take eight days to prepare freshly pressed, pure olive oil, divided the oil in the jug into eight parts. Thus, even on the first night, the oil burned miraculously as if the cups of the *Menorah* had been completely filled.

3. The jug of oil immediately refilled itself after the *Kohanim* poured its contents into the *Menorah.* Thus, on the first day they were already witness to a miracle.

Rambam lends added insight toward an understanding of מַאי חֲנוּכָּה, *What is the essence of Chanukah?*

> During the era of the Second *Beis HaMikdash,* the Syrian-Greek kings decreed laws against the Jews, forbidding them to practice their religion, and they did not permit them to toil in the study of Torah or perform *mitzvos.*
>
> They desecrated the *Beis HaMikdash* and persecuted the Jews, until the G-d of our forefathers had mercy on them and saved them. The family of the *Chashmonaim Kohanim overcame* the enemy and destroyed them, and rescued the Jews from their hands.

In the following paragraph, *Rambam* briefly writes of the miracle of the oil as stated in the *Gemara.*

Thus, whereas the Talmud stresses the miracle of the oil, *Rambam* emphasizes the incredible military victory of the few *Chashmonaim* against overwhelming odds.

We come to a similar observation in studying *"Al HaNissim,"* which is inserted into *Shemoneh Esrei* and *Bircas HaMazon* during Chanukah. It clearly stresses the miracle of the military victory, and only hints to the miracle of the oil.

In answering the question of why Chanukah is eight days and not seven, the *Pri Chadash* answers that the first day commemorates the miraculous military victory, while the next seven days commemorate the miracle of the oil. Thus, the eight days of Chanukah commemorate both miracles. The two miracles go hand in hand; the miracle of the oil was an open miracle that no one could deny. It demonstrated to all that the victory of the *Chashmonaim*, a victory where Hashem gave over the "many in the hands of the few; the impure in the hands of the pure," was clearly a miracle as well.

⋖ "Chalos HaNeis"

It is mentioned in the *Zohar* that Hashem does not bring about a miracle without something tangible to which the miracle can attach itself so that it should appear as if it were a natural occurrence. In the case of Chanukah, it was the jug of oil. G-d's blessing came to rest upon that small jug of oil so that it could last eight days instead of one. This concept is referred to as חֲלוֹת הַנֵּס, the "taking effect" of the miracle upon a given object.

In *Melachim II,* Ch. 4, we read of another miracle:

A widow poured out her tale of woe to Elisha, the prophet, saying that she was unable to pay her debt. The creditor wanted to enslave her children as a method of payment. Elisha asked the woman what she had in the house. She told him that all she had was a jug of oil. He told her to bring the jug of oil to him, as well as all the empty jars she had in the house. From this small jug of oil she was able, through a miracle, to fill all the empty containers she had. She then sold these containers filled with oil. The woman not only paid up her debt with the money she earned, but was able to support herself and her children as well. This was her reward for her righteousness.

> Thus, we can see that, even though she deserved and merited a miracle, there had to be something tangible upon which the *chalos haneis* could occur. In this case, that object was the woman's jug of oil.

> On Chanukah, the first jug of oil was there to begin with. That jug was the *chalos haneis;* the following seven days' miracle occurred as if they were an extension of the first day's lighting.

After the Jewish nation left Egypt, the Egyptians pursued them and caught up to them at the Sea of Reeds. *Klal Yisrael* seemed trapped. The Egyptians were chasing them from behind. The sea was in front of them. They did not know what to do. Hashem told Moshe *Rabbeinu* to tell the people to go forward.

> Did the sea split at that point? No!

The miracle of *krias Yam Suf,* the Splitting of the Sea of Reeds, was the greatest miracle of all time, that Hashem brought about when the Jews were redeemed from Egypt. The *Midrash* describes the miracle in great detail.

The Jews were divided according to tribes and each tribe crossed the sea through its own path of dry land. The people could peer through the transparent walls of water, which stood upright between them, and see each other as they walked.

The miracles of the Exodus, which were climaxed by the Splitting of the Sea, demonstrated to the entire world that nothing is beyond Hashem's power. Nevertheless, Hashem did not allow the miracle at the sea to occur until there was something to which the *chalos haneis* could attach itself.

> When was the *chalos haneis* at the Sea of Reeds? When Nachshon ben Aminadav, *nasi* (prince) of the tribe of Yehudah, fearlessly jumped into the raging sea. Once he jumped in, the miracle began and the waters split. From that moment, the miracle of the Splitting of the Sea began to unfold.

~§ A Miracle in Our Time

We hope that we will merit to witness miracles, with the coming of *Mashiach.* In truth, *we have* seen a miracle in our time.

Between 1939 and 1945, six million Jews were destroyed, annihilated, brutally slaughtered. We lived through it. Many of your parents or grandparents were in concentration camps. Everyone who was living during the Holocaust knew someone who was killed or whose property was destroyed in Europe. When the war finally ended and the embers were still smoldering, everyone was concerned as to what would happen to *Klal Yisrael.*

Our greatest and finest men, women, and children were murdered most cruelly. *Roshei Yeshivah* and their student bodies were no more.

How would Judaism carry on?

Would Judaism falter and disappear? G-d forbid!

A miracle was needed to save the future of our people. But for the miracle to occur, there had to be something to which the *chalos haneis* could attach itself.

> The yeshivah students in America and Israel were the cruse of oil for the miracle of a rejuvenation of Torah, for

the flame of Torah study to be rekindled, *both here and in Israel.*

Years ago, people said that America is a *"treif medinah,"* an "unkosher land." They claimed that there cannot be true, unadulterated *Yiddishkeit* in America.

But a miracle occurred in America and in *Eretz Yisrael.* The miracle is the rebirth and continued growth of yeshivos, as well as the growth of Torah learning among laymen. This is the miracle, in our time, of the continuation of *Klal Yisrael,* a miracle that is living proof of the eternity of the Jewish people as a Torah nation.

From where did the miracle in our time begin? How did it happen? How did the *chalos haneis* occur?

> The miracle attached itself to "the jug of oil" — you, the students who are studying Torah in yeshivos.
> *You are that jug of oil.*

Sadly, there are many millions of Jews who are far removed from the essence of Judaism, Torah, and *mitzvos.* Yet, there is still that jug of oil through which the miracle has already taken effect and hopefully, will grow greater and greater. The young yeshivah students are the ones upon which the entire miracle of *Klal Yisrael* is dependent. They are the "jug" upon which the *chalos haneis* has occurred.

In short, the miracle that is taking place in our time revolves around one small but very powerful group:

> the *"yeshivah students"* of the world.
> Upon your shoulders lies the future of our people.

It does not rest upon the shoulders of boys and girls who unfortunately are attending public schools or an afternoon Talmud Torah.

How many children are attending yeshivos in New York City? There are two million Jews in our city. Perhaps there are 60,000 or 70,000 yeshivah students.

You, boys and girls who are attending yeshivos, are the *chalos haneis.*

I look at a class of 25 students and I say to myself:

> All of you will become *talmidei chachamim* in various degrees. Perhaps five of you will become future *rabbanim.* It is my hope that several of you will become *roshei yeshivos.*

But, *all of you* will become ambassadors of Torah in your own community.

We exhort our students to attend *minyan* regularly, to learn well, and to review their studies at night, with the hope that they will continue to do so when they are older. It is through you that the miracle of *Klal Yisrael* will continue. Each one of you should aspire to be a complete *ben Torah,* to spread *Yiddishkeit,* to fight for the honor of Hashem. In this way, every Jew will be enhancing *K'vod Shamayim,* the glory of Heaven, and will add yet more to the miracle.

- You will increase the miracle of *Klal Yisrael* in our time.
- You will add to the rejuvenation of *Klal Yisrael.*

It will not be easy. Fight with yourself to become better in every possible way. Come to *minyan* on time, learn well, and review your studies at night. Stay away from television. Call a failing student and learn with him.

- The future is in your hands.
- You can be the miracle of *Klal Yisrael* in our time.
- Who knows where you will be
  when you become adults?
- Who knows where you will live?
- Who knows what profession or business you will enter?

Wherever one lives, wherever one works, he takes his education with him.

For example:

One of our graduates became a physician and moved to San Palo, California, a suburb of San Francisco. He is a renowned heart specialist. Today, there is a yeshivah there, because this doctor, our graduate, helped organize it. Eventually, he became president of the yeshivah. He sets aside time each day to study Torah.

One does not know what he will be doing in the future. You might become a *rebbi,* work for a yeshivah in some other capacity, or teach Torah outside the realm of the yeshivah. If one is a business person, he can also work for Torah causes and, of course, must study Torah every day. Not everyone becomes a *rav* or a *rosh yeshivah,* but, whatever one does, he must realize his responsibility to *Klal Yisrael.* Wherever you will be, you can and must help to build the future of *Klal Yisrael.* However, first, *one must build oneself.* You must be the "jug of oil," so that the *chalos haneis* can occur.

Being the "jug of oil" means to give light to the world. Oil gives light, and the greatest light is the light of Torah. As our Sages teach (*Megillah* 16b):

אוֹרָה זוֹ תּוֹרָה

"Light" — this refers to Torah.

⋅§ *Doing Our Part*

In *Al HaNissim* we say: You in Your great mercy stood by them in their time of distress. You fought their battle, judged their claim, and avenged their wrong. You delivered

- the strong into the hands of the weak,
- the many into the hands of the few,
- the impure into the hands of the pure,
- the wicked into the hands of the righteous,
- the sinners into the hands of those who toil in Your Torah.

For Yourself you made a great and holy Name in Your world . . .

All this Hashem did. An incredible miracle, but then again, nothing is beyond Hashem's power.

We may suggest that the greatness of *Al HaNissim* does not lie in these sentences. It is found at the end of the prayer:

וְאַחַר כַּךְ בָּאוּ בָנֶיךָ לִדְבִיר בֵּיתֶךָ וּפִנּוּ אֶת הֵיכָלֶךָ וְטִהֲרוּ אֶת מִקְדָּשֶׁךָ
וְהִדְלִיקוּ נֵרוֹת בְּחַצְרוֹת קָדְשֶׁךָ . . .

Thereafter, Your children came to the Holy of Holies, cleansed your Temple, purified your *Beis HaMikdash,* and kindled lights in the Courtyards of Your Sanctuary.

These words are, perhaps, the most important part of this prayer.

V'achar kach, and afterwards, after all the miracles that Hashem had performed,

the people did something.

They purified the Temple of any impurities. They lit the *Menorah* with pure oil. They established these eight days to express thanks and praise to Hashem's Great Name.

Hashem will do everything for us, but we have to know that there is a great responsibility on our part to do our share. If we do not exercise our responsibility, then we have no right to ask Hashem to do it for us.

בָּא לְטַהֵר מְסַיְּיעִין אותו (יומא לח:)

Our Sages (*Yoma* 38b) tell us that if anyone wants to become *tahor*, if he wants to purify himself, Hashem will help him. But the individual *must do something* first.

> If you do something about it, then Hashem will do something about it as well. He will help you far, far beyond your own natural abilities.
>
> You have to take the first step, even a tiny small step. Hashem will then take a Giant Step towards you and help you on to greater heights.

GET STARTED *NOW!*
Do not wait for tomorrow.

Index

Index

∾§ Scriptural and Talmudic Index

Scriptural and Talmudic Index

Torah

Neviim and Kesuvim

Mishnah and Talmud

This volume is part of
THE ARTSCROLL SERIES®
an ongoing project of
translations, commentaries and expositions
on Scripture, Mishnah, Talmud, Halachah,
liturgy, history and the classic Rabbinic writings;
and biographies, and thought.

For a brochure of current publications
visit your local Hebrew bookseller
or contact the publisher:

Mesorah Publications, ltd

4401 Second Avenue
Brooklyn, New York 11232
(718) 921-9000